A HISTORY OF
Transport

A history of

Transport

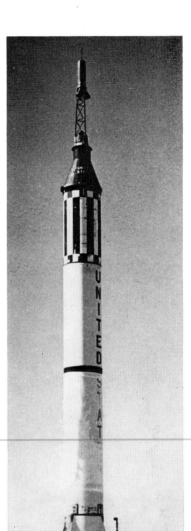

edited by
G. N. Georgano

with over 400 illustrations
including 16 pages in colour

J M DENT & SONS LTD
LONDON

First published 1972

© Text J. M. Dent & Sons Ltd 1972

Made in Great Britain
at the
Aldine Press · Letchworth · Herts
for
J. M. DENT & SONS LTD
Aldine House · Bedford Street · London

ISBN 0 460 03951 2

Contents

PART SIX
Aviation, by David Mondey

Illustrations

Introduction

It has often been said that transportation and civilization go hand in hand. Whether a civilized society develops appropriate transportation, or whether existing transportation contributes to (and spreads) civilization is a question as difficult to answer as that of the chicken and the egg. Certainly the growth of material civilization has only been possible as a result of constantly improving means of movement, for it is only when men can move freely and fairly rapidly that any interchange of ideas is possible.

In this book we have only touched in passing on the civilizing effects of transportation, since it has been our purpose to describe the means by which men have moved around. For this reason also we have had largely to ignore military developments, except where they have directly contributed to general improvements. It is interesting to note that in the infancy of a new system military developments loom large; fighting galleys gave the lead to commercial ones in the early Mediterranean civilizations, while the war chariot was the fastest land vehicle in the days of Julius Caesar. The roads themselves would not have been built as the Romans built them had there not been the need to communicate rapidly with garrisons and outposts. As a means of transportation settles down and matures, so military and commercial needs diverge and the interchange of development becomes less. The eighteenth-century East Indiaman was both a fighting and a transport ship, but the modern war vessel is really a floating fortress rather than a means of conveyance. The rocket received its first impetus as a secret weapon in the Second World War, but now its importance in space exploration has come to the fore, and it is hoped that circumstances will reduce or eliminate the need for ballistic missiles. The submarine and the tank are two forms of transportation that have remained entirely military, despite Jules Verne's prophecies about the former, and these find no place in this book. These considerations apart, and bearing in mind the extremely limited space available for such a vast subject, we hope that readers will find a balanced and interesting account of transportation on, and indeed beyond, this planet.

Acknowledgments

As General Editor I would first like to thank all my contributors for their prompt delivery of copy and readiness to incorporate modifications and extra material where it was thought necessary. Thanks are also due to the following, for help and advice in providing information and illustrations.

E. Albertini, State Papers Dept, British Museum

B. W. Bathe, Science Museum, London

R. E. Braithwaite, Chief Engineer, Birmingham & Midland Motor Omnibus Co. Ltd

Erik Eckermann, Deutsches Museum, Munich

Tony Hamilton-Baker

Patrick Hickman-Robertson

Arthur Ingram

Miss Juanita Kalerghi, Editor, *Hovering Craft and Hydrofoil*

Miss Susan Maguire, Cunard Line Ltd

W. B. Nodwell, Vice-President, Foremost Tracked Vehicles Co. Ltd

S. Otsuka, Ishikawajima-Harima Heavy Industries Ltd

John F. Parke, Editor, *Buses*

Kenneth G. Pope, Press Officer, London Transport

Michael Preston, National Maritime Museum, Greenwich

E. Schacher, Lake Lucerne Navigation Company

A. G. Simmons, British Hovercraft Corporation Ltd

John W. R. Taylor, Editor, *Jane's All the World's Aircraft*

Mrs E. Tucker, National Maritime Museum, Greenwich

Bart H. Vanderveen

Michael Ware, Curator, National Motor Museum at Beaulieu, Hants.

G. N. G.

Note on Sterling/Dollar Rates

When quoting equivalent figures for British and American currency, we have followed the exchange rate prevailing at the time referred to. This has varied as follows:

Before 1900, the figure fluctuated, but we have chosen a rate of £1 = $4.

1900–1931: £1 = $4.80

1931–1939: £1 = $4.50 (in fact there were small fluctuations during this period)

1939–1949: £1 = $4.03

1949–1967: £1 = $2.80

after 1967: £1 = $2.40

PART ONE

Before the Machine
by A. A. Dent

The history of mechanical transport runs to rather less than two centuries in extent. The history of transportation—not before the machine existed, but before the machine was adapted to locomotory use—goes back about a hundred centuries from the present day. This section must therefore be the merest sketch of the stages by which the world into which the railways were born was formed.

1

Man Alone

The masculine, to adopt the legal formula, shall hereinafter imply the feminine. If it be asked how the movable goods of primitive man were transported, the answer is quite simple and based on copious evidence: on the shoulders or head of primitive woman. Bands of primitive hunters or food-gatherers either in primeval times or such as survive into the present day, moving across the face of the land seeking what they may devour, are alike in that the men carry only their weapons because they must at all times be ready to attack the game or defend the band from predators, unencumbered. The women carry everything else—including the next generation. A baby can be carried in the folds of clothing, but if there are no clothes in this stage of culture there must be some sort of sling instead, and perhaps this is where it all began, with a primitive baby-carriage rather than a primitive goods wagon.

Human porterage, whether on the head or the back, survived for a very long time on the African continent because the presence of tsetse fly, and other insects carrying endemic disease of some grass-eating animals, has made the use of horse, ass or mule impossible. It is inexplicable that the potential of the ox as pack or riding animal was not further exploited in Africa. There are rare Saharan rock-paintings over five thousand years old showing oxen carrying packs: none, from that area, of ridden oxen. At the other end of the continent, Hottentots rode their cattle in recent times. Livingstone rode an ox on his last expedition. But, in Africa as a whole, man-pack was the only carriage for goods, and the man-borne litter for passengers. The highest development of the man-borne litter was achieved independently and at about the same time in Europe and North America. There is a well-known picture of Queen Elizabeth I in such a litter identical in pattern with that used by the paramount chief or Great Sun of the Natchez Indians, as depicted by French explorers, about 1700. In both continents the litter had carrying-poles fore and aft as in the modern stretcher, and another pair athwartships, giving scope for eight bearers.

Wheelbarrow, here used as an ambulance, ultimately of Chinese origin. From the Luttrell Psalter, c. 1340.
British Museum

The American version was much superior. Her courtiers carried Gloriana at a walk, but the Natchez subjects conveyed the Great Sun *au pas de gymnastique*, and in relays, which were trained to take over, a whole fresh team at a time, without stopping or even slowing down to a walk. The state litter today survives only in one instance, and that processional; at certain seasons and on certain occasions the Pope progresses through the Vatican City in a litter virtually identical with that used by Queen Elizabeth I.

The palanquin was the oriental man-borne conveyance that was brought back by the earliest seventeenth-century travellers from India to become the town-conveyance—'sedan chair'—of London, where its history stretches from the reign of Charles I to that of George IV. In narrow streets it had many advantages over the coach, but its occupants were signally vulnerable to the attacks of footpads, especially if the chairmen were in league with the latter. When they were not they usually ran away—it was virtually unknown for a London chairman to stand and fight in defence of his fare. Footmen who were permanent employees were of course another matter; really the last vestige of the medieval retainer whose functions as bodyguard were most in demand while the retainee was travelling, and particularly when moving about after dark in a strange town.

Travel on foot on ice and snow brought the invention of the snowshoe, the ski and skates. The first does not permit a speed faster than walking, but it allows the wearer to make headway across snow that would otherwise be impassable. The snowshoe is now confined to North America, but was once in use throughout the entire sub-arctic rim of the Old World. Very different is the ski, which facilitates travel at a speed far in excess of

Queen Elizabeth I's litter, in use on the occasion of her visit to Lord Hunsdon. British Museum

The manner in which the Great Sun was carried to the harvest festival of the Natchez. Smithsonian Institution National Anthropological Archives, Bureau of American Ethnology Collection

that put up by a running man, over great distances. The same can be said of skating, in which the great speeds attainable are counter-balanced by the necessity to stay on smooth waterways. All three devices are of pre-historic origin, the first two originating in northern Scandinavia and the White Sea area, while skates made of the shin bones of sheep or goats have been found in central European lake-dwellers' sites, as well as in the far north. Ski-ing in particular was primarily an aid to the hunter after fur-bearing game, and bow-bearing skiers are depicted in the rock drawings of the north. Only on skis could a man run down a wolf, alone and without a dog.

2
Animal Aids

It is assumed, though the material evidence for the belief is scanty, that the first animal to be domesticated was also the first to be used for draught; that is the dog, first tamed in the Mesolithic, or Middle Stone, Age. Certainly those people who notoriously on first contact with Europeans had only the dog among domestic animals—the Eskimo and the Red Indians—used dog teams to pull sleighs (on ice rather than on snow) and single (presumably the largest available) dogs to pull the *travois* (called in Devon, where it was seen until about 1800 behind single ponies, the 'truckamuck'). This was simply an A-shaped frame consisting of two poles almost but not quite converging from rear to front, with cross-pieces forming a platform on which the load was carried.

The presence of the same vehicle in primitive northern societies in both Europe and America might indicate that it was a product of the sub-arctic peoples whose material culture is very much the same all around the Pole. It is assumed that early Eurasian users of dog-drawn sleighs also used the dogs to hunt reindeer, until it occurred to them that the reindeer might be caught alive and made to pull the sleigh, leaving the dog free to do more hunting. The most important fact supporting this assumption is the similarity of design between the dog and reindeer harness and the extent to which they differ from that used on all other animals. This type of harness is best described as a net, with only one large mesh, which fits round the shoulders of dog or deer close to the base of the neck and is joined to a single trace which runs back between the animal's legs to the front of the sleigh. Dog-teams in the Canadian and Alaskan Arctic are today only just holding their own in the face of the 'skidoo', or snowmobile, a tracked motor scooter, and probably the present generation will see the last of them. Perhaps the reindeer will last a little longer because it is edible (at least, more edible than the dog), and as long as the Lapps find it worth while to keep reindeer for the sale of the meat—which, smoked, is eaten all over Scandinavia—they might as well work them also. Hard travel with dog-teams is easier than with reindeer or with any other ruminant since

Norwegian pony with container, used to bring down milk from mountain dairies (saeter). *Example of various specialized fittings for pack transport of special loads. A similar container is shown in use in Sussex on the Bayeux Tapestry, 1086.* Mary Aiken Littauer

dog-feed can be carried in very concentrated packs which occupy little space, such as pemmican or even frozen fish; or the dogs can be fed on fresh game shot on the march. But in country where there is nothing to graze on, the problem of carrying forage and fodder for draught animals is daunting. There is also the fact that the dog can gulp down its daily rations in a matter of minutes, whereas horses and ruminants not only have to be fed several times a day, but have to have time to masticate their feed properly, and must rest to digest it.

In the comparatively thickly populated Antarctic of today, its coast littered not only with whaling bases but with government-run meteorological stations and observatories of many nations, dog-teams are still used for journeys that do not justify the employment of snowgoing tracked vehicles, the fuel consumption of which is rather high; but dogs can only be economically used on coastwise journeys, for there is no animal life in the interior of that continent, though the coast abounds in seals and penguins. And if dog-feed has to be taken on a journey, then the sleigh cannot be carrying its maximum payload.

Polar travel affords one point of departure for the history of riding, draught and pack animals. The origin of these uses is multiple, and in most regions the first two are a development of the last. The ass, for instance, was first domesticated in North Africa, and did thousands of

Pack-saddle as used on donkeys and mules in Greece today. This pattern was formerly much more widely distributed in Europe. It differs radically from that used on horses.
Mary Aiken Littauer

years' service under the pack before being ridden. The reindeer, it seems, was domesticated at least as early, and originally was a pack-carrier as much as a sleigh-hauler. But at an early date the ridden reindeer was depicted in the rock drawings of the White Sea coast; according to one theory the riding of horses is an imitation of reindeer-riding by nomad herdsmen living in Central Asia south of the reindeer belt and already keeping mares for milk and their foals for meat, occasionally packing their tents and other gear on the backs of the quieter mares. It has been held that the use of *all* larger grass-eating animals for work is a development of this meat-and-milk stage of pastoralism. This would apply also to cattle, first harnessed to the plough in Mesopotamia, then to the sled, which by the addition of wheels became the cart. Side by side with the ox-drawn cart in Sumeria was the onager-drawn processional wagon, and from the meeting of the Sumerian masters of the onager (Asiatic wild ass, *Equus hemionus*) with southward-migrating horsemen arose the final stage in a complicated process whereby the horse, having first been a pack animal, then a riding animal and possibly also a sleigh-hauler, was harnessed to what

Battle of Egyptians and Philistines, second millennium, showing, exceptionally, ox-transport actually mixed up in the fighting, not in transport echelon. J. H. Potratz

Mediterranean type chariot, racing (?) model. Tomb of Tutankhamen. British Museum

Pair of draught oxen, South Germany, 1960. Central European versions of horns yoke, retained instead of the adaptation to horse harness and single traction with shafts. Daphne Machin Goodall

became the war-chariot—the universal vehicle of the fighting aristocracy of Western Asia, Europe and North Africa, from its beginnings before 2000 B.C. to its final eclipse about A.D. 500.

This double shifting from one working animal to another, and from one kind of work to another, brought with it a complicated train of adaptations, new inventions, re-inventions and transferences in the fields of harness and saddlery. Thus if we suppose a shift from reindeer-drawn sleigh to horse-drawn sleigh, the harness could be adapted to fit the horse instead of the reindeer (as it had once already been adapted to fit the reindeer instead of the dog), but the halter used on the driven reindeer was of no possible use in connection with the horse. Something quite new had to be invented—and it was: the first bridle, with bits made of bone and deer-antler. When the horse underwent its second change of use, however, the new owners, in Mesopotamia, used with it a type of bridle identical with that current in Siberia. But their horse-harness bore no relation at all to the reindeer-harness of, say, the Lena basin, being simply an adaptation of the ox-yoke, originally designed for ploughing, and which had been used on the onager and the ass with fair success. This leads to the conclusion that the peoples from whom the Sumerians acquired horses must have been riders and not drivers, and it is at this point that two diverging streams in the exploitation of equines of all species take their rise. From the Mesopotamian system of the pole and yoke arose a 'school' of chariotry and a system of pair-harness in draught which was diffused westward over the whole of the Near East, Europe and North Africa. Farther east and farther north the nomads of the steppe for the most part confined themselves to riding, and when they finally took to driving they found their own solution to the problem of harnessing which owed nothing to the ox-yoke tradition. These streams did not again meet and merge until the early Middle Ages, the divergence lasting some thirty-five centuries.

Owing to the shape of the withers in the respective animals, the use of the ox-yoke on the ass, the onager and the mule had been reasonably effective, but when it came to be applied to the horse its efficiency was limited; the horse could be prevented from walking 'out from under' the yoke only by the provision of a neck-strap which, because throughout antiquity it was too flexible and placed too high, exercised a throttling effect, and by forcing the head into a certain position precluded galloping. Moreover the yoke, a legacy of plough-oxen working in pairs, could not be adapted in any way to accommodate the single horse. At first this did not matter because the available horses were so small that they were better used in pairs, but a system which posed the alternatives 'double or nothing' had grave inherent disadvantages. For some reason which is still not clear to us the ancients were able to adapt harness for the use of a single animal in the case of the mule only, and this is only one of the reasons why this hybrid was so highly valued

*Wheeled cage drawn by zebus, showing Late Roman
solid-disc wheel of unusual construction: built up out of
six planks instead of the customary three. Piazza
Armerina, Corridor of the Great Hunt (detail). Foto del
Gabinetto Fotografico Nationale, Rome*

in antiquity for 'civilian' use, and why one of the most
expensive prizes offered for the famous race in Homer's
Odyssey is a mare due to give birth to a mule shortly. It
is impossible to understand the limitations of ridden and
driven animals in 'classical' antiquity unless these
lacunae of technique are appreciated. There were, for
instance, no traces, so that however the team was
harnessed, no matter how many animals it comprised
and no matter how powerful they were individually, they
could exert no direct tractive power on the body of the
vehicle. Again, the size of the team was limited by the fact
that the maximum number of animals that could pull
abreast under the ancient yoke was two; four could be,
and were, put to the vehicle, but still abreast, so that the
outer pair were drawing askew with enormous loss of
mechanical efficiency. Throughout the rise, the flourish-
ing and the decadence of the Roman Empire, no Roman
ever learnt the simple technique whereby two animals or
two pairs of animals can be harnessed one in front of

another by means of a chain or cable or articulated
draught-pole of double length.

Similarly in riding, the saddle in any form recognizable
as such today was unknown to the Western world until
about the second century A.D., and no European people
had stirrups of any kind before the incursion of the Avars
in 568. The lack of stirrups, besides its obvious disadvantages in terms of military potential, severely affected the
ability of the messengers, etc., to ride long distances at
fast paces. The complacency of the Romans in leaving to
the Outer Barbarians such vulgar matters as the design
and *exploitation* of a wagon with a fore-carriage that
would turn on a 50-degree lock is almost Chinese: but
this is an insult to the Chinese who themselves, having
adopted the use of the horse from the Huns beyond the
Great Wall, proceeded to invent shafts for the single
harness horse, which invention was transmitted to the
West only half way through the Middle Ages. The real
weakness of classical draught systems is brought out by

not infrequent representations in sculpture, such as that in the church of Maria Zell in Carinthia showing a Roman wagon drawn by two enormous and powerfully muscled horses such as would be capable of drawing three tons between them in modern gear. Yet the capacity of the wagon, in this obviously realistic composition, is perhaps 10 hundredweight (which is indeed the maximum permitted load laid down in an ordinance of the late Empire under Theodosius II).

By contrast, in the primitive and impoverished Anglo-Saxon kingdom of Mercia, where only faint echoes of Mediterranean culture survived, and these only in ecclesiastical circles, five centuries later, the tax records for the Cheshire salt-works reveal as a matter of course that a normal wagon-load was 24 hundredweight.

These wagons on which, all over Europe from the fall of the Roman Empire down to the lifetime of Dr Johnson and later, the real economic 'burden of the day' was carried behind teams of oxen, were a legacy of the northern barbarians whose women, children, provisions, spare weapons and dry socks had been carried in them, behind the battle line, at the crises when they broke through the Roman frontier zones and founded such kingdoms as those of the Franks and the Burgundians. The difference was that now, after about a century of life in the run-down Roman provinces, they stopped travelling in them. Again, we do not know really why. Only it seems that, once having become used to driving on the highly efficient Roman highway systems, when these fell into disrepair people travelled only on horseback and the wagon went back to where it started—the means by which the harvest is got out of the fields and into the barn, or at most as far as the mill. Outside the immediate Mediterranean region, four-wheeled wagons with swivel-

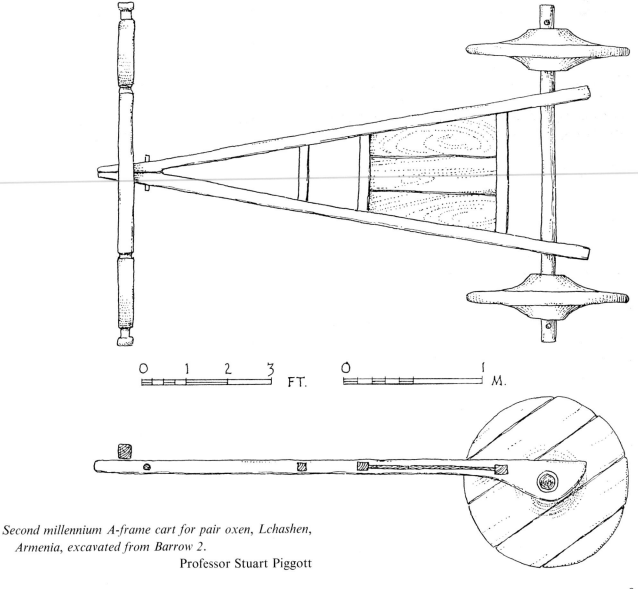

O 1 2 3 FT.

O 1 M.

Second millennium A-frame cart for pair oxen, Lchashen, Armenia, excavated from Barrow 2.

Professor Stuart Piggott

9

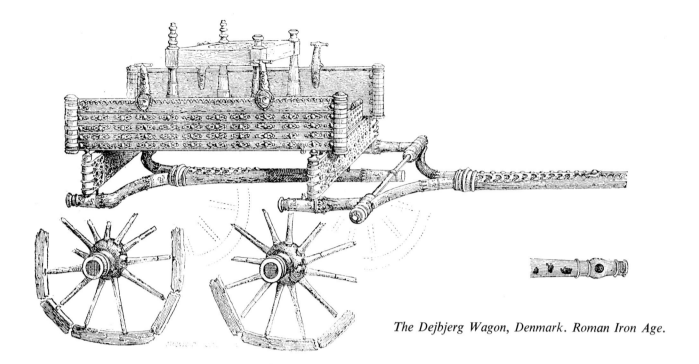

The Dejbjerg Wagon, Denmark. Roman Iron Age.

ling fore-axle, a pole to take the yoke on the 'wheeler' pair of oxen, and a chain producing it forward to take further yokes *ad lib.*, are common form. All derive from such early Iron Age models as the famous one found at Dejbjerg in Denmark. Few attained such elaboration, such running efficiency and such beauty of form as the English wagons with their characteristic county variations displayed at the period when they were being adapted to horse-draught.

Once again the wind of change blew out of the steppes and across the desert. The eighth, ninth and tenth centuries of our era saw the threefold and partly simultaneous but never concerted assault on Western Christendom of the Vikings from the north, the Saracens from the south on the broadest front from Sicily to Spain, and the Magyars from the east. With these apocalyptic ravagers came technical innovations that were to make rapid and efficient travel, both riding and driving, again possible. The Magyars and the Vikings brought the stirrup to those nations who had not yet adopted it (perhaps to all Europe outside the bounds of the Byzantine Empire). The Vikings brought the breast-collar, and shafts also, borrowed from the Turks.

Rapid and efficient are relative terms. Neither could have much meaning until the road network again reached something near the standard, all over Europe, that had been acceptable in the heyday of the Roman

Empire, the time when the province of Britain contained 5,000 miles of *via strata* suitable for fast wheeled traffic. This figure was reached again in Britain, in terms of 'turnpike roads', about 1780. By about 1830 it had reached 20,000 miles. The English post-chaise, the best but also the most expensive method of travel available before the Railway Age, travelled at about the speed and with the same reliability as the Roman *cursus publicus*.

The coach takes its name from the Hungarian village of Kocs, famous for its skilled wainwrights, who in the late fifteenth century produced a model of four-wheeled wagon with smaller fore-wheels and larger hind-wheels that permitted the fore-carriage to turn with a very full lock. The body had as yet no roof, was higher behind than before and consisted of basketwork covered with leather. To add a leather roof was a simple matter. Such vehicles soon became articles of export, principally by way of Bohemia and Germany, and the first one reached England in the reign of Elizabeth I. For long the trade to England remained almost a German monopoly, and English wainwrights could not compete with the prices quoted by German builders of forty guineas, f.o.b. London, including spare wheels. While in German hands the coach designs became heavier and heavier, and lost the flexibility which their original light construction had imparted. This was only rectified by two later Hungarian inventions, the sling (leather) on which the body was supported hammock-wise between corner-posts, and later multi-leafed elliptical springs.

Coaches for public use—'stage-coaches'—first took the English roads about 1650, having been preceded about 1550 by stage-wagons, which were entirely springless and windowless. The latter proceeded at a foot-pace, the wagoner walking alongside the team at an average 2½ mph.

The great flowering of the English coach traffic came to pass because of a fourfold improvement which arose within the second half of the eighteenth century—in roads, harness, vehicles and horses. Similar improvements took place in various continental countries, but in none of them simultaneously. English craftsmanship in coachbuilding overtook that of the Germans in the reign of George II. Harness became lighter, stronger and more flexible from about 1750 onwards. But the most impressive improvement was a by-product of racing. The English thoroughbred horse had by 1770 about a century of history behind it, counting from the importation by Charles II of the royal mares from Barbary who are the ancestresses of most horses in the General Stud Book. By 1770 thoroughbred propagation had begun to 'boil over'. Blood stallions no longer covered exclusively blood mares. Increasingly they were put to hunter mares and to coach mares such as the Cleveland Bays (which cross produced the famed Yorkshire Coach Horse). Moreover, such was the over-production of thoroughbred horses that the surplus of animals which had no success on the turf began to find its way between the traces. Only in this way could a team be got together that could, about the beginning of the nineteenth century, attain speeds of 20 mph on flat stages.

In England the mail was first carried by coach in 1784 (London to Bath) and the employment of thoroughbreds enabled great improvements in speed to be made. Another factor contributing to the supreme performance of the mail-coach was simply a matter of drill. Whereas in the reign of George I it took half an hour to change the team, during the Regency it took one minute. By 1800 it was no longer a matter of waiting to hear the post-horn, sounded perhaps a furlong short of the post-house; the

Anglo-Saxon cart, A-frame as in that illustrated on page 9, from a psalter, c. A.D. *1000.* British Museum

Rhineland pattern of general utility wagon, used as military transport. In use with Highland regiment, probably of Jacobean mercenaries at Mainz, 1743.

National Gallery of Scotland

Northern English farm tumbril, showing detail. W. Howitt,
c. *1800.* Anthony Dent Collection

An epitome of transport history. Toy from the nursery of the railway magnate Sir Joseph Pease. The car is the 'coup' or tumbril that replaces the wagon in England north of the Tees, drawn by a Durham ox (natural hide) and modelled in 1815–1821. The name of this ox, 'Billy Ruffian', handed down from one generation of Pease children to the next, was the seamen's rendering of 'Bellerophon', the frigate that carried Napoleon to St Helena. Solid or clog wheels survived late in Teesdale. A pair is still preserved at the Bowes Museum, Barnard Castle, a dozen miles upstream from the terminus of the first English railway. Photo: Anthony Dent Collection

grooms were standing-to, horses harnessed and in hand, five minutes before the coach was due to arrive.

What the English were able to overcome, by the use of abundant Thoroughbred stock, was the baneful legacy of chivalry. All coach-horses in Western Europe were derived from the slow, heavy war-horse of feudal times, and its descendants the Neapolitan, the Frisian, the Flemish, the Old Lincolnshire Black, the Breton, etc. East Central Europe was free of this burden because there the 'feudal' method of armoured cavalry combat had never been practised. The only coach-horses comparable with the English were not to be found in the nearest countries such as France and the Low Countries but in the Habsburg Empire whose reservoir of horse stock lay farther east, in Transylvania, in Poland, in Wallachia, where speed had priority over weight-carrying. This is

true to a certain extent of riding-horses also. The performance of the Hungarian Count Sandor (143 miles in 8 hours 10 minutes) is really more creditable than that of Osbaldeston (200 miles in 8 hours 40 minutes), which was purely experimental, being fifty circuits of Newmarket racecourse, because Sandor rode along roads under normal travelling conditions. Both feats were for bets; Sandor's journey was made in 1820, and Osbaldeston's ten years later.

Stage-coach travel in England cost the passenger 1s. per 5 miles throughout the eighteenth century until about 1780, when fares rose from 2d. to 3d. a mile. Only 14 lb. luggage went free, the remainder was charged at a prohibitive 3d. per lb. Mail-coach fares, after 1784, were more like 1s. a mile, minimum acceptable tip to a crack driver was half-a-guinea, and half-a-crown to the guard.

Highland pony and cart in the 1880s. Harness almost entirely of vegetable origin, halter of willow withes. Wheels of second millennium 'clog' type.

Highland Museum, Kingussie

Even so, the trade operated on a fairly narrow margin. Keep of a pair of coach-horses cost £2 a week, and one horse per mile of route had to be maintained. Thus a coach service from London to York could not make do with less than two hundred horses, a running expense of £10,400 a year. Replacements to the team cost, on an average, only £25 each. Even so, the posting yards of Hounslow or Barnet, in the year of Waterloo, would contain between them some £60,000 worth of horse-flesh. At these prices the teams could be horsed with blood animals only by accepting every sort of vice and every kind of infirmity which did not actually preclude a horse drawing for ten miles, flat out, daily for the three years or so which was computed as the average life of a horse in the mail-coach business. 'Working to death' was a commonplace expression, objectively used, in the

coaching trade. So was 'three blind 'uns and a bolter', literally meant for a team of four.

The economics of post-chaise travel, an alternative (and a much better one for those who could afford it) to the public coach, were easier for the contractor, who only had to provide two horses at every stage. Charges in 1832 were about half-a-crown a mile—about four times the cost of a similar equipage in Germany, at that time.

The alternative for those who could not afford the post-chaise remained, until the coming of the railways, 'coming up with the carrier'. The carrier was there, as a long-haul goods conveyor, before the stage-coach and before the stage-wagon. He was a survivor of the medieval pack-train operator, and he began to run wagons on some routes in the early sixteenth century. But to the end these slow carrier wagons ran, on some routes, side by side with pack-trains, essentially the same sort of caravan as had plied the Great Silk Road from China to Byzantium before the Christian era. Even the pack-horses took passengers on top of the normal load; this was the cheapest conveyance of all, but was it worth it? Let Tobias Smollett in his realistic autobiographical novel, *Roderick Random*, answer for all: 'I determined therefore to set out with the carriers, who transport goods from one place to another on horseback; . . . on the first day of November 1739, sitting upon a pack-saddle between two baskets, one of which contained my goods in a knapsack. But, by the time we arrived at Newcastle-upon-Tyne [from Edinburgh], I was so fatigued with the tediousness of the carriage, and benumbed with the coldness of the weather, that I resolved to travel the rest of my journey [to London] on foot . . .'

In towns the ordinary people had no transport provided for them until well into the nineteenth century, if one excepts the short-lived coach service started by Blaise Pascal in Paris in 1662, and even this was forbidden to *les gens du peuple*. The omnibus owes its origin as well as its name to a French source. When the contractor Stanislas Baudry was trying out his scheme for a general passenger service in Paris, his experimental routes, in 1828, were set up at Nantes, where one of the termini was outside the business premises of a certain M. Omnes. The Parisian enterprise was speedily copied in London, where Shillibeer's first service ran on 4th June 1829. By 1839 there were 62 London buses in service, and by 1850, 1,300. About the middle of the century the London bus traffic was dominated by French interest, and the 'Compagnie Generale des Omnibus de Londres', incorporated in 1855, was not fully anglicized in name or in capital until 1862. The first omnibuses were drawn by two or three horses, with not more than seven outside passengers, and four-horse buses carrying twenty-eight passengers in all were not on the streets before 1855. Overall, the horse-bus era lasted some seventy years, and was almost coterminous with the horse-tram period. The horse tram lasted in peripheral form as a seaside novelty in such places as Douglas, Isle of Man, long after the horse trams of large cities had been replaced first by the electric tram,

Post-chaise (left) and cabriolet outside a West Country inn, c. 1790. Devon Archives Office

then by the trackless trollybus, and finally superseded altogether. The diffusion of the omnibus system through the capital cities of the world was probably a result of the Great Exhibition of 1851, for which occasion the number of vehicles in service on routes leading to the site was increased by 250.

The mail-coach had its second wind, after the railways had displaced it in England, in other countries before the construction of a rail network, and in some cases until the advent of the internal combustion engine. In the United States and Australia these were called 'stage-coaches', but in fact are comparable with the English mail-coach rather than with the much slower and heavier English stage-coach, being drawn by faster horses. In terms of coach-building, they differ not at all from English models of the 'classic' period (1790–1830). Only the much longer distances involved made them 'stages' in the strict sense insomuch as the passengers slept the nights (or *some* nights) at inns.

That other monument of the American Far West, the Pony Express, is the last legitimate descendant in the West of the English post service (which went on horseback until 1784), deriving ultimately through the Roman Imperial system and the courier services of Alexander the Great and the Persian King of Kings from the messenger services maintained by the nomad rulers of the Asiatic steppes, described by Marco Polo but in existence thousands of years before his time. In Outer Mongolia, almost certainly the country where this system was born, it survived into the 1920s. William Russell, the last surviving Pony Express rider, died at Stockton, California, in 1934. So vivid is this American legend of the Pony Express that few people realize that it existed for less than two years. It first ran in April 1860 from St Joseph, Missouri, through Kansas, Nebraska, Colorado, Wyoming, Utah and Nevada to Sacramento, California. The last run was made in October 1861. The fastest was by Bob Haslam, who carried the mail 120 miles from Smith's Creek to Fort Churchill, Nevada, in 8 hours 10 minutes in March 1861.

It was not a federal nor yet a state service, but a contract undertaken by the transport firm of Russell, Majors and Wadell, who were also engaged in goods and passenger haulage by road and employed five thousand men. Although there were only about two dozen riders at any given time, the service was uneconomic because the ancillary services required to support the actual riders took up too many man hours of the labour force as a whole. Four hundred horses were used, including spares, to cover the 1,966 miles of route. It was a Pony Express

A coach in Covent Garden, 1640. Engraving by Hollar.
British Museum

Winter travel in Russia c. 1526. Short ski, and sleighs, probably derived from a reindeer-drawn model. Harness of this distinctive design is still in use in Russia.
J. M. Dent & Sons Ltd

'Sleigh Racing on the Zaan', by Verschuur, c. 1840. The scene shows the obvious influence of Arab blood on the Dutch trotting-horse strain. Rijksmuseum, Amsterdam

Trotting match against time, with an American 'Match Cart': 45 miles were covered in 2 hours 55 minutes 30 seconds. Comparable performances at this period in England, by single horses in harness, are of the order of 100 miles in $10\frac{1}{2}$ hours. Lithograph after J. F. Herring Sr, c. 1840. Anthony Dent Collection

Dog cart, built new in Arkansas in 1961 by the one firm surviving in all the U.S.A. who flourish, untroubled by competitors, and are barely able to keep up with the demand caused by a mild boom in driving.

Anthony Dent Collection

De Tivoli's patent omnibus, 1860. Access to the knifeboard seats on the roof was by the precarious steps at the rear offside of the vehicle; proper stairs came later.

Anthony Dent Collection

literally inasmuch as few of the animals were over 14 hands high, and none were materially above this height. But they were of greatly superior quality and price to the general run of Western cow-pony. They had to be because sometimes, at the very end of their stage, they had to out-distance hostile Indians mounted on fresh ponies. This risk also added to the weight carried. Saddle, bridle and mailbag together only weighed 13 lb., whereas the common Western saddle of that day weighed more than that by itself. Twenty pounds of mail (say 300 ordinary letters) were carried. Since most of the men were smallish and lightly built, their all-up weight unarmed would be about 168 lb. But since the Pony Express era coincided with that of one of the most dangerous Indian risings, each man carried a carbine as well as two revolvers, with ammunition. The entire route was almost exactly equal to ten times the distance by road from London to York, and was covered in ten days. At its peak, the London–York

mail-coach did the run in one day and one night (record twenty hours). Parts of the Pony Express route corresponded exactly to that of the Wells-Fargo Overland Stage. The service cost $100,000 to equip initially, and $30,000 a month to run. The company finished operations $200,000 in the red, but this is a case where success, and service to the public, cannot fairly be measured in financial terms.

The English stage-wagon or carrier-wagon and its continental equivalents had no exact counterpart in the New World. Here speed was not the object and the vehicle was not necessarily horse-drawn. The carrier-wagon, in England, was simply the adaptation to road use of various types of four-wheeled harvest wagons, with the addition of an arched tilt; just as in the settlement of the American West and in the Great Trek of the Afrikaners from the Cape to the Orange River and the Transvaal, the 'prairie schooner' and the 'ossewa' are simply the normal

Two-horse bier, used until fairly recent times for carrying the dead along narrow bridle paths and mountain tracks to the parish church of Llangywair on the shores of Lake Bala, North Wales. William Meredith

Ohio wagon train. Mules out of draught mares by 'Mammoth' jacks. Betsy Hutchins

farm wagon fitted with racks, lockers and weatherproof tilt.

Mule-teams often drew the wagons of the migrants across the Great Plains of the Oregon Trail. Although these wagons were not all of one type, they derived with few significant exceptions from English and German patterns, the German type being recognizable from the fact of the sides raking outwards to give a V-shaped cross-section. There is nothing specifically American about the 'Conestoga' wagon, or about the 'Red River' cart. The Ohio Wagon Train Association, which is today primarily a club for mule-breeders and amateurs of the harness (as opposed to the riding) mule, has seasonal rallies and parades in which fair numbers of authentic 'Prairie Schooners' can be seen. Sometimes these are replicas, sometimes genuine bygones, but perhaps most are examples in which various parts have been replaced one by one, so that they are like the old axe which has had three new shafts and two new heads—'but still it's my old axe'.

In South Africa the prototype was the Dutch 'long wagon', usually drawn by oxen, since these were immune from the ravages of African Horse Sickness (though it is true that they were vulnerable to rinderpest), but sometimes by mules. These mule-drawn (four-pair) wagons are still exhibited competitively at agricultural shows in South Africa, but stripped of the tunnel-like tilt which makes the *voortrekker* image. Slow cross-country travel in South Africa was still a reality in the childhood of our contemporaries; my cousin in Natal remembers going to boarding-school from his home in back-country Zululand just after the First World War in such a wagon, drawn by pair after pair of donkeys, for many days' journey.

PART TWO
Land Transportation: Roads

by G. N. Georgano

1

The Pioneers in Steam

The idea of the self-propelled vehicle is a very ancient one. In Homer's *Iliad*, written about 700 B.C., the blacksmith god, Vulcan, is said to have built twenty tripods that

'. . . placed on living wheels of massy gold
(Wondrous to tell) instinct with spirit roll'd
From place to place, around the blest abodes,
Self-moved, obedient to the beck of gods.'
(Book XVIII: Alexander Pope's translation)

The later Greeks certainly knew of the power of steam, and Hero of Alexandria designed a steam turbine in 130 B.C. However, these and other ideas found no practical application, and it was not until the eighteenth century that a self-propelled vehicle appeared, large and powerful enough to carry men and pull loads.

Nicolas Joseph Cugnot was an engineer in the French Army who began to experiment with steam-driven machines in the 1760s. He built two vehicles, and fortunately the second, dating from 1770 or 1771, is still in existence. It is a clumsy-looking three-wheeled machine with an enormous boiler projecting ahead of the front wheel. Intended as a tractor for towing heavy cannon, its maximum speed without a load was only 4 mph, and it had to stop every fifteen minutes in order to build up a fresh head of steam. The two cylinders, with a bore of 13 inches each, were mounted vertically, and drove the front wheel by a ratchet and pawl mechanism. This was one of the remarkable features of Cugnot's machine: steam power had been used in stationary engines, largely for pumping water from mines, for sixty years, but no one had thought of a satisfactory means of converting the up and down motion to a rotary one. Cugnot not only overcame this problem, but he also built up steam under pressure, whereas the previous steam engines worked by atmospheric pressure, the steam only serving to cause, by condensation, a partial vacuum in the cylinder. It is remarkable that Cugnot, working on his own, in a country whose industrial revolution came later than England's, should have made an engine compact and efficient enough to drive a vehicle. It is also curious, but sadly typical of inventors, that such a pioneer should have devoted less than ten years of his life

Model of Cugnot's second steam carriage, 1770.
Crown Copyright. Science Museum, London

Model of Goldsworthy Gurney's steam carriage, 1827.
Science Museum, London

John Scott Russell's steam carriage, 1834. One of six built
at the Grove House Engine Works, Edinburgh, and used
on a service between Glasgow and Paisley.
Road Locomotive Society

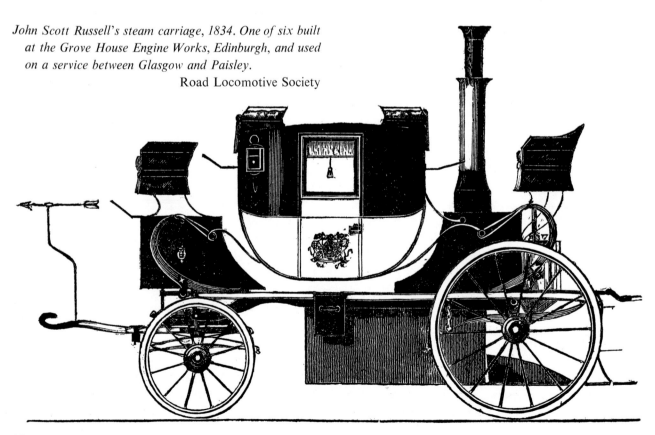

to the motor vehicle. He was a man without great means, and it seems that the only person of influence to be interested in Cugnot's experiments was the Duc de Choiseul, Minister of War. After his dismissal in 1771 no one else was prepared to give Cugnot financial backing, and he abandoned his work.

England had a considerable lead over France in industrial development. By 1784 the Birmingham firm of Boulton & Watt were already making stationary steam engines for commercial sale to factories, particularly breweries and cotton mills. However, because this business was so profitable, little interest was shown in the moving vehicle. Watt's assistant, William Murdoch, built a model steam locomotive in 1784, whose boiler was heated by a spirit lamp, but he never made a full-sized vehicle. Although several other steam carriages were projected in the 1790s, it was not until the beginning of the nineteenth century that a full-sized steam vehicle was built in England. This was the work of the Cornish engineer Richard Trevithick. In 1803 he built a three-wheeler with an enclosed carriage-type body capable of carrying eight people. The driving wheels were 10 feet in diameter, and the machine was said to achieve a speed of 12 mph with a full complement of passengers. However, like Cugnot and so many of the pioneers, Trevithick could find no financial backing, and after 1804 he turned his attention, with great success, to the railway loco-motive.

In the year that Trevithick abandoned his road vehicles an American inventor called Oliver Evans was construct-ing a steam-powered barge for dredging the docks of Philadelphia. This would have been a remarkable enough machine anyway, but in order to move it from the shed where it was built to the Schuylkill river, Evans fitted four iron-shod wooden wheels and by a system of belts and pulleys arranged for the barge's vast single-cylinder engine (19-inch stroke) to drive one of the front wheels. The resulting contraption, known as *Orukter Amphibolos*, the Amphibious Digger, can be thought of as America's first self-propelled vehicle, the world's first amphibious vehicle, and the world's first front-wheel-drive four-wheeler. However, having accomplished the mile-and-a-half journey to the riverside, *Orukter Amphibolos* settled, one imagines rather gratefully, into the water and, so far as is known, never ventured on land again.

For the next fifteen years no more self-propelled vehicles of any significance appeared. This may have been due to the European preoccupation with the Napoleonic Wars, but is more probably explained by the fact that most engineers were devoting themselves to the stationary engine or to the railway locomotive. Road vehicle

Walter Hancock's steam carriage, 'Era', built in 1834.
Road Locomotive Society

experiments had been so sporadic and unsuccessful that they had no immediate imitators. The 1820s, however, saw a sudden surge of interest in road steamers, and during the next twenty years at least fifty vehicles were built, the majority in the British Isles, and nearly all of them passenger-carrying. It is often forgotten that steam buses operated regular services in London six years before Queen Victoria came to the throne, and that steam coaches ran regularly between Gloucester and Chelten-ham, and made long-distance journeys (though not on a normal fare-carrying basis) from London to Brighton and from London to Bath.

During the period 1825 to 1840 two Englishmen did more to advance the road steamer than all the others put together. They were Goldsworthy Gurney (later knighted for work unconnected with transport) and Walter Hancock. Gurney built six vehicles, two carriages and four 'drags', or tractors, which pulled ordinary horse-drawn carriages. The latter went some way towards assuaging the layman's fears of fatal explosion. One of these drags was demonstrated in 1829 to the Duke of Wellington who said: 'It is scarcely possible to calculate the benefit we shall derive from this invention.' In 1831 Gurney's drags were operating a regular service between Gloucester and Cheltenham, covering 9 miles in 45 to 60 minutes. Between February and June 1831 the company covered 3,600 miles of successful transport, but a broken axle brought this run of luck to an end, and on 23rd June the service was suspended. Presumably public demand was not very high, or a small mishap like this would not

*Another Hancock carriage, 'Automaton', built in 1836.
Because of its open sides, 'Automaton' was used only in
fine weather.* Road Locomotive Society

have been allowed to halt this enterprising service, the
first in the world to carry passengers by mechanical means
on the road.

The most successful builder of steam vehicles at this
time was Walter Hancock. At his works in Stratford,
then an Essex village reached by leafy lanes from London,
he built a total of twelve machines, the largest a twenty-
two seater bus. Although he made a number of long-
distance runs, including London–Brighton and London–
Marlborough, his greatest fame came from the regular
services he operated in London. Between 1831 and 1833,
and again in 1836, Hancock's buses ran from Stratford to
the Bank of England, and from Paddington to Moorgate,
Islington and Pentonville. They were gaily painted
vehicles, each carrying its individual name, such as

'Infant', 'Era', 'Enterprise', 'Autopsy' and 'Automaton'. Each carried a crew of three; driver, engineer
who oiled and generally looked after the engine, and a
lad at the rear who kept the fire supplied with coke.
Largely because of good boiler design and construction,
Hancock's buses were reasonably reliable, and one would
imagine that he, if anyone, could have made steam
successful on British roads. And yet after 1836 all the
regular services were withdrawn, and the only further
vehicles he built were two steam cars for his own use. By
the early 1840s there were no steam coaches running
regular services anywhere in the British Isles, and
practically all the experimenters had turned to other
fields. It was to be over fifty years before London had any
other self-propelled buses.

2

The Traction Engine

No sooner had the steam coaches become moribund than the precursor of another form of transport appeared, this time in an agricultural district. During the 1830s a number of engineering firms built portable steam engines which provided power for threshing and other purposes, but had to rely on horses to be moved from place to place. In 1841 J. R. & A. Ransome of Ipswich (now the well-known firm of Ransomes, Sims & Jefferies) made their first portable, and the following year converted it to self-propulsion. The resulting machine could now move itself from one place of work to another, but it still relied on a horse for steering, having ordinary shafts in front. It was not long before the traction engine proper appeared, steered by the driver and capable of pulling loads. The first such machine was built by Robert Willis in 1849. It was very similar to the contemporary railway locomotive in appearance, even down to the four-wheeled tender.

From the 1860s onwards traction engines were made in increasing numbers, and for nearly thirty years they were the only self-propelled road machines to do useful work. Their most valuable service was to the farmer; teams of men took threshing tackle from one farm to another, and specially adapted engines were used for ploughing. Two engines were used, one on each side of the field. On the

Three-wheeled traction engine built by Tuxford of Skirbeck, Lincolnshire, using Boydell wheels for working on soft ground. Taken in 1857, this is one of the first photographs to show a self-propelled road vehicle.

Science Museum, London

Chain-driven traction engine built by William Tasker and Sons of Andover, Hampshire, in 1869. This is one of the few photographs to show the 'man with the Red Flag' in action. Taskers of Andover (1932) Ltd

Some of the largest traction engines in the United States were the three-wheelers built by the Remington and Best companies. This is a Remington 'Boss of the Woods', at work in a logging camp in 1891.

F. Hal Higgins Collection

A special Best traction engine of 1900. It had wood-covered driving wheels fifteen feet wide and nine feet high. Total weight was 41 tons. Caterpillar Tractor Company

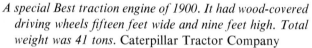

A Fowler Compound Road Locomotive built in 1896. Traction engines like this looked after most heavy haulage on Britain's roads until after the First World War. 'The Engineer'

roads, traction engines were employed on every conceivable work, including long-distance furniture removal where they had the advantage over the railway of giving a door-to-door service, albeit a very slow one. The most powerful road locomotives developed over 100 hp, and a team of two or three could haul over 120 tons. As late as the 1930s in Britain the largest loads were pulled by traction engine. Pickfords, the well-known hauliers, had a few in service up to 1950. Another well-known use of the traction engine was the Showman's Engine, mainstay of travelling fairs from the 1880s until the Second World War. It was basically similar in design to the ordinary traction engine, but its appearance was quite different, with brightly painted canopy supported by twisted brass columns and festooned with lights, and big dynamo in front of the chimney. They were dual-purpose engines, being used to tow all the fair's equipment from place to

place and, once installed, to generate electric current for the stalls, dodgems and other attractions. Merry-go-rounds were driven by centre-engines which, when all the surrounding machinery was dismantled, could be used for traction purposes. Showman's Engines are among the most valuable traction engines today, and one in good condition will fetch over £4,000 ($9,600).

The first traction engine in America was that built by John Reed of New York in about 1862, to the order of Major-General Joseph R. Brown of Minnesota. General Brown planned a road train to deliver supplies to the frontier territories, but unfortunately the engine broke down after seven miles of its first day's journey. Traction engines were never so numerous in America as in England and were mostly confined to farm work. Some of the most impressive were the enormous three-wheelers built by the C. L. Best Company of San Leandro, California.

27

These were used in the logging industry of north-western America and Canada, towing loads of up to 30 tons. Some American traction engines burned wood or straw, fuels more immediately available than coal. Straw-burners were also used in Latin America and in Russia.

The traction engine had a short life in military service, beginning in the Franco-Prussian War of 1870-1, when two British-built Fowlers were used by the Germans during the Siege of Paris. In the Russo-Turkish War of 1878 the Russian Army used twelve traction engines, including two locally built Maltzefs. The Boer War, 1899-1902, saw over forty engines in use, but already the lighter steam truck was proving more effective, and Lord Kitchener pronounced in favour of the latter. The French Army, who had used traction engines since 1875, replaced them with trucks after 1900.

3

The Passenger Car, 1858–1972

Thomas Rickett's steam carriage built for the Earl of Caithness in 1860. This photograph shows the Earl and Countess, and the Rev. William Ross of Kintore on the front seat, with Rickett on the rear platform. It was taken on the occasion of a 146-mile drive from Inverness to Barrogill Castle, Thurso, which involved the ascent of the Ord of Caithness, a climb of nearly 900 feet in 5 miles.

A. S. Heal Collection

The object of the earliest pioneers had been no more than to produce a machine that would move under its own power, and their successors had been largely concerned with commercial transportation in one form or another. With the exception of a light steamer built by Walter Hancock for his own use, nothing that could be called a private car appeared until the middle of the nineteenth century. In 1858 Richard Dudgeon of New York built a steam car which resembled a small traction engine with a bench seat on each side of the boiler. The engine consisted of two single cylinders, each driving one rear wheel. These wheels were of solid wood, red cedar, and were shod with iron tires. The car seated eight passengers, and was said to 'proceed at a lively gait'. The first car was destroyed in the New York Crystal Palace fire, but Dudgeon made a replica which still exists.

In 1859 Thomas Rickett, an ironfounder of Buckingham, built the first of a number of light steam cars. It weighed only 2 tons, could carry three passengers as well as a stoker, and all three wheels were independently sprung. It was demonstrated to Queen Victoria and Prince Albert, but there is no evidence that they actually rode in it. However, a machine of this size offered opportunities for amusement which the heavy steam coach could not, and for the first time the British aristocracy began to show an interest in mechanical vehicles. Rickett's second car, or possibly the same car that was demonstrated to Victoria and Albert, was bought by the Marquess of Stafford, while later customers included the Duke of Sutherland and the Earl of Caithness. Rickett could be considered as the first private car manufacturer, for he advertised that he would take orders for cars at £180 to £200 each. However, he does not seem to have made any more, and within a few years was experimenting with a traction engine which was eventually sold to Spain.

Between 1860 and 1880 at least forty steam cars were built in the British Isles, all by private inventors, and few being made in more than one example each.

So far all the road vehicles had been powered by steam engines, usually coal- or coke-fired, but in 1860 Etienne Lenoir of Paris patented an engine in which the piston was moved in the cylinder by the explosion of a gasoline/air mixture—internal combustion. It differed from all later internal combustion engines in that there was no compression of the mixture: as the piston moved forward (the cylinder was horizontal) the mixture was drawn in, and at half stroke it was ignited by an electrically induced spark. The explosion drove the piston to the end of the stroke, and the return of the piston drove out the burnt gases. Lenoir patented his engine in 1860, and two years later built a car powered by it. This made a few short journeys, but was too slow to be of practical use. Lenoir engines were later used with more success in motor boats.

If one has to select one pioneer vehicle as the father of the automobile, the choice must fall to the three-wheeler built by Karl Benz in 1885. Benz planned his car as an organic unit of chassis and engine, not as a conversion of a horse-drawn vehicle, but, more important, it had direct descendants which were on sale within a few years. The 1885 car was powered by a single-cylinder horizontal engine developing $\frac{3}{4}$ hp, and had a speed no higher than

A typical light steam carriage of the 1860s, built by H. Percy Holt in 1867. 'The Engineer'

Steam carriage designed by Alfred Yarrow and James Hilditch, and built by Cowan & Company of Greenwich in 1862. Both designers were under twenty years old at the time. 'The Engineer'

The first four-wheeled Benz car, 1893. This photograph shows clearly the vis-à-vis seating arrangement.
The Veteran Car Club of Great Britain

1896 Duryea 4-hp motor buggy. Kenneth H. Stauffer

1903 Curved Dash Oldsmobile 5-hp two-seater.
The Veteran Car Club of Great Britain

8 mph. At first Benz could not find anyone who was interested in buying his car. His partners in his gas engine firm thought he was wasting his time, and begged him to concentrate on a product from which they could all make money. However, he persevered; in 1888 he published a catalogue (the first automobile catalogue ever produced) and the following year began to sell a few cars. They still had three wheels, but power was up to 2 hp, and speed to 15 mph. The first four-wheeler Benz came in 1893, by which time he had sold a total of sixty-nine cars. In 1894 alone he sold sixty-seven, while in 1896, 181 cars left the factory. By this time Gottlieb Daimler had also begun to build cars in Germany, and sold the rights to build his engines in France to two firms who became well-known car manufacturers—Panhard et Levassor and Peugeot Frères.

There are several claimants to the title of First Gasoline Car to be made in America. The Lambert three-wheeler from Ohio City, made in 1891, has a well-attested claim to be the first, but the most successful, and the first to result in a production car, was the Duryea. In 1892 the brothers Charles and Frank Duryea fitted a single-cylinder 4-hp motor to a horse buggy. Charles said of it: 'It ran no faster than an old man could walk . . . but it did run.' The following year improved Duryeas were made, and by 1895 the brothers were turning out cars for sale from their small factory at Springfield, Mass. A Duryea buggy driven by Frank won the 1895 Chicago to Evanston Race. He took 9 hours to cover 50 miles, but even so finished ahead of a Benz which was the only other car to complete the course.

During the decade 1890 to 1900 the building of automobiles became an obsession with a large number of amateur mechanics and small bicycle and engineering works. By 1900 there were about two hundred firms throughout the world offering cars for sale, and already quite a number of 'makes' had fallen by the wayside. The market was still more limited than many optimists thought, and, having little mechanical knowledge, buyers wanted a product that was reliable and simple to maintain. Amongst the hordes of indifferent cars, some began to establish themselves as reliable and good value, and these makes were rewarded with excellent sales. The first car to be produced in anything approaching large numbers was the Curved Dash Oldsmobile, built from 1901 to 1906. It was a light, simple machine, easy to

1909 Waverley Electric runabout. Burton H. Upjohn

operate and sturdy enough to plough through muddy roads. The price was $650 (£130), and in the first year the plant turned out four hundred. In 1902 the figure was 2,100, and in 1904 over five thousand of the Curved Dash were made. In Europe the most popular car was the De Dion Bouton single-cylinder *voiturette*, originally with 3½-hp rear-mounted engine and *vis-à-vis* (face to face) seating, and later with an 8-hp engine at the front. Cheap cars such as these were the mainstay of the middle-class motorist, the doctor, solicitor or clergyman who drove and looked after his car himself. For the wealthy owner a great variety of powerful machines was already available by 1904. The 60-hp Mercedes had a 9·2-litre 4-cylinder engine, a speed of over 70 mph, and a price tag of £2,200 ($11,000) for the chassis alone. The purchaser then had to pay at least £600 ($3,000) for a good body, making a total cost of £2,800 ($14,000). Taking into account the fall in the value of money, this represents about £14,000

in today's terms. But at least our wealthy motorist had less income tax to pay!

In the early days the gasoline car was challenged by the steamer and the electric. The first steam automobiles made for sale in America came from the Newton, Mass., works of the Stanley twins in 1897. They were a vast improvement on the cumbersome machines of the 1860s, being neat-looking little two-passenger buggies with wire wheels. Top speed was about 25 mph, and the cars cost $700 (£140). The steamer had two great advantages over the gasoline car at this time; it was almost silent, giving a quiet hiss when accelerating, and it needed no gear changing, as the steam engine can work efficiently at any speed. The biggest drawback of the steamer was that it took a long time to start up from cold. To build up enough pressure in the boiler the burners had to be operating for at least ten minutes, often longer. By 1903 there were over forty firms making steamers, most of them light buggies of the Stanley pattern. Two years later the boom collapsed, and only a few makes were left. The most important of these were the Stanley and the White from Cleveland. The latter was a bigger and more expensive car than the Stanley, costing up to $3,700 (£740) for a seven-passenger touring car. Over the years the price of gas cars went down, thanks to mass production, but the steamers became more costly as design became more complex. White turned to gas cars in 1910, but Stanley went on making steamers in small numbers until 1927. By this time there was only one other steam car made in the United States, or in the world for that matter. This was the Doble. It was a superb automobile, with lines as good as those of any gasoline car. The flash boiler could raise steam in less than a minute. Maximum speed was 95 mph, and the car could travel 750 miles on one filling of water. Prices ran from $8,200 to $11,000 (£1,640 to £2,200) making the Doble one of the most expensive American cars. Only forty-five were sold, and production ended in 1930. In the past few years there has been some stirring of interest in the steam car again, but nothing near a production car has yet been announced.

The electric car has had a much less dramatic career than the steamer, although one made a sensation in 1898 when the Marquis de Chasseloup-Laubat drove a Jeantaud at 39·3 mph, a speed record for that time. The following year Chasseloup-Laubat and his rival Camille Jenatzy built specially streamlined cars and engaged in a series of speed trials. Jenatzy eventually achieved 65·75 mph in April 1899. However, on the whole the electric car was valued for its silence and ease of driving rather than for speed. Electric carriages, open and closed, were used in most countries, but to a greater extent in America than in Europe. The most famous American makes were Baker, Detroit, Milburn and Rauch & Lang. Milburns were used by President Wilson's secret service men

Scene at the finish of the New York to Boston Endurance Run, March 1907. The three leading cars are Aerocars, followed by a Packard and a Model K Ford.
Automobile Manufacturers Association

around 1918, and electric broughams were still to be seen in the early 1920s. The possibilities of an electric car revival are discussed later in this chapter.

From the earliest days of motoring, owners and builders wanted to test the speed and endurance of their machines. By 1900 competitions had divided into two categories: there were races, held on open roads with cars which were originally standard machines but were becoming increasingly powerful and specialized; and there were reliability trials. The races attracted the lion's share of public attention, but the trials were more important for demonstrating the capabilities of the average car. Two of the best-known were England's 1,000 Miles Trial, held first in 1900, and the American Glidden Tours. These began in 1905 with a tour of 870 miles from New York to Bretton Woods, New Hampshire, and return, and were extended to as much as 2,600 miles by 1909. The first motor trip across the American continent was in 1903 when Doctor H. Nelson Jackson and his chauffeur, Sewell Crocker, drove a Winton from San Francisco to New York in 64 days. Five years later the incredible New York to Paris race was held; the winning Thomas car covered a total of 13,341 miles in 88 days. The struggles of the Thomas through the mud and snow of America, Canada and Siberia highlighted what every American motorist knew already, the appalling state of country roads. Most rural roads had dirt or corduroy surfaces, the latter being a row of logs laid across the road as closely as possible. These roads began a mile or two outside the towns, so a 12-mile journey could represent an almost impossible challenge. The first rural mile of concrete pavement was laid in July 1909, in Wayne county, Michigan. Poor roads encouraged a peculiarly American type of car, the high-wheel buggy. Based on the horse buggy so popular with farmers, the high-wheelers had simple 2-cylinder engines, final drive by chain or even rope, and large wheels with solid tires. Their heyday was 1908 to 1911, when there were nearly ninety different makes, the best known being Holsman, International Harvester and Sears. The last-named were sold by the famous Chicago mail order company, Sears Roebuck.

The high-wheelers and many other more conventional autos were doomed with the appearance in October 1908 of the Model T Ford. It was a medium-sized five-passenger touring car with 22-hp 4-cylinder engine. With this car Henry Ford began mass production on a scale quite unheard of at that time. By June 1909 a hundred cars a day were being made. More than 100,000 were made in 1913, 300,000 in 1914, and in 1922, when the Model T was becoming outdated, yearly production

1911 Sears high-wheel motor buggy.

Harrah's Automobile Collection

1917 Ford Model T coupé. The previous autumn the famous brass radiator had been abandoned as a war-time economy measure and all subsequent Model Ts bore black-painted radiator shells as seen here.

Ford Motor Company

passed the million mark. When it was finally replaced in 1927 more than fifteen million had been turned out. Because of this mass production, Ford was able to reduce the price from the original $850 to an all-time low of $260 (£52) in 1925. Despite these reductions he was also able to *raise* the daily wage rates in 1914 from the industrial average of $2.40 (9s. 6d.) to $5.00 (£1). It is a cliché to say that the Model T put the world on wheels, but it undoubtedly spread the motor car in seven years to a phenomenal extent. In 1908 there were 458,000 cars registered in America, but by 1915 the figure had reached 2,332,000. Fords were made in England from 1911, and in 1919 it was calculated that two out of every five vehicles on British roads were Fords. Other firms soon saw that the only way to bring their prices down to Ford levels was to go in for mass production too. Annual sales of Chevrolet's '490' reached 126,000 in 1917, and nearly half a million in 1923. In 1928 Chevrolet sales overtook those of Ford, and it has remained in the lead of world car sales for almost every year since.

The impact of mass production was not felt immediately in Europe, but after the First World War there were a large number of motor-minded men who would leap at the chance of becoming car owners if a car were available at a low enough price. At first numerous cyclecars appeared to satisfy this demand. They had 2-cylinder engines of motor-cycle type, final drive by chain or belt rather than by shaft, and minimal weather protection. The breed had appeared first before the outbreak of war, and up to about 1923 hundreds of small firms in England, France and Germany sold cyclecars to those who could afford nothing better. However, three European manufacturers had learnt Henry Ford's lesson: William Morris, Herbert Austin and André Citroën. Morris introduced his Cowley in 1915, and for the first year and a half after the war sales were quite encouraging. Then, towards the end of 1920, there came a slump in the British motor industry which hit sales badly. In February 1921 Morris decided to cut the price of his Cowley touring car by £100 ($500) and was rewarded by a leap in sales to the pre-slump figures within one month. Over the next two years Morris led the industry in price cuts, and by 1925 the car which had cost £525 ($2,625) in 1920 cost only £195 ($975). The result was that in that year Morris sold 54,151 cars, or 41 per cent of all British car production. Herbert Austin's Seven, the famous 'Baby Austin', appeared in 1922; with a wheelbase of only 78 inches, and engine of 698 cc and 10 hp, it was no larger than a cyclecar, but it had four cylinders and shaft drive, was much better made and more reliable. Within a year Austin was selling two hundred a week, and drove the cyclecar makers out of business almost overnight. A similar success was achieved in France by André Citroën, whose famous 5 CV with 856-cc engine and three-seater clover-leaf body appeared in 1922. Two years later daily production of all Citroëns was 250, while in 1925 the first cheap all-steel sedan bodies to be made in Europe came from the Citroën factory, made under American Budd patents. Europe was gradually taking to the automobile, but not on a scale comparable to America. The factory car park filled with workers' cars was not to be seen in Europe until a decade after the Second World War, when the mixed blessing of a truly motorized society became a reality on both sides of the Atlantic.

It has been said that the first decade of the motor car was devoted to making it run, and the second to making it run well. The 1920s saw a consolidation in which the

The famous Bullnose Morris Cowley. This is a 1924 tourer owned by the National Motor Museum at Beaulieu.

G. N. Georgano

1923 Citroën 5 CV, showing the clover-leaf arrangement of the three seats. S. A. André Citroën

The ultimate in pre-war sports cars—the Alfa-Romeo 8C-2900B, which had a top speed of 140 mph with rear-axle ratio of 4.16 : 1.

34

*The car that set the fashion for the mid-engined GT coupé—
the Lamborghini Miura P.400.*

Carrozzeria Bertone S.A.S.

cheap car became reliable as well, while for those who could afford them, the expensive cars were as luxurious and magnificent as anything that has been seen since. The Depression dealt a blow to the hand-built car from which it has never recovered, yet some of the finest machines were made during this sad era. The Rolls-Royce Phantom II, Hispano-Suiza V-12, and Duesenberg Model J all flourished during the years 1929 to 1935, all magnificent survivors from the booming 1920s. The Duesenberg cost up to $20,000 (£4,000) but for this one received a four-passenger car which could do 116 mph, and even more in supercharged form. By 1937 it was possible to buy a sports car (the Alfa Romeo 8C-2900B) capable of 140 mph, which is attained by only a select handful of cars in 1972. More important than speed to the average motorist were comfort, reliability and ease of driving, all of which improved immeasurably during the inter-war years. Closed cars sales exceeded those of open cars for the first time in 1925 (in the United States), and by 1935 the four-door open touring car had virtually disappeared. Its place was taken by the convertible, a two-door car with wind-up windows making it almost as snug as a sedan. The 1939 Plymouth had a vacuum operated top, while power operation of windows and top became familiar features of many of the more expensive post-war American cars. The spread of syncromesh to popular cars took the terror out of gear-changing, while in 1939 Oldsmobile introduced its Hydramatic Drive, an automatic transmission. This was another feature which became widespread after the war, reaching the popular European cars in the early 1960s.

After the Second World War wage rates in Europe rose well above pre-war levels, enabling far more ordinary men and women to become car owners. At the same time taxation of high incomes rose sharply, and it seemed as if the luxury motor car might disappear. But this has not happened. True, the custom-built limousine is all but extinct, but the dowager has been replaced by the successful young (or would-be young) executive as the typical customer for the higher-priced car. They have created a market for a fast, comfortable closed car to carry two, or at most four, persons. Usually known as GT (Gran Turismo) coupés, the first examples were seen shortly after the war in the new Italian make, Ferrari. Since then many variations on the theme have appeared; the British Aston Martin, Jaguar E-type and Jensen, the Italian Iso Grifo, Maserati and Lamborghini, and the Swiss Monteverdi. In the late 1960s the front-engined GT seemed to be on the way out, with the highest performance cars adopting the mid-engined layout favoured by racing cars in the past decade. Examples of these are the Ferrari Dino, Lamborghini Miura, and the more modestly priced Porsche 914/6.

In earlier days almost every European country attempted manufacture of cars of their own design, but in the smaller countries the trend since 1945 has been towards assembly of well-known products from the major countries. Thus Spain built over 450,000 cars in 1970, but none was of Spanish design; although bearing local names, they were in the main of Fiat, Renault, Simca, Dodge or Morris design. A similar situation prevails in Belgium, Switzerland, Bulgaria, Yugoslavia, South Africa and India, to mention a few of the countries which assemble or build foreign cars under licence. Two countries which have vastly increased their share of world markets are Germany and Japan. In 1939 Ger-

The fastest Wankel-engined car so far built is the Mercedes-Benz C.111, with top speed of 162 mph.
Daimler-Benz A.G.

many came fourth in production, after the United States, Great Britain and France. Their industry was devastated during the war, and up to 1950 production was very restricted. Since then their growth has been phenomenal; led by the Volkswagen, both production and export have forged ahead, and Germany is now in second place behind the United States in car production. In 1970 Volkswagen alone exported more cars than the entire British motor industry. The growth of the Japanese industry is in some ways even more remarkable because before the war Japan had very little tradition of car building. Only 856 passenger cars were turned out in 1939, and production did not reach five figures until 1954 (14,472). In 1970 it was over three million, bringing Japan into third place in world production. In the fields of trucks, buses and motor cycles she leads the world. Japanese car design is still conventional, with front-engined, rear-driven medium-sized sedans in the majority, but the little Honda sports has one of the fastest turning engines of any road car (8,500 rpm, at which speed the 791-cc engine develops 78 bhp), while Mazda now make three models using the Wankel rotary engine.

Although rationalization and mergers have reduced the number of makes of car, there is a far greater variety of design now than thirty years ago. Then practically all cars had front-mounted engines in line with the chassis frame driving the rear wheels. This layout still exists, but in addition we have transverse engines driving the front wheels, rear-mounted engines and horizontally-opposed engines. These are not freak designs, but are found on many mass-produced European cars. American cars are generally more conventional, but the Chevrolet Corvair broke all the rules, with a rear-mounted horizontally-opposed air-cooled engine. A radically new design that has appeared recently is the Wankel engine, a rotary unit with three-faced piston which rotates eccentrically inside a specially designed chamber known as an epitrochoidal housing. Any number of rotors can be combined on the same shaft; the original N.S.U. Spider sports had one rotor, the N.S.U. Ro 80 sedan and Japanese Mazda 110 sports coupé have two, while the experimental Mercedes-Benz C. 111 had three rotors in its original form, and later four. The Wankel engines are very compact and have excellent power/weight ratio, but so far exhaust emission prevents them from being sold in the United States.

Turning to motive powers not yet on sale to the public, the first gas-turbine car appeared in 1950. This was built

Ford of Great Britain's experimental electric car, the Comuta. Ford Motor Company Ltd

by the British Rover company, and an open three-seater reached 152 mph on test. Later Rover gas-turbine cars included an attractive sedan, but none went into production. Turbine cars were also made by Renault, Fiat and Chrysler, who built fifty convertibles in 1963 for evaluation under varying conditions. However, the cost of the engine and a lag in acceleration are serious drawbacks to the gas turbine, and it is more likely to find an application in trucks and buses. Increasing traffic congestion in towns has led to many suggestions for an ultra-small city car; some of the proposed designs have used electric motors. These have the advantages of silence and simplicity of driving and, most of all, freedom from air pollution. But they are slow, with a maximum of about 45 mph, and batteries must be recharged frequently, limiting their range to about forty miles in most cases. Anything like enterprising driving reduces this sharply, so that two or three bursts of acceleration above the normal may mean failure to return to the charging point. Electric cars may be used in towns over short distances as electric delivery vans are already, but unless the anti-pollution lobby becomes powerful enough to overcome the vested interests of the oil industry, the majority of cars will continue to run on gasoline.

Experiments have been made over the years with cars which can take to the air, but so far none has approached production. The designer has to compromise on too many factors, and generally if you get a good aeroplane you get a bad car, and vice versa. Retired U.S. Navy Commander Molt B. Taylor of Longview, Washington, has built several prototypes of his Aerocar, a four-passenger sedan with ground speed of 70 mph, and air speed of 150 mph, and says that he could sell them for $10,000 (£4,100) if enough buyers came along. Another combination vehicle is the amphibious car which has attractions as a weekend machine for those who live near rivers or lakes. An amphibian was made as early as 1918 (the Hydrometer from Seattle, Washington), and many were used during the Second World War, but the first to be sold in any numbers was the German Amphicar, made from 1961 to 1968. It had a four-passenger body, a road speed of 68 mph and a water speed of $6\frac{1}{2}$ knots. It was intended only for inland waters, but in 1962 two Frenchmen were rash enough to cross the English Channel in one. Interesting though these hybrids are, they are unlikely to have much future, if only because increasing affluence means that more and more people will be able to afford a car *and* a boat, and some of them an aeroplane too.

4

Trucks and Trucking, 1875–1972

Apart from isolated experiments in the 1820s, the load-carrying vehicle made a much later appearance than either the traction engine which pulled its load, or the bus which carried passengers. In 1875 the Wiltshire traction engine builders, Brown & May of Devizes, built a steam van capable of carrying 4 tons; it had a vertical boiler working at 70 lb. per square inch, and final drive by chain to a differential in the centre of a live rear axle. Despite this advanced specification, it had no successor. The traction engine was often too heavy to negotiate the loose, soft-surfaced roads of the time, and if one added several tons of load to the overall weight the problem simply became worse. Thus the first vans and trucks to be used commercially were not descendants of the traction engine, but were much lighter machines, powered by internal combustion, or oil-fired steam engines.

In 1892 Maurice Le Blant built a number of steam vans for the Paris store, La Belle Jardinière, which were the first goods-carrying vehicles to be sold for commercial use. They had Serpollet boilers and 3-cylinder engines. Like many contemporary steam vehicles they needed a 'chauffeur' or stoker as well as a driver who steered; engine, boiler and chauffeur took up more than half the interior body space. Nevertheless they ran well and saw service for several years. Their use encouraged rival stores such as the Galeries Lafayette and Grands Magasins du Louvre to try the new machines which made such excellent publicity even if they were no faster, and probably less reliable, than horse-drawn vans. By 1896 there were quite a number of these vans running in Paris, the most popular builders being de Dion Bouton for steamers, Panhard and Peugeot for gasoline and Jeantaud for electric vans.

In England goods vehicles were slow to appear, and when they did it was not Bond Street and Piccadilly that first saw them, but the cobbled streets of industrial Lancashire. In 1897 the Royal Agricultural Society

Moving house at the turn of the century. A Foden overtype steam wagon with two trailers which had been built for use with horses. Arthur Ingram Collection

offered two prizes of £100 ($500) for self-propelled vehicles to carry up to 4 tons. Only one claimant put in an appearance at the trials, built by the Lancashire Steam Motor Company, of Leyland. This ancestor of the vast British Leyland empire of today did not distinguish itself, retiring after 30 miles. No prize was awarded. At the Liverpool trials in 1898 three machines took part, a Leyland and two vehicles from the south of England, a Lifu from the Isle of Wight and a London-built Thornycroft. The latter was interesting because it was an articulated six-wheeler, a four-wheeled tractor pulling a two-wheeled trailer. This was seen as the only means by which the 1,150 sq. ft platform space demanded by the 5-ton class could be achieved. Although it had no immediate successor, the articulated system has since become universal for really large loads. It gained a Premier Award in the Liverpool Trials. Meanwhile, Thornycroft had made their first commercial sale, of two dustcarts to Chiswick Vestry, and Leyland followed this up by selling a steam wagon to a Somerset wool merchant. Experience with this led Leyland to turn to coal rather than oil for fuel, and from then onwards nearly all British steam wagons used solid fuel, coal or coke.

Steam-wagon design soon diverged into two main classes, which could be distinguished by the most casual observer. The early machines just described were undertypes, with engine mounted on the chassis frame, and usually having a vertical boiler either in front of, or behind, the driver. Both the first and the last steam wagons were undertypes, but in the intermediate years there were large numbers of overtypes. These had horizontal locomotive-type boilers with the engine mounted above them, driving by a long chain to the rear axle. They had the appearance of traction engines with a load-carrying space behind, and generally there was less space than on the undertypes. However, the overtype had the advantage of being a proven design, as well as giving better accessibility to the engine. It was more reliable in the early days, and lasted in production until 1927. The most famous maker of overtypes was Foden, but other well-known firms included Aveling & Porter, Burrell, Clayton and Foster. Like the traction engines, the earlier steam wagons were shod with steel tires, solid rubber coming in during the decade up to 1914, and pneumatics during the late 1920s. Rubber tires posed a curious problem, that of the build-up of a high charge of static electricity, caused by steam escaping at high pressure. As the tires insulated the wagon from the ground, this could give the driver a nasty shock. The solution was to trail a short length of chain from the wagon to the road, thus

Undertype steam wagon—this 1900 3-ton Thornycroft was the twentieth wagon to be made by the company.
Transport Equipment (Thornycroft) Ltd

*One of the earliest delivery vans built in Britain was this
2-cylinder Daimler of about 1898.*

The Veteran Car Club of Great Britain

*Unlike the Daimler van, which used a passenger car chassis,
this 1899 Panhard et Levassor is a proper truck with
forward control and a really useful carrying capacity.*

S. A. André Citroën

conducting the charge safely to earth. Most steamers
carried enough fuel for a journey of 50 or more miles,
but water was a more serious problem. However, every
driver made it his business to know where water could be
found on his route, from horse-troughs, ponds and half-
hidden streams. R. W. Kidner * remarks that as late as
1930 one could see the steam wagons coming in from
Kent queuing up to get their last fill before London at a
shallow stream on the Eltham bypass.

If these paragraphs seem to be over-British in content,
it is only because the steam lorry was itself a largely
British phenomenon. France pursued the steam bus with
some enthusiasm, but apart from the undertype wagons
built by Valentin Purrey of Bordeaux (later H. Exshaw et
Compagnie) the French steam lorry was virtually non-
existent. Even fewer were made in Belgium, Germany or
Switzerland and, so far as is known, none in Italy.

* *The Steam Lorry, 1896–1939.* Oakwood Press, 1946.

America had perhaps a dozen small makers, but their products were never a significant part of the transportation scene: this in contrast to the steam car picture, where America had over fifty makes, and England fewer than a dozen.

The internal combustion-engined truck developed logically from the passenger car from 1896 onward. Such well-known firms as Daimler in England, Panhard and Peugeot in France, Cannstatt-Daimler and N.A.G. in Germany, were all selling goods vehicles in fair numbers by 1900. The earliest examples were simply passenger car chassis with a box-van or platform body in place of the rear seats, but by 1900 the wheelbase had been lengthened to make a genuine goods-carrying chassis.

By 1914 an enormous variety of motor vans and trucks was available in all industrialized countries. Their carrying capacities ranged from a few hundredweight to, in some cases, 10 tons, although 5 tons was the normal limit. On the whole they did not engage in long-distance haulage, which was still the preserve of the railroads at this time. When really heavy indivisible loads had to be hauled, this was done by the traction engine. Apart from local delivery from shop to home the greatest value of the motor truck before 1914 was to act as a feeder to the railheads. These services were often operated by the railroads themselves, a condition being that only goods destined for further carriage by rail would be handled. Distances covered by these feeder trucks were seldom more than 30 miles in Europe, but they brought inaccessible valleys and remote fishing villages into the orbit of railroad services. In the same manner, motor trucks toured the farms, collecting eggs and other produce, and taking them to a distribution centre in the nearest town. This medium-distance haulage of fresh fruit and vegetables changed America's eating habits, providing more fresh meat, vegetables and milk at the expense of sauer-

One of the more ingenious conversions of the Model T Ford. The tractor is a chain-drive conversion known as the Form-a-Truck, and attached to it is one of the earliest Fruehauf trailers. The tractor dates from 1911, the trailer from 1914. Owned by the Henry Ford Museum, Dearborn, Michigan

The Pierce-Arrow was one of the better-known American trucks used in Europe during the First World War.

Arthur Ingram Collection

kraut and cured ham. The railroads were all right for long-distance haulage, and horses could look after town deliveries, but only the motor truck could visit a large number of outlying farms within a radius of 30 miles or more, and bring the produce to market the same day. Apart from general transportation, trucks were used in road construction, and in the arduous logging industry of the north-western states of America from about 1913 onwards.

In 1911 the British War Office announced that motor trucks were to replace horses on a large scale in the British Army. This decision led to the subvention or subsidy scheme, whereby owners of suitable vehicles were paid an annual sum of money in return for purchasing and maintaining them. This scheme not only provided the Army with a fleet of transportation available in time of war, but also encouraged the spread of motor vehicles. A small tradesman or carrier debating the outlay of £500 ($2,500) on a truck would be tempted by the thought of an annual subsidy of £110 ($550). When war did break out in August 1914 the War Office was able to assemble immediately over 1,200 well-maintained trucks. Similar schemes operated in France, Germany and Austria. America supplied large numbers of basically similar trucks by Pierce-Arrow and other makers to the British and French armies. In 1917, the year that America entered the war, production began of a standardized vehicle, the U.S. Standard Military Truck, generally known as the Liberty truck. Another widespread truck was the Model AC Mack with radiator behind engine, introduced in 1915. It was christened 'Bulldog' by the

American troops in France because of its aggressive and rugged appearance, and this name remained with it after the war.

On active service the 3-tonners (Class B) were the most widely used trucks in all armies. As in civilian life they conveyed food, ammunition and other materials from the railheads to the front lines. They also supplemented the buses in carrying troops. Specialized bodywork carried mobile workshops, radio and photographic vans, water tankers and anti-aircraft guns. The needs of all the warring nations were much the same, but Germany built a large number of artillery tractors, whereas Britain and the United States tended to use ordinary trucks to pull their heavy guns. The German tractors were enormous machines, some with rear wheels over 8 feet in diameter, and a number used four-wheel drive. This system, so widespread in the Second World War, was employed by two American trucks, the F.W.D. and the Jeffrey/Nash Quad.

The end of the war meant that an enormous number of trucks of all kinds became surplus to requirements, and available to the civilian user. In England Government Motor Sales were held throughout 1919, and thousands of War Department trucks, cars and motor cycles were sold to the public.

The decade after the Armistice saw vast improvements in goods vehicle design, and by 1930 long-distance road haulage was beginning to play an important part in

F.W.D. B-type four-wheel-drive truck 'somewhere in France' during the First World War.

B. H. Vanderveen Collection

The famous Mack Model AC or 'Bulldog'. This articulated unit dates from about 1930. Note the solid tires on the driving axle, although at the front and on the trailer pneumatics are worn. Arthur Ingram Collection

the economies of industrialized countries. Carrying capacity was increased from 5 tons to 12 tons or more, thanks to more powerful engines and greater platform area. The wheelbase of a two-axle truck could not be extended indefinitely, and the answer was either to increase the number of axles on a rigid chassis, or to built an articulated truck with trailer attached to a turntable. This had been seen on the 1898 Thornycroft, but the first firm to establish the system was the newly formed British manufacturer, Scammell. Using tractors powered by 47-hp 4-cylinder engines, the first articulated Scammell of 1920 was quite capable of handling a 7½-ton load, which represented a 50 per cent increase in capacity for the same size engine as the standard 5-tonners had used. In 1924 Scammell built their first frameless tanker, another articulated vehicle in which the tank was self-supporting, requiring no separate chassis. These frameless tankers were widely used for the transport of gasoline, milk, molasses and many other liquids. Scammell also built three-axle trucks on a rigid chassis, but the

pioneer work on this layout was done by the Goodyear Tire & Rubber Company of Akron, Ohio. Up to 1920 all heavy trucks ran on solid rubber tires, and, to prove that pneumatics were equally suitable, Goodyear built several six-wheel trucks in which the four rear wheels transmitted power. Goodyear built seven or eight of these trucks between 1918 and 1920, as well as some buses with three and even four axles. One of their trucks made a coast-to-coast run, 3,507 miles in 12 days 14½ hours. The actual running time was 6 days 15½ hours, during which time the engine turned 3,113,156 times. Goodyear did not build trucks for sale, but within a few years rigid six-wheelers with one or two axles driven were being built by Mack, Safeway, White and other truck and bus makers.

In 1926 the U.S. Quartermaster Corps built a modified Liberty 1½-ton truck in which the front axle drove as well as the rear pair. This layout became known for convenience as the 6 × 6, as opposed to the 6 × 4 in which only the rear axles drove. Both were widely used during the Second World War. In Europe the popularity of the

A striking example of multiple trailer operation in America;
the Canadian Kenworth 6 × 4 tractor is pulling a two-
axle semi-trailer followed by two four-axle full trailers.
Williams Air Controls Divn: Omark Industries

An unusual example of rigid eight-wheeler used in conjunction with a two-axle semi-trailer; A.E.C. Mammoth
Major at work in New Zealand. A.E.C. Ltd

three-axle layout spread also, sometimes in a 6 × 4 arrangement, sometimes a 6 × 2, in which the rear axle was simply a non-powered extra support for the chassis. After the Second World War some of these trailing axles were made so that when the truck was empty they could be lifted completely clear of the ground. In 1929 the British steam wagon builders, Sentinel, introduced a rigid eight-wheeler, with twin axles at front as well as rear, and a capacity of 15 tons. By 1939 most British heavy vehicle builders offered a rigid eight in their range, although the design never caught on in other countries. Their popularity survived until the 1960s and, at the time of writing, several makes, including A.E.C., Atkinson, Leyland and Scammell, are still offering rigid eights, now with a capacity of 22 tons. All the rigid eights had forward control, generally known in America as cab-over-engine. In this layout the driver and his mate sit on each side of the engine, which is situated partly, or entirely, inside the cab. This arrangement clearly allows a greater load-carrying space, without an extension of wheelbase, and was increasingly favoured by British manufacturers of larger trucks. In Europe and America the 'normal control' or bonneted layout lasted for many years longer, and still prevails in hot climates where an engine inside the cab would prove exceedingly uncomfortable.

One of the most important developments of the inter-war years was the introduction of the compression-ignition, or diesel, engine. At the 1924 Berlin Motor Show three firms, Daimler, M.A.N. and Benz, exhibited varying designs of compression-ignition oil engines. The 50-hp 4-cylinder M.A.N. engine was the first to go into everyday use in a truck, followed by the 30-hp 2-cylinder Benz unit. During the early 1930s well-known British firms such as Crossley, A.E.C. and Leyland turned to the oil engine, which also attracted firms such as Foden and Fowler who had made only steam wagons up to that time. The steamer was fast losing popularity, for the oil engine had the same advantages of cheap fuel and aptitude for heavy work, combined with much simpler operation and maintenance. In America, land of cheap gasoline, the oil engine did not find favour until many years later. In 1938 Dodge and International Harvester offered diesel engines as options on some of their trucks, and since the war more and more American truck builders have included diesel engines in their ranges.

We have seen that during the first twenty years of its life the motor truck was confined to relatively short-distance work, acting as an adjunct to the railroad network. During the inter-war years it gradually became a rival, even over the longest-distance routes. Speeds were rising, and although never as fast as the railroads the trucks had

The first oil-engined rigid eight-wheeler to be built in Britain, the A.E.C. Mammoth Major was introduced in 1934. A.E.C. Ltd

the advantage of door-to-door service, and were always cheaper. In Britain firms such as Pickfords and Fisher Renwick began to operate regular services three times weekly, and then daily, from London to Cardiff, Plymouth, Manchester, Edinburgh and other centres. In France a regular van service was inaugurated in 1930 between Paris and Marseilles, using Bernard trucks. A Bernard advertisement claimed that peasants no longer looked to the sun to tell the time, they waited for the Bernard van. In Germany the growth of the *autobahn* system in the 1930s encouraged enormous road trains consisting of a two-axle truck pulling one or two two- or sometimes three-axle trailers. Capacity of such a train could be as high as 30 tons, and speeds were 40 to 50 mph. In America the time for a transcontinental truck journey shrank from forty-six days for a Packard in 1912 to five days for a G.M.C. in 1931. Such men as E. G. 'Cannonball' Baker who had broken long-distance records in passenger cars were employed to make high-speed truck journeys too.

The Second World War saw motor vehicles used to a far greater extent than in its predecessor of 1914 to 1918. Probably the most important influences of the war on vehicle design were in the field of all-wheel-drive, and of the general purpose light vehicle which became known as the Jeep. The first 6 × 6 truck was built by the U.S. Quartermaster Corps in 1926, but it was not until the Second World War that many such trucks were made. They varied in size from 1½ tons to 8 tons, although 12-

tonners were used as tractors. Although 8 tons does not seem a particularly large capacity by civilian standards, these 6 × 6 trucks, chiefly made by Mack, Federal and Reo, had to be very powerful to cope with poor surfaces, cross-country work and gradients of up to one in three. The largest had 6-cylinder engines of 895 cu. in. displacement (14·7 litres).

The first of the line of vehicles which became known as Jeeps was built by the Bantam Car Company of Butler, Pennsylvania, although the great majority of the 639,245 made up to 1945 came from the factories of Willys and Ford. The Jeep was officially called a 'quarter-ton Command Reconnaissance Vehicle' to carry personnel and light cargo, and to tow a 37-mm gun. An open four-seater, or two-seater with cargo space, with short wheelbase and four-wheel-drive, it found innumerable uses during the war, and is still in production today. What is more, it inspired imitators in other countries; over the past twenty-five years Jeep-type vehicles, sometimes heavier and more sophisticated, have been built by twenty manufacturers in Great Britain, France, Italy, Germany, the Soviet Union, Brazil and Japan. The Jeep was also produced in amphibious form, being one of the first vehicles to operate successfully on land and water. Other, larger, amphibious vehicles were also built, such as the American DUKW on a 6 × 6 G.M.C. truck chassis, and the British Terrapin, an 8 × 8 5-tonner powered by two Ford V-8 engines.

With the end of hostilities in 1945 the world began to pick up the pieces and restore road transport services to normal. As in 1919, the thousands of ex-Army trucks performed invaluable service, especially in Europe where U.S. Army Dodges, Internationals, F.W.D.s and Macks were the mainstay of many truck operators until they could buy new vehicles again. Changes in truck design since the war have been gradual rather than spectacular, and probably the greatest strides have been made in overall capacity of two-, three- and four-axle trucks, and in driver comfort. In most countries gross vehicle weight loadings on a given number of axles have been raised, so that whereas a typical two-axle truck of 1945 had a capacity of 6 tons, the figure in 1972 is more like 9 or 10 tons. The four-axle rigid eight has remained an almost exclusively British preserve, and even there is now beginning to lose ground to the articulated eight-wheeler. The articulated vehicle has several advantages which have led to its increasing adoption all over the world; a higher loading per axle is allowed in some countries, it is more flexible in operation since one tractor can be used with different trailers, and for its size it is more manœuvrable than a rigid chassis. Up to the early 1950s the usual layout

was a two-axle tractor and single-axle trailer; now two-axle trailers are much more common, and larger combinations are frequently seen, such as a three-axle tractor and two- or three-axle trailer. Sometimes the third axle on the trailer is self-tracking. In many parts of the world, though not in Great Britain, there are road trains with one or two full trailers behind an articulated trailer. An extreme example of this is an American Diamond T unit with a total of forty-two wheels on eleven axles. For a rigid chassis the record is held by another American truck, the Oshkosh Model D-3466 which has six axles and drives on five of them. Its gross vehicle weight is 100,000 lb. or over 44 tons. For really large loads which have to be taken by road, a low-loading multi-wheeled trailer is used, towed by two or three specially designed tractors. In this way loads of up to 300 tons may be carried.

The comfort of the truck driver and his crew has improved greatly over the past twenty-five years. Cabs are much more accessible, and on not so many does the driver have to clamber over the front wheel to reach the door. Heating and air-conditioning are luxuries no longer confined to the passenger car, while long-distance trucks have comfortable sleeper cabs with points for electric razors.

The growth of international truck traffic has been very marked since the end of the Second World War, and especially in the past ten years. National frontiers in Europe have been crossed for some time, but the Channel formed a more effective barrier. Now it is by no means rare to see European trucks in England, not only from Western Europe, but from as far afield as Hungary and Turkey. Sometimes a trailer alone is shipped across, being hauled to its destination by a British tractor. When complete vehicles are not shipped, the bulk container is frequently used. Trucks designed to handle containers work in conjunction with container trains running from Europort at Rotterdam to Frankfurt, Mannheim and other German cities. Another post-war trend has been the spread of bulk transport trucks, especially tankers. Whereas previously milk and beer had been carried in churns or barrels, now they are carried in tankers of up to 4,000 gallons, and delivered to bulk storage units. This principle has been extended to powders and grains, and trucks are specially built for carrying flour, cement and so on in tanker bodies.

Mechanically the truck has not undergone dramatic change. Except in tropical climates the cab-over-engine layout has become almost universal, and the diesel engine has spread more widely than ever. British units, especially Perkins, are available in a number of American

Still known as the Mammoth Major, this is A.E.C.'s current rigid eight-wheeler. A.E.C. Ltd

Mack Model NO 7½-ton six-wheel-drive truck for the U.S. Army, Second World War

B. H. Vanderveen Collection

A 'road train' used for the long-distance transportation of cattle in Australia. The truck is an export model A.E.C. with normal control; all A.E.C.s for the domestic market have forward control. A.E.C. Ltd

A real multi-wheeler, this G.M.C. Diesel has eleven axles and twenty-two wheels. General Motors Corp.

truck chassis, and conversely the powerful American Cummins oil engines are found in British chassis such as Atkinson, E.R.F. and Scammell. The gas turbine has fascinated truck designers for some time. An experimental turbine chassis appeared at the Paris Motor Show as long ago as 1951, while a turbine-powered Kenworth truck was running in the United States in the mid 1950s. In the last decade Chevrolet and Ford have built experimental turbine articulated trucks, but the first to go into production is likely to be the Leyland GT. This is a 6 × 4 tractor designed for trailers of 38 tons gross train weight. The turbine develops 400 hp for a unit weighing under 1,000 lb., or half the weight of a comparably powerful conventional engine. With a total weight of 38 tons, a speed of 70 mph should be possible. Clearly the greatest advantage of such a truck would be on straight long-distance routes in the United States, Australia and South Africa, but with the growth of motorway systems everywhere the gas turbine truck should find enough applications to sell two thousand to three thousand units per year.

5

Buses and Streetcars

After the disappearance of the Hancock and Gurney steam buses of the 1830s passenger transport on roads was left entirely to the horse for some sixty years. Alongside the horse buses, many cities installed horse-drawn tramway systems, and it was these that were mechanized before the ordinary bus. Britain's first steam tram was built in 1873 by Merryweather of Greenwich, underwent trials in London's Vauxhall Bridge Road, and in 1876 went into service on the Wantage tramway in Berkshire, where a steam tram was operated until 1925. This was a self-contained unit, but a number of early operators preferred a steam tractor with separate trailer, on the same principle as Gurney's drags. By 1890 many steam tramways had been opened in industrial England, and there were a few services in London and rural districts. No more than one trailer was allowed in Britain, but this rule did not apply on the Continent where many systems opened using two or more trailers. In northern France and Belgium these were extended from town to town, forming a light railway system. Apart from steam, compressed air was used as a motive power; Paris had over two hundred double-decker trams powered by the Mekarski compressed air system, and some of these survived until 1914. For steep gradients trams were unsatisfactory because they could not obtain sufficient grip; the obvious answer to this was the cable-car, where the vehicle is hauled up the incline by an endless rope wound round pulleys at either end of the track. Power for the pulleys came originally from a steam engine, later from electricity. Cable-cars were first used by Andrew Hallidee on Clay Street, San Francisco, in August 1873, and were soon adopted in Philadelphia, Washington, New York, Chicago and other American cities. Chicago had the most extensive cable-car network in the world, but there were two services in London, and a big system in Edinburgh. They were also used in Melbourne and Sydney, the former surviving until 1940. San Francisco still preserves

Metropolitan Electric Tramways Car No. 279, Class H, built 1909–12 period, seen at Enfield, Middlesex.

Arthur Ingram Collection

49

A.E.C. three-axle trolleybus of the type familiarly known as the Diddler. First introduced in May 1931, these vehicles were not withdrawn until after the war. The one illustrated was scrapped in September 1948.

Arthur Ingram Collection

its famous cable-cars, and they are found on a number of short Swiss mountain routes such as that between Treib on Lake Lucerne and Seelisberg, where the gradient is over 45 degrees.

Most people associate the tram with electricity, and certainly the majority of tramways throughout the world have used this motive power. The first electric tram ran in Berlin over a 1½-mile route, using the rails as conductors of current. This was clearly very dangerous, and if an alternative had not been found the system would have had to be abandoned. Various methods of overhead delivery were tried, including a trolley, two wheels running along an overhead wire, connected to motors in

the car by flexible wires. The familiar trolley pole was introduced by an American, Frank Julian Sprague, and used in Richmond, Virginia, in 1888. Five years before this Magnus Volk had built a light electric tramway along the front at Brighton, which still runs. During the period 1890–1900 electric tramway systems spread across America and Europe with lightning speed. By the end of the century America had 75,000 miles of urban tramway which were soon extended to a considerable network of inter-urbans. On these services, which reached their peak mileage in 1916, speeds of up to 80 mph were sometimes achieved. Urban electric tramways came to Britain in 1891 (Leeds), and France in 1896 (Paris), while

50

1933 A.E.C. three-axle trolleybus with experimental centre-entrance body, seating 74 passengers. This was the first London trolleybus to use the full-width cab, in contrast to the motor-bus-type half-cab of the Diddlers.
Arthur Ingram Collection

by 1900 most European countries had at least one tramway system, and they were also found in Australia, South Africa and Argentina. They rapidly replaced the steam trams, just as their rivals the motor buses replaced horses. In Britain the trams were mostly double-deckers, the lighter vehicle running on four wheels, with two four-wheeled bogies for the heavier. Trailers were rare in Britain, although widely used in the United States, where most trams were single-deckers.

After the end of the war in 1918 the tramways began to feel the challenge of the motor bus and trolleybus. Tramway mileage reached its peak in Britain in 1924, Paris in 1925 and America in 1926, after which a decline set in.

The last Paris tram ran in 1938, while the London system carried on until 1952. Before the Second World War no fewer than forty-three municipalities in Britain still ran trams, but all had gone by 1961. American cities were abandoning their streetcars too, but on the continent of Europe the tram is by no means dead even now. Single-decker cars, often articulated, are in wide use in German cities such as Stuttgart, Frankfurt and Düsseldorf, often running out into the country to form inter-urban services on the lines of the American routes of the early 1900s. In Switzerland the Locarno–Domodossola tramway not only becomes a mountain-climbing inter-urban but crosses the frontier into Italy in the course of its 35-mile

51

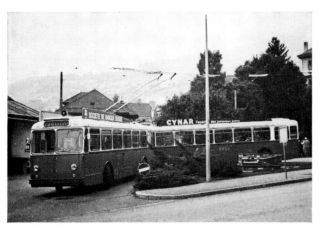

Swiss articulated trolleybus, seen at the lakeside terminus of the Vevey-Mont Pélerin funicular railway.

G. N. Georgano

journey. Other cities employing trams of modern design include Copenhagen, Brussels, Moscow and Tokyo.

Before turning to the motor bus it is worth looking briefly at that hybrid vehicle, the trolleybus. In 1882 Dr Wernher von Siemens designed a railless electric vehicle drawing current from overhead wires, and the first trolleybus service began in 1901 at Bielethal in Saxony. By 1914 some eleven German towns had tried the trolleybus, some only to abandon it within a few years, while the first British service began at Leeds in June 1911. The 1920s saw the greatest expansion of trolleybus routes, which generally, though not always, replaced existing tram routes. London was late in turning to the trolleybus, where it did not arrive until May 1931. When the trams

One of the first motor buses to operate a regular service in London; a German-built Daimler on Westminster Bridge, 1899. The Veteran Car Club of Great Britain

finally disappeared from London in 1952, London Transport ordered a new fleet of trolleys. However, ten years later these too had gone, and Britain's last trolleybus system, at Bradford, was replaced by diesel buses in February 1972. Several factors have contributed to this decline. The inflexibility of the trolleybus has become increasingly awkward where one-way traffic schemes are introduced, while the cost both of overhead equipment and of electricity has grown very rapidly. Some undertakings made considerable use of former tramway overhead equipment and sub-stations, but these gradually wore out, and the cost of replacement was prohibitive. On the Continent a number of advanced trolleybuses have been built. In Switzerland three manu-

facturers have combined to produce a standard articulated vehicle with three axles, the centre and rear axles each being driven by a 140-hp motor. As in many continental buses, there is far more room for standing (107) than for seated passengers (30). Articulated trolleybuses are also in use in Vienna and Moscow.

The motor bus, relying neither on rails nor on overhead wires, is obviously the most flexible and attractive form of passenger transport, but for some time was not a serious rival to the tram because low power limited its carrying capacity. Between 1889 and 1899 a number of experimental buses powered by gasoline, steam and electricity were tried in London, but none operated a regular service. The honour for that achievement is due to two German-

1905 Milnes-Daimler double-decker bus operated in London by Birch Brothers Ltd. From 1904 to 1906 there were more Milnes-Daimlers running in London than any other make of bus.

The Veteran Car Club of Great Britain

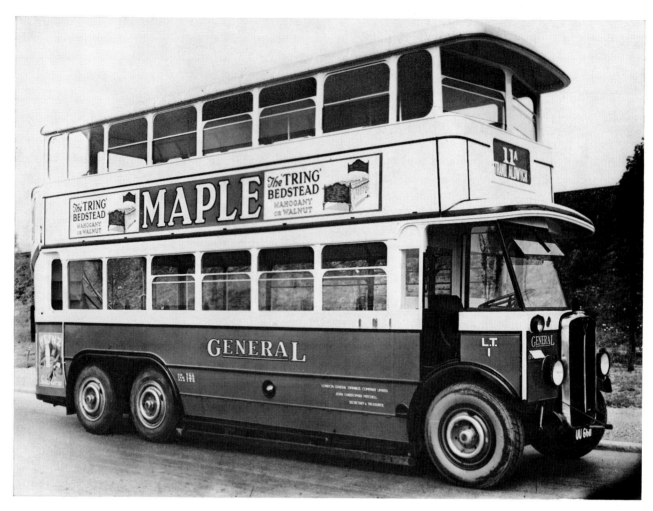

The first of the LT class of A.E.C. double-decker bus built for London Transport in 1929. Although the top was enclosed the stairs were still open to the elements.

A.E.C. Ltd

built Daimlers with twenty-six seater horse-bus bodies which ran from Kennington to Victoria station (later to Oxford Circus) between October 1899 and December 1900.

Between 1905 and 1914 the use of motor buses increased dramatically all over the world. In the former year London had only twenty buses working, while by the outbreak of war the figure was over 2,500. In November 1910 motor buses outnumbered horse buses for the first time, and in 1914 the last horse bus ran in London. A wide variety of makes were used in London in the early days, but the most celebrated was the B-type built from 1910 to 1920. Like many successful designs it was a conventional machine with 30-hp 4-cylinder gasoline engine, shaft drive and an open-top double-decker body seating thirty-four passengers. Over 2,900 were made, of which

more than a thousand went to France with the B.E.F. in 1914. Many continued to run in Flanders mud carrying their route cards 'Piccadilly–Strand–Bank', and advertisement boards announcing the latest revue at the Empire Theatre.

It was not only in the capital cities that buses were seen. The first recorded excursion by charabanc, as the early pleasure buses were called, ran from London to Clacton in 1898. By 1905 many holiday centres were featuring excursions by charabanc; the English Lake District, where they were not deterred by steep hills, Interlaken in Switzerland, the Black Forest in Germany and the French watering resorts of Annecy and Aix-les-Bains. The early charabancs were steeply banked to the rear, as in a cinema or theatre, and as they had no gangways this called for mountaineering abilities from the rear-seat passengers. On steep hills the conductor or guide would walk behind with a large chock to slip behind a rear wheel if necessary, and sometimes the male passengers would have to get out and walk too. Local bus services often carried mail or goods as well as passengers; milk churns in particular were often carried from outlying villages to the nearest station by bus. In Germany, Austria and Switzerland the Post Offices still operate passenger services, carrying sacks of letters in the back of the bus. In Britain the railroad companies often ran local bus services, and in some cases, such as that of the Great Northern Railway, built their own buses. Because trains were infinitely faster and more comfortable, there were few town-to-town bus services before 1914.

The decade 1920 to 1930 saw vast improvements both in bus design and extent of routes. Pre-war buses had generally been built on truck chassis, which necessitated several steps up to the platform. During the 1920s the purpose-built bus chassis appeared with lowered frame, so that one step sufficed to enter the vehicle. This not only made things easier for the elderly, but improved appearance and lowered the centre of gravity. Two developments in the truck field which spread to the bus were the cab-over-engine layout and the three-axle chassis. As with trucks, Europe took to the cab-over-engine before America, and British manufacturers made a speciality of the half-cab in which the driver sat alone in a small cab to the offside of the engine. This remained a characteristic of British buses and coaches up to the 1950s, and the majority of London buses still have half-cabs.

Probably the greatest strides were made in the rural and long-distance buses of the period. In America in particular, rural bus operators grew in number from only a handful before 1914 to 6,500 in 1925. Admittedly most of these were small operators owning not more than two buses each, but it was the beginning of a network in which amalgamations led to a number of famous lines. In 1929 Pickwick Stage Lines of Los Angeles and Pioneer Yelloway Systems merged with the bus section of the Southern Pacific Railroad to form Pacific Greyhound Lines. Between California and the Mississippi the company was known as Pickwick-Greyhound Lines, and further mergers meant that by 1930 nearly every state was served by coaches bearing the name Greyhound. In 1928 the Pickwick company built a sleeper coach with toilet, bar and kitchen, and was operating a coast-to-coast service. Sleeper coaches were tried out in England too. Land Liners Ltd ran a London–Manchester service by three-axle double-decker Guy buses, with seats convertible to bunks for thirty-one passengers. They were slower and less comfortable than the trains, and the service was soon discontinued. For medium-distance journeys, however, the coach was an attractive proposition, and by 1930 had reached a level of comfort and service not improved on since. The London–Bristol coaches had a small buffet for the preparation of light meals, which were served on folding tables as in a modern airliner. Each seat was provided with a bell to summon the steward, and the coaches carried a clock, barometer, cigarette cabinet and flower vases.

Apart from the regular town-to-town services, the excursion coach improved immeasurably between the wars. In 1919 open charabancs began to flood the roads of Europe, often owned and driven by ex-service men who sank their gratuities into the purchase of two or three second-hand chassis. The bodies which were mounted on these were not a great improvement on those of the early charabancs of pre-war days. They seated more passengers, but they seldom gave any protection from the weather, and were entered by rows of doors along the side. With solid tires they offered little in the way of comfort or speed, but they did take the working man away from his immediate surroundings for the day, and at a price that he could afford. From the East End of London, and from other industrial cities, on Bank holidays the 'charras' poured out to the country and the seaside. It was not only the townsman who enjoyed the new-found mobility; for the poorer people of an inland

'Off to the seaside'; a Tilling-Stevens petrol-electric charabanc with full complement of passengers, about 1919.
Arthur Ingram Collection

A long-lived rural bus, this 1936 Ford was photographed thirty years later in the Spanish town of Murcia from which it operated a regular service to the mountain villages near by. G. N. Georgano

A typical British coach of the late 1930s, this Tilling-Stevens illustrates clearly the half-cab favoured by British designers at this period. Duple Coachwork Ltd

village, the church outing by charabanc was often their only opportunity ever to visit the seaside.

By 1925 pneumatic tires and covered bodies appeared; the charabanc became the saloon coach, and excursions of several days' length were offered. The first continental tour from Britain was started in 1920; Chapman of Eastbourne ran a six-day tour of the battlefields of France and Belgium. In 1921 they went to the South of France, and by 1925 tours were available to Holland, Germany and Spain, the last being a twenty-two day excursion which included Gibraltar. Another firm, Motorways of London, ran luxury tours between Calais and the French Riviera, using ex-U.S. Army Whites with armchair seats which could be moved around the car, kitchen and toilet. In 1924 they went to North Africa, while by 1935 their

list of itineraries included Russia. In Germany the growth of the *autobahn* network encouraged rapid coach services operating at speeds unknown elsewhere in the world. By 1938 thirty-seater coaches were averaging 50 mph between cities such as Darmstadt, Munich, Frankfurt and Düsseldorf. These speeds included negotiated city traffic at each end of the journey, so that on the *autobahn* they had to be capable of over 70 mph.

In 1927 a remarkable vehicle was built by the Twin Coach Company of Kent, Ohio. It looked almost identical at front and rear, and its two engines were mounted under the floor, between axles, instead of in front under a bonnet. Driver-operated doors were mounted ahead of the front, and behind the rear, axles. It looked quite revolutionary at the time, but what is more remarkable is that it does not appear particularly old-fashioned today, forty-five years later. The removal of the engine to a side, underfloor, or rear position was slow to establish itself, but has been one of the most fundamental changes in design and appearance of the bus and coach. In 1932 the British A.E.C. company introduced the Q-type single-decker bus with engine at the side, immediately behind the front wheels. Only 250 were made, as well as a handful of double-deckers, and it was not until 1948 that A.E.C. again moved the engine away from the front, this time on the Regal IV underfloor-engined chassis. By 1950 underfloor engines were becoming quite familiar. Some of the most advanced work in England was done by the Birmingham & Midland Motor Omnibus Company, an operating company who have built their own vehicles since 1924. They developed their own diesel engine in 1936, a horizontal underfloor-engined bus and coach in 1941, and chassisless single- and double-deckers in 1953 and 1958. In 1958 the Leyland company introduced an advanced chassis named the Atlantean. This was designed to take double-decker bodies seating seventy-eight passengers, and had a 6-cylinder engine mounted transversely at the rear. The entrance was ahead of the front axle. The appearance of this bus immediately made conventional front-engined double-deckers seem old-fashioned, but the latter are still made,

1935 Büssing streamlined coach for autobahn work.
Neubauer Collection

A typical post-war design of Fageol Twin Coach, seen here at Lucerne, Switzerland. G. N. Georgano

especially for London Transport who have made only limited use of Atlanteans. Rear-engined double-decker chassis are also made by Daimler and Bristol, while rear or underfloor single-deckers are made by a large number of manufacturers throughout the world. Except for small buses for fewer than twenty-five passengers, or certain special vehicles for underdeveloped countries, it seems that the front-engined bus is on the way out.

A striking difference between British and continental practice is that the latter consider seating in urban buses to be of lesser importance. For this reason European buses have higher capacities than any in Britain. A Moscow articulated trolleybus has capacity for two hundred passengers, but seats for only forty-five. A rare example of this system in England is the Red Arrow single-decker bus operated by London Transport on certain routes. This has a single flat fare, standing room for forty-eight, and seats for twenty-five passengers.

The economics of bus operation have been affected in all industrialized countries by the growing prosperity of the working man. This is especially true in the United States where in some communities almost every household has a car. Suburban services have been withdrawn

as their use was minimal, but this trend ignores the needs of a small number of people, elderly, maimed or blind, who will always depend on public transport. As with some train services, it seems that bus routes will have to be operated as a community service, with no expectation of profit. The long-distance inter-city coach would seem also to be threatened by the private car, but, by offering really good value, it continues to flourish. With the growth of the motorway network all over Europe it can now challenge the railroad in speed, and is invariably cheaper. In America the Greyhound network extends throughout the United States, Canada and parts of Mexico. The fleet consists of seven thousand vehicles, most of them the twin-engined 1½-decker 'Scenicruisers' seating forty-three passengers, with air-conditioning and toilet. The sleeper coach has not been employed to any great extent recently, as a satisfactory hotel can always be reached in a day's journey. However, an alternative is the mobile hotel which has been developed in Germany and Czechoslovakia. The coach tows a trailer with sleeping accommodation for about thirty passengers. This can be parked in a town and meals taken in a restaurant, or meals can be served in the coach. It is not the most com-

The first B.M.M.O. vehicle to use a horizontal underfloor engine was this coach, an existing vehicle modified in 1941 to take the new engine. Production of underfloor-engined buses and coaches began in 1946.
Birmingham & Midland Motor Omnibus Co. Ltd

B.M.M.O. chassisless double-decker, Type D9, built from 1959 onwards.
Birmingham & Midland Motor Omnibus Co. Ltd

1968 G.M.C. experimental gas-turbine coach, the RTX (Rapid Transit Experimental). For stops without kerbs, the coach can 'kneel', reducing the step height by three inches. General Motors Corp.

fortable form of holiday, but undoubtedly it is a cheap way of visiting foreign countries, and has good possibilities for school or student parties.

It is never easy to predict the future, but there are some trends which are likely to continue. The overall size and capacity of urban buses is unlikely to grow very much, but the movement towards a larger number of standing passengers will be maintained. Some cities such as Paris and Madrid are already running smaller single-decker buses with limited stops and one-man operation. This may well be copied in other countries, as shortages both of staff and of space on the roads are not likely to

decrease in the foreseeable future. As in the truck field, experiments have been made with gas-turbine power. A G.M.C. turbine coach built in 1968 had a three-axle layout, disc brakes all round, and a system of air-conditioning in which the passengers on the sunny side could be cooled, while those on the shady side were not affected. Thus in the world of the touring coach passenger needs and comforts will be of major importance; for the urban bus traveller the outlook is not so good. The signs are that the economics of operation will take a very definite first place over travelling comfort.

6

Transportation on Two Wheels

Considering its simplicity, it is surprising that the two-wheeled man-propelled vehicle did not appear earlier than it did, for the first such machines were not made until about 1790, twenty years after Cugnot's steam tractor was built. They were very crude, and lacked both pedals and steering, two pretty basic amenities of the later bicycle. Known as the *celerifère*, they often were made in the form of a horse or lion, with a saddle half way along the back, and a simple grip behind the animal's neck. Propulsion was by trundling the feet along the ground. They achieved some popularity in Paris, but it was not until steering was developed that they became at all widely known. In 1817 the German Baron von Drais de Sauerbon built a steerable velocipede which became known as the Draisine, and within two years it had been taken up by fashionable young society in France, Germany and Britain, where it was known as the Pedestrian Curricle or, more usually, the Hobby Horse. It came to New York in 1819, but was apparently not popular there. No improvements were made until 1838 when a Scots blacksmith named Kirkpatrick Macmillan

made a machine with treadles and lever cranks connected with the rear wheel; this was the first use of pedals. In 1861 Ernest Michaux of Paris began to build for sale bicycles with pedals acting directly on the front wheel, and for some years front-wheel drive was the generally adopted principle. In order to raise the gearing the front wheel was increased in size until it was more than twice the diameter of the rear. Known familiarly in England as the 'penny farthing', this was properly called the High Bicycle, and later the Ordinary, to distinguish it from the new Safety which appeared in the 1870s. The High Bicycle was made in different sizes according to the rider's leg length, from 44 to 52 inches in most cases, although the well-known sporting cyclist H. L. Cortis rode a machine with 62-inch wheel. The Safety Bicycle, with chain drive to the rear wheel, was introduced by H. J. Lawson, later famous for automobile promotion, in 1877. Early Safeties varied in wheel size, some having larger rear wheels (Humber) and some larger front ones (Rover). J. K. Starley's Rover Safety of 1885 set the pattern for the modern bicycle, and was one of the most successful commercially. The High Bicycle was practically obsolete by the early 1880s, but was kept going for sport for a while longer. In 1888 the pneumatic tire came in, and the following decade saw the bicycle reach the peak of its popularity. It had something of the effect of the later charabanc in liberating the townsman from the confines of his streets, although this was mainly a pleasure of the middle class. For a brief period before the arrival of the motor car, the bicycle became a fashionable toy for the rich, and society was regularly to be seen awheel in Hyde Park.

The idea of fitting an engine to a two-wheeler seems to have occurred to cartoonists as early as 1818, with the

Johnson's Hobby Horse, 1819
Science Museum, London

Macmillan's bicycle, 1839
Crown Copyright. Science Museum, London

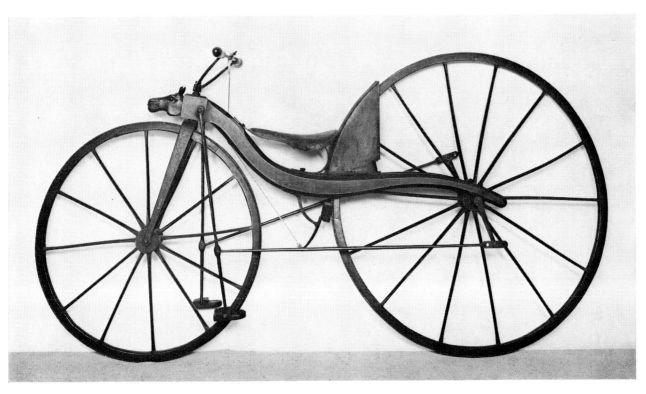

appearance of the first Draisines, but an actual motor bicycle was not made until 1869 when a steam engine was mounted in a Michaux. The American inventor Sylvester Roper made a similar machine in about 1870, while L. D. Copeland of Philadelphia fitted a steam engine to a High Bicycle in 1884. Copeland and several other inventors also made steam conversions to tricycles, and from these came some of the earliest motor cars. Gottlieb Daimler built a motor cycle in 1885, powered by a gasoline engine, but it was not successful, and in any case does not rank as a proper two-wheeler, as it needed small wheels at the side to stabilize it. In 1892 the Germans Hildebrand and Wolfmüller built a genuine gasoline-propelled motor cycle, and two years later they put it into production, the first firm to sell motor cycles to the public. It had two horizontal cylinders driving directly to the rear wheels, and a top speed of about 28 mph. This was faster than almost any car at this date. The H & W was sold in England as the Duncan-Superbie, but for some unknown reason the makers went out of business in 1898. It may have been because the motor cycle had a very bad name

Matchless Ordinary bicycle, 1883.
Crown copyright. Science Museum, London

Hildebrand & Wolfmüller motor cycle, 1894.
Crown copyright. Science Museum, London

62

F.N. 3½-hp 4-cylinder motor cycle, 1905.
Lent to the Science Museum, London, by Mr. P. A. Clare

for skidding, and for a few years was eclipsed by the safer motor tricycle, of which the 2¾-hp de Dion Bouton was the most famous. During this period two-wheelers sold in small numbers; the 1899 Werner had a 1½-hp engine mounted over, and driving, the front wheel by belt. It also had pedals to the rear wheel, just in case. Cyclemotor attachments were popular in the early days. They weighed no more than 40 lb. and gave a top speed of about 20 mph from a 1¼-hp 143-cc engine. Some of the best-known were the French Clement, Swiss Motosacoche and Belgian Minerva, of which over three thousand were sold in 1901. One of the most famous British makes, Triumph, began as a Minerva-engined bicycle in 1902, and emerged as a motor cycle proper with engine built into the frame from 1904. The London firm of J. A. Prestwich built their first engine in 1903, a 293-cc single-cylinder unit. They made a few motor cycles of their own, but became chiefly famous as suppliers of engines of all kinds to other makers. American production began with the Indian in 1901, and Harley-Davidson in 1903, both becoming America's most famous machines.

V-twin engines began to appear in about 1905, and vertical twins at the same time, although the latter were soon abandoned and not revived for thirty years. The horizontally opposed twin was made famous by Douglas from 1907 onwards, while the Belgian F.N. had an in-line 4-cylinder engine. The 2-cycle engine came in 1908 with the Yorkshire-built Scott, although the firm had experimented with such engines since 1900. The 1909 Scott had all-chain drive, kick starter and expanding clutch type of 2-speed gear. Up to about 1910 final drives were mostly by belt, which was smooth and simple, but suffered from slip in the wet. Chains were free from this disadvantage, but were noisier. The F.N. 4-cylinder motor cycle had shaft drive to a bevel gear; curiously this make was little more expensive than a belt-driven single-cylinder machine. By 1914 motor cycles could be had with engine sizes up to 500 cc and even 750 cc, and the fastest machines were capable of over 80 mph. By contrast there were some very small cycles too, such as the Guernsey-built Pacer with 49-cc 1-hp engine. Chain drive was becoming more popular, and there were a number of shaft-driven machines such as the American Pierce-Arrow, and the British Wilkinson with worm gear. Side-cars were introduced in about 1903, and by 1914 were widespread, some of them large enough to carry two

63

passengers. With the rider and a pillion passenger, this meant that a motor-cycle combination could carry four people, which was more than the average light car of 1914 could do.

During the 1920s engine speeds went up to 6,000 rpm in some cases (overhead camshaft J.A.P.). Engines were still mostly singles or V-twins, but Douglas continued their horizontally opposed twins, and F.N. their fours. Other 4-cylinder machines included the American Militaire of 1,145 cc, Henderson of 1,168 cc and Indian Ace of 1,229 cc. There were a few unusual layouts which became popular for a time; the German Megola had a 5-cylinder radial engine mounted on the front wheel and a seat rather than a saddle for the rider. Another machine which approached the car in design was the American Ner-a-car, with low-built frame, 269-cc 2-cycle engine and 5-speed friction transmission. It was also built in England between 1922 and 1926. Motor scooters appeared just after the First World War. The A.B.C. Skootamota had a 1¼-hp engine, speed of 20 mph and

consumption of 150 mpg. The Autoped was literally a scooter, with no seat at all; power came from a small electric motor, or a 155-cc gasoline engine. Later, in 1938, the Belgian Socovel company made larger electrically powered motor cycles but they never became popular. One of the biggest milestones of the 1930s was the introduction of the vertical twin 500-cc Triumph which set the fashion for modern vertical twin engines. Performance was improved considerably in the decade up to the war; the 1938 500-cc Norton developed 48 bhp at 6,500 rpm, and lapped at 91 mph in the 1938 Tourist Trophy race.

Two important developments of the post-war period were the cyclemotor and the motor scooter. The former was a revival of the engine attachments of the early 1900s, but with increased power per cubic centimetre the capacities could be as small as 25 cc, and still give 25–30 mph and the amazing fuel consumption of 200 mpg. Self-contained motorized wheels were popular for a while, replacing the rear wheel of an ordinary bicycle. The

1911 Pierce single-cylinder motor cycle. Built by a sister company of the well-known car makers, Pierce-Arrow, these motor cycles had tank frames, fuel being contained in the wide-diameter tube on which the name is written.

John Price

revived scooter achieved a tremendous success which had always eluded the scooters of the early 1920s. Appearing first in Italy with the two makes which are still the most popular, Vespa and Lambretta, scooters were being made in a wide variety of countries within a few years. With a 125-cc 2-cycle engine, the average scooter had a speed of about 45 mph. Weather protection was better than on a motor cycle, and they extended the appeal of two-wheel motoring to those who did not want to dress up in leather and goggles, equipment which the ardent motor cyclist will always have to use. More elaborate scooters had engines of up to 250 cc and speeds of 75 mph.

On the Continent the most successful sporting motor cycle has been the Italian M.V. Augusta, various models of which have won twenty-five world championships during the firm's lifetime from 1946 to the present day. M.V. are among the largest motor-cycle makers in Europe today. The largest producer in the world is Honda of Japan. This is another example of the incredible rise in importance of the Japanese motor industry. In 1950 only 2,633 motor cycles were built; less than ten years later the figure was 592,752, while the 1968 total was 2,242,135. Japanese motor cycles are made in a wide variety from 49-cc mopeds upwards. Among technical developments have been torque converter transmissions even on the smallest models, shaft drive and air suspension. Exports of Japanese motor cycles and scooters have penetrated even more widely than those of their cars, so that in many markets the names Honda and Suzuki have become synonymous with motor cycling.

In terms of numbers on the road, the motor cycle reached the peak of its popularity in England in 1953; since then it has had to yield to the car for practical and comfortable transport, and numbers have dropped sharply. In America the same process took place twenty-five years earlier. However, in both countries, as well as elsewhere, it has retained an enthusiastic following as a sporting machine. There are certainly much more camaraderie and technical expertise among motor cyclists than are found in the world of those who motor on four wheels.

Harley-Davidson 7/9-hp motor cycle with sidecar, 1925.
Crown Copyright. Science Museum, London

7

Transportation without Roads

There have been many attempts to provide satisfactory mechanical transportation across sand, mud, snow and other difficult surfaces, and we have only space to look at a few of them. Almost certainly the first were the ice locomotives ordered by Russia in 1861 for use on the frozen River Neva between St Petersburg and Kronstadt. They were similar to the railway locomotives of the day, but had steerable sledges in place of the front wheels. A 'track' was cleared on the ice, and signals provided. They drew a train of several carriages, for passengers and goods, and on occasions are said to have left the river and travelled into the country on sleigh roads. At least two locomotives were used, both built in Great Britain. About forty years later ice locomotives were used in the lumber industry of Wisconsin, Montana and Saskatchewan. They ran not on frozen rivers, but on specially prepared ice tracks made by sprinkling the rutted roads generously with water which, at more than 30 degrees below zero, froze immediately. The speed was 4 to 5 mph, and each loco could haul a train of fifteen sledges, making a weight of about 420 tons. They were used in America and Canada from 1904 until at least 1920, and one was employed on similar work in Finland. Gasoline-propelled snow vehicles were prepared for the Antarctic expeditions of Ernest Shackleton (1907–8) and Captain Robert Scott (1912), the former being an Arrol-Johnston with four wheels and wooden tires, the latter a fully tracked machine built by Wolseley.

The first fully tracked vehicle was a kerosine-engined tractor built by Richard Hornsby & Sons Ltd of Grantham, Lincolnshire, in 1907. It weighed 23 tons and was steered by track braking, like its descendant the tank. Built for the War Office, it was not developed by them. However, it attracted the attention of an engineer in the Yukon who wanted to draw coal trucks from his mine to Dawson City over 40 miles of rough virgin country. Working in co-operation with the steam engineers Fosters of Lincoln, Hornsby built a 40-ton steam tracked machine which worked successfully in the Yukon for several years. Hornsby sold the American and Canadian rights for the design to the Holt Caterpillar

1907 Hornsby kerosine-engined tractor, the first full-track vehicle in the world. B. H. Vanderveen Collection

U.S. Army M3 half-track personnel carrier. This type of vehicle was made during the Second World War by Autocar, Diamond T, and White.

B. H. Vanderveen Collection

Steyr RSO/01 full-track truck-cum-tractor, used by the German Army mainly on the Eastern Front, but later in the West as well. B. H. Vanderveen Collection

Company of Peoria, Illinois, who built their first gasoline-engined tractor in 1912. It had two tracks at the rear, and a single front wheel; many were used by the U.S. Army during the First World War and it was the ancestor of the many thousands of bulldozers and crawler tractors which have made Caterpillar synonymous throughout the world with this type of vehicle. A number of Holt tractors were imported to England when the first tank was being planned (1914–15), and in fact these were built in the works of William Foster who had helped to make the 1909 Yukon tractor. As tanks are fighting rather than transportation vehicles they have no place here, although it should be mentioned that at least one tank was used to give joyrides on Southend beach in 1920.

Between the wars many experiments were made with tracked vehicles. They ranged from the Fowler Snaketrac of 1923, which was a traction engine on tracks, to conversions of passenger cars and trucks. The most famous of the latter were the Citroën-Kégresse machines. Designed by Monsieur Kégresse, who had been manager of the garage of Czar Nicholas II, they were half-track cars with conventional front wheels which steered in the normal way. In 1923 Kégresse cars made the first successful crossing of the Sahara, and followed this up with journeys across French Equatorial Africa to Mozambique in 1925, and from Beirut to Peking in 1931–2. Citroën-Kégresses were made in various sizes, both as passenger cars and as trucks. In 1934 the Linn Manufacturing Company of Morris, N.Y., built a half-track 3-ton truck for the U.S. Army, powered by a V-12 American La France engine. During the Second World War the tracked transport vehicle was made by many countries in a wide variety of designs. The U.S. Army M Series half-track personnel carrier was one of the best-known; over 41,000 were made, with and without armour, and some equipped with gun turrets. The American, German and Russian armies used half-track conversions of trucks, and other vehicles were full-track trucks and tractors, and even an amphibious full-track tractor, a 16-ton German machine powered by a 300-hp Maybach engine.

In peace-time conditions there is less demand for cross-country vehicles, but nevertheless a number of interesting ones have been made. Some of the most impressive have been built in response to the needs of the oil industry which has been pushing farther and farther into northern Canada. The need was for a truck with maximum carrying capacity but able to negotiate the marshy muskeg of the area. Previously the oil companies worked only in winter when the muskeg was frozen solid. Beginning in 1953 the Bruce Nodwell Company has developed an extensive line of tracked vehicles with capacities from 2 to 30 tons. The smaller have full tracks and steer by track braking, but the larger trucks have two separate pairs of tracks at front and rear. At first only the front track steered, but on the latest models both steer, giving maximum manœuvrability with a carrying capacity of 30 tons. Truly a remarkable machine. Now known as Foremost Tracked Vehicles Ltd, the makers have recently supplied the Russian Oil Ministry with fifty-two tracked vehicles.

An alternative to tracks on certain types of soft ground is the use of large tires. Numerous trucks have been converted to use these, but the most spectacular, and one of the most incredible vehicles in the whole world of transportation, is the U.S. Army Overland Train Mark II, built by R. G. Le Tourneau Inc. of Longview, Texas.

A development of the past few years in North America is off-road transportation for pleasure and sport. This

Yukon 9-ton all-track truck, built by Foremost Tracked
Vehicles of Calgary, Alberta
Foremost Tracked Vehicles Ltd

*One of the largest tracked trucks made by Foremost is the
Dawson Seven with 20-ton capacity and steering on both
front and rear tracks.*
Foremost Tracked Vehicles Ltd

The Le Tourneau Overland Train Mark II is the longest vehicle in the world. Each of the fifty-four 10-foot-diameter wheels contains its own electric motor, power for which is generated by two 1,170-hp gas turbines in the rear trailers. The complete train is 572 feet long and can carry tonnage equal to sixty standard 2½-ton U.S. Army trucks. B. H. Vanderveen Collection

The versatile 'Amphicat', first of a new breed of all-terrain vehicles. Crayford Auto Development Ltd

new family of vehicles includes dune buggies, snow-mobiles and all-terrain vehicles such as the Amphicat. Dune buggies are light, open two- or four-passenger cars, mostly Volkswagen-powered, although enthusiasts have fitted Porsche, Volvo and Corvair engines. They were used originally on sand dunes for the sheer pleasure of open-air motoring away from traffic lights and speed restrictions, but now clubs organize races of all kinds up to the 700-mile trans-desert Nevada Stardust Race. Auto sport on snow is provided by the snowmobile, a two-passenger machine not unlike a motor scooter, with single track transmitting the power, and steered by skids at the front. They can be used by children as no licence is needed, although this presents problems when they are taken onto the roads. Like the dune buggies, the snow-mobiles were originally built for sheer amusement, but now serious competition models have been evolved, with engines tuned to give 60 hp and 80 to 90 mph. They can even be used for slalom contests and long-distance jumping, up to almost 70 feet. The third of the new off-road vehicles is the light amphibian, of which the Amphicat is the best known. This is a small go-anywhere vehicle with six wheels, all driven. Power comes from a 281-cc Sachs 2-cycle engine, giving a speed of 35 mph. The most practical of the new breed, the Amphicat can be used for mountain rescue work, or as a farm vehicle where rough country and rivers have to be crossed. In addition, the Amphicat is invaluable for shooting in marshy terrain, and cross-country races have been organized for them as well.

PART THREE
Land Transportation by Rail
by J. B. Snell

1

Railway Prehistory

The word 'Railway' or 'Railroad' has two syllables; and each one illustrates a different aspect of the whole. The most important is that the word refers to a 'way'—a prepared path, driven continuously from one point to another, with a surface suitable for the movement of heavy vehicles. The second aspect is that it is not an ordinary way, but one with rails; means are provided not only to carry the vehicles, but also to guide them. An adult has usually lost sight of this distinction of meaning; the concept is familiar to him and forms one package. But the child who asks where the steering wheel is in the cab of a locomotive has tripped up on what remains a rather important point.

The earliest ancestors of railways were the rutways of ancient times. On these, the idea of guiding a wheel was not fundamental; the point was to provide a practical path for it as economically as possible, without going to the trouble of smoothing a surface for the whole width of passage. At several places round the Mediterranean, but most notably in Malta and Cyrenaica, are series of rutways cut in the limestone (which, bar a light covering of soil here and there and scanty vegetation, forms the surface of the ground). Some of them certainly date back to Neolithic times, when they were used by carts carrying earth and water to defensible hilltop sites which would otherwise be barren. A typical track would have twin ruts 10 to 20 inches wide at the top, 12 inches or so deep, tapering down to a width of some 4 inches at the bottom, and some $4\frac{1}{2}$ feet apart. Sidings and passing places can be found here and there; the stone is not worn away by horses' hooves between the ruts, so probably haulage was by manpower. On the other hand, iron horseshoes were not very common before about the eighth century A.D., so we cannot be sure. The close correspondence between the distance apart of these ruts and the 4 ft $8\frac{1}{2}$ in. standard railway gauge of modern times is interesting; the distance between the ruts in a tunnel of Roman date between Grenoble and Valence is 1·44 metres, which is within 0·2 of an inch of standard gauge.

However, these rutways were used by ordinary carts which could also run on roads; and except where the rock lay near the surface, a road was easier to build and maintain and more convenient to use. Thus they were fairly uncommon, and used only in special circumstances. Perhaps they were not really the ancestors of the railway so much as of the system of providing specially smooth and reinforced strips running along roads to carry wheels —either wood planks laid on bare earth, or long ashlars of granite built into cobbles or stone pavement, which can still sometimes be seen. Valencia (Spain) was remarkable in having until very recent times a system of tracks of this kind for the use of peasants' carts, finished with steel plates and so considerably smoother and easier to draw a load on; it is only now, with the growth in the number of rubber-tired lorries in farmers' hands, that these are falling out of use.

The more readily traceable ancestry of the railway began in the mines of Austria and Hungary, probably about the fifteenth century. In the cramped darkness of a rough-hewn tunnel, with the need to roll continuous heavy loads of stone to the surface, it became important to devise some system to make the drawing of small trams and tubs easier, and at the same time to devise some method of guiding them so that they followed the twists and turns of the road. Mining was very much a guild industry, with trade secrets kept hidden; it was not until Georg Bauer, 'Agricola', wrote his remarkable treatise on mining methods, *De Re Metallica*, published in 1556, the year after he died, that any public account was given of how this particular problem was dealt with. The book is a very considerable work, illustrated with many woodcuts, going in great detail into mining methods, and in fact it remained the standard authority on the subject for two hundred years. Only one illustration is given of a mine-car, but from this and the accompanying account it is clear that Agricola's system involved the use of two planks laid side by side and secured to the rough floor, while a pin in the leading end of the car steered it by engaging in a rough slot which could be formed by the gap between the planks. But from other accounts it seems

One of the earliest pictorial representations of a railway: part of the frontispiece to Brand's 'History of Newcastle', 1783, showing a wagoner followed by his horse coasting downgrade towards the River Tyne.

Science Museum, London

clear that an alternative system also existed, then or soon after, which involved the use of rails of plain squared timber on which ran wheels with flanges.

The most famous, but by no means the only, set of early railways of this kind existed in the coal-mining districts of Tyneside and Durham from the seventeenth century; since the matter was regarded as one of purely rude and mechanical interest, there are few literary references to them. One refers to Huntingdon Beaumont, who commenced mining operations in the district in 1608 and was said to have introduced the use of railways, on which ran wagons carrying coal from the pits to the river, at that time; he may have brought the idea from Nottinghamshire. But certainly it seems to have been Britain that fostered the invention most notably, to the extent that when railways began to be built in the Ruhr in the eighteenth century they were known as 'Englischer Kohlenweg'. By the second half of the eighteenth century the English lines were common enough and important enough to have been the subject of lawsuits over such

matters as wayleave rights; they were often considerable works several miles long, with some substantial bridges and embankments or cuttings. The track was wooden, usually laid with timbers salvaged from dismantled ships (since in those days large wooden beams in new condition fetched a very good price); and the carts or wagons which ran on them carried over 2 tons of coal. From about 1760 cast-iron wheels, which were cheaper than wooden ones, began to be used. In order to lessen the resulting wear, the rails were then made in two sections, a stout beam below to bear the weight, and a thin renewable plank above to take the rough usage. The purpose of the engineering and earthworks was to limit gradients in a fairly hilly area, not so much to allow the horse to haul the empties back uphill easily as to ease the problem of getting the loads downhill safely. This was not too difficult on an ordinary road, where the friction of loose gravel or the worse-than-friction of axle-deep mud often made it unlikely that a cart would ever get out of control on the downgrade. But the penalty of reducing obstacles to movement is always that you have to improve your brakes (especially in wet weather). A horse is unhappy holding back a load pressing down behind him; the wagons had to be fitted with good brakes, and there had to be boys throwing sand or cinders on the rail in rain or frost, lest the wheels skid.

Iron rails were first used by Richard Reynolds at Coalbrookdale in 1767; these were no more than cast-iron plates, made during a period of slack trade at the foundry in order to avoid blowing out the furnace, and laid on top of the wooden rails existing already. But the vast increase in a horse's haulage capacity which resulted convinced Reynolds, and others, that they were worth while. However, it was not until about the turn of the century that the wooden beam supporting the plate was dispensed with, and self-sufficient iron rails commenced to be cast.

All these early lines used plain rails and flanged wheels; the disadvantage that wheels of this kind could not run on ordinary roads, and the vehicle fitted with them was therefore confined to a prepared track, was accepted. The opposite system, with plain wheel on flanged rail, was certainly known and at one time popular. It is not quite certain who invented it: some authorities say John Smeaton about 1756, but although he used the system it may well have been older. However, it was not much used with wooden rails, and achieved its greatest success with some of the cast-iron rails made in the early nineteenth century; railways of this kind were favoured by certain engineers of the school of Benjamin Outram, closely connected with the building of canals (at that time considered to be the best form of long-distance inland transport for freight), and a good number of lines using L-shaped rails were built as feeders to the inland waterways, serving hilly parts where many locks would otherwise have been needed. The coalmining industry of South Wales used this pattern of railway at first almost exclusively. It was practical enough up to a point, but suffered from two disadvantages; the more serious one was that the lip on the rail tended to retain dirt and gravel kicked up by horses' hooves, which greatly increased friction. The other was that the cast-iron rail was inevitably fundamentally weakened by the fact that its vertical part, giving strength to bear weight, had to lie in a different plane to the path of the wheels, and so did not provide the support where it was needed. These factors caused the gradual abandonment of this pattern of railway; one last survivor continued to work, with horse traction, in the Forest of Dean into the 1930s, but the big changeover in South Wales had taken place by the 1850s.

By 1800 the idea of a railway was quite well known, and some far-sighted people were beginning to wonder if perhaps it offered better possibilities than canals for the national transport network, made more and more necessary by the increased trade and traffic which industrialization was bringing about. One of the long-sighted ones was the greatest canal-builder of all, the Duke of Bridgewater, who remarked shortly before his death in 1803, 'I see mischief in these demned tramroads'. Certainly a railway was very much cheaper and quicker to build than a canal; it was maybe more expensive to work per ton-mile, but transits were faster even with horse haulage. A horse might haul some 50 tons on a canal, but at only about $2\frac{1}{2}$ mph. On a railway it depended on grades, but with iron rails 10 tons was a very reasonable proposition, and speeds could easily be three times as fast. It was a very nice point. Canals continued to be built until the 1820s, and remained a commercial proposition for some time after that; but people made remarks on such cases as the Brecon Canal, which paid a mere $\frac{1}{2}$ per cent dividend, while a tramroad which fed into it (running from Brynmawr down to Govilon) earned 5 per cent from a purely tributary traffic.

However, men are slow to change their ways. It was not until the advent of mechanical power that the railway really began to grow.

A plain wagon from the horse-powered Stratford & Moreton Railway (1826), now preserved at Stratford-on-Avon. Note the primitive handbrake acting on one wheel only.
Stratford Trust

75

2

The Beginnings of Steam Locomotion

The idea of building a steam engine which moved itself along was not particularly new; the first person actually to do it was the Frenchman Nicolas Cugnot, in 1769, though his experimental vehicles did little work. The same year James Watt, the very businesslike British inventor who did more than any man before him to make the steam engine a satisfactory power source, took out a strategic patent for a self-propelling engine, and followed it with another in 1784. But he had no intention of actually building one; merely of stopping anybody else, or of being able to claim royalties if they did. For one thing, Watt's engines were low-pressure ones, which derived their power as much from the vacuum created in a bulky separate condenser as from the steam, at about 5 lb. per square inch, fed into the cylinder. They could hardly be considered portable in any way; they had to be set up with a building erected round them. Again, most boilers at the time were made of cast-iron, which was a brittle material prone to fracture. It was bad enough if a cast-iron rail broke under a wagon, but nothing very desperate usually resulted, and a bit of hearty lifting and levering would set matters right again. But a boiler explosion was another matter, even at low pressure, and to have cast-iron boilers running up and down the public highway was not a happy thought at all, in Watt's view. So his pupil William Murdoch, who built a model of Watt's 1784 engine and set it off along the road, got a severe wigging.

However, contrary views on steam-engine design were held by the Cornish engineer Richard Trevithick, who was a believer in 'strong steam', at a pressure of 25 or even 50 lb. per square inch. He did not mind the thought of cast-iron boilers either, although he took good care to make them pretty substantial. He dispensed with the condenser, sending his exhaust steam straight to the atmosphere, and he found that he could build an engine weighing no more than 2 or 3 tons which was much cheaper in first cost and also cheaper to operate than a

A model of Trevithick's third locomotive, the 'Catch-me-who-Can', which ran on a circular line in London during 1808. Note the single vertical cylinder.

A.T. & S.F. Railroad Co.

Watt engine. Furthermore, it could develop the same power. However, having set a number of his engines to work in Cornwall pumping and lifting in mines, Trevithick turned his attention to locomotives. He built one, running on the road, in 1802; the following year he built another, or rather modified one that had been intended to power a hammer at an ironworks, and set it on a railway at Penydarran, near Merthyr. (It was, as it happened, like most others in South Wales, one with L-shaped rails.) The main motives for doing this had been to win a wager for Samuel Homfray, the owner of the ironworks, who had bet that the engine could haul a 10-ton load over the 9½-mile Penydarran Railway. It could, and it did, so he won; but thereafter it was set to driving its hammer. Trevithick built two more locomotives, as well as a number of road vehicles, but had little success with them; one ran on a circular demonstration line in London, and caused a great deal of public interest, but for some years no commercial result followed. The weight of a loco-

76

William Hedley's 'Puffing Billy' of 1813, photographed when it made its last run on the Wylam Railway in 1862.
Science Museum, London

motive seemed to break too many of the cast-iron rails, and it was not clear that there was any economic case for replacing horses. There was also a fairly considerable academic dispute about whether a smooth iron wheel on a smooth iron rail could possibly grip well enough to haul a useful load; there was no shortage of pundits to say that it could not.

As a result, the first locomotives to enter commercial service had a toothed driving wheel, which engaged in a rack cast into the outer edge of one rail. John Blenkinsop, who was the responsible designer, had wished for a more symmetrical and balanced arrangement with two driving wheels and both rails fitted with teeth, but this was refused him on the grounds of expense. The railway concerned was the Middleton, near Leeds, three miles long; and the experiment of adopting steam power was decided on partly out of a spirit of adventure but largely because of the increasing price of fodder for horses. Two locomotives were ordered from Matthew Murray, the

owner of a nearby engineering works, and placed in service during 1812; they followed Trevithick's final design fairly closely, and in fact the inventor received a royalty under his patent. They proved able to haul trains of 100 tons at $3\frac{1}{2}$ mph, and, together with two more built shortly afterwards, they handled the busy coal traffic of the railway uneventfully for the next thirty years. Few mechanical devices so entirely new have had such a trouble-free entry into commercial service as the steam locomotive!

The ice having been broken, and the commercial possibility of steam haulage proved, several other engineers soon tried their hands. Two of them continued in the belief that the simple adhesion of a plain wheel on a plain rail was insufficient, and devised substitute systems of traction. William Chapman built an engine that hauled itself along on a chain; but the weight and friction of the chain was so great that it could do little more than just that. William Brunton built another, tried in 1815, that

The conjectural replica of George Stephenson's first loco-motive, the 'Blucher' of 1814, built for the St Louis Exposition of 1892. The original's wheels would certainly have been cast-iron and not built up, like these.
Association of American Railroads

The Stockton & Darlington's first power: George Stephenson's 'Locomotion' of 1825. This machine took the Blenkinsop/Trevithick layout as far as it would go.
British Railways

propelled itself along on a pair of mechanical legs working behind it; an ingeniously complicated mechanism, but apart from being unable to walk backwards it spoilt its chances by exploding. William Hedley, the manager of the Wylam colliery, however, decided to put the matter to the test, and built an experimental car whose wheels could be turned by cranks worked by men riding on it; he found that the adhesion of plain wheels was quite sufficient to haul a train. Between 1813 and 1815 he built four loco-motives, three of which remained in service at Wylam for nearly fifty years, quite successfully. In their original form, these 'Puffing Billies' were four-wheelers running on flanged rails, for which they were too heavy; they had to be rebuilt as eight-wheelers on two bogies. About 1830 the railway was converted, and the engines rebuilt on four flanged wheels. Two still exist, in museums at South Kensington and in Edinburgh.

George Stephenson, at that time the head enginewright of the Tyneside collieries owned by a group headed by the Earl of Strathmore, and a man with some record of engineering achievement already, was at that point also set to the task of building a locomotive. His first ran in 1814. Like Hedley's, it was a fairly close copy in most

respects of the Middleton engines, with vertical cylinders set into the boiler along its centre line, driving the flanged wheels by beams and rods. But for the following ten years Stephenson was the only person who built any locomotives, and was therefore responsible for all the improvements made during that time, with considerable assistance from Nicholas Wood, who as manager at Killingworth had working responsibility for many of the engines built. Stephenson's main improvement, apart from matters of detail, was in evolving the method of powering more than one pair of wheels by coupling as well as connecting rods; Wood's contributions were the first study of valve performance demonstrating the important economy that could be made by allowing the steam to expand during the greater part of the stroke of the piston, together with the manufacture of the first sufficiently strong steel springs.

Till 1825 all locomotives had run on private railways, most of which were solely intended to serve coal mines. In that year the world's first public railway, intended for all kinds of traffic and laid out for steam haulage, was opened: the Stockton & Darlington. George Stephenson, assisted by his son Robert, had engineered it; in charge of the stable of locomotives was Timothy Hackworth. The first four engines, including the famous *Locomotion*, were all of standard Killingworth type, and so still fairly close to Trevithick's final pattern. But with the strains and stresses of working by steam power for the first time on a public railway 22 miles long, certain shortcomings began to be felt. Cast-iron wheels would no longer do; cast steel was seventy years ahead, but Hackworth devised a built-up construction of cast-iron segments wrapped by a wrought-iron band, introducing for the first time the idea of a separate tire standard on most locomotive and carriage wheels since. Vertical cylinders involved awkwardly large unbalanced weights and forces, so that speeds had to be kept low to avoid the engine dancing off the track; the search for a more satisfactory layout of the machinery therefore began. More important still, boiler power had to be increased. The plain Stephenson boiler had a barrel pierced by a large tube containing the fire; this was wasteful, as much heat escaped, and the older arrangement used by Trevithick and Hedley, where the large tube was doubled back to emerge at the same end of the boiler as the firedoor, was found to be considerably better at raising steam, yet still not good enough. But in spite of all these troubles, the S & D showed that mechanical power was cheaper per ton-mile than horse power. And this was the important lesson.

The Liverpool & Manchester, opened in 1830, was the world's first railway linking two cities. It was a double

The Rainhill Contestants: Robert Stephenson's 'Rocket', Timothy Hackworth's 'Sans Pareil', and Braithwaite and Ericsson's 'Novelty'. Author's Collection

A cutaway model of Marc Séguin's first engine for the St Etienne–Lyon railway (1829), showing the underfired multiple-tube boiler and the belt-driven blower fans.
Crown Copyright. Science Museum, London

track line 30 miles long, and again George Stephenson was responsible for its construction. There was considerable force in the argument put forward by some of the directors that locomotives had not yet proved themselves sufficiently; the line should therefore be worked by stationary engines, winding the trains along by ropes. Yet again the argument was, at bottom, a financial one. Maybe rope haulage would be somewhat cheaper—figures could be produced to show it, though not beyond controversy. But fifty-four winding engines would be needed at once, at vast capital cost. Locomotives cost less to build, and while the capital cost of a fleet would not be far short of the cost of the winding engines, the whole railway could be worked by a much smaller number which could be increased as traffic grew, while if they proved unsatisfactory they could be abandoned without ruinous loss. It was therefore resolved to try locomotives, and to encourage improvements the company advertised a contest for a prize; the famous Rainhill trials of 1829.

Three engines contended: Timothy Hackworth built a smaller version of the types used on the Stockton & Darlington, the *Sans Pareil*; Braithwaite and Ericsson built an intriguing but insufficiently powerful one on the lines of Gurney's steam road coach. Easily the winner was Robert Stephenson's *Rocket*, partly because it had cylinders which were not vertical but inclined at about 30 degrees, which allowed full springing without consequent loss of efficiency due to excessive clearance volume in the cylinders (on the other hand his father had already built two engines, one for America, with this feature); but mainly because of the great step forward in the design of its boiler. It had a water-jacketed firebox, and the hot gases from the fire were led forward through the water space in many small tubes, giving a great increase in steam-raising power. The *Rocket*'s boiler was the first ancestor of the modern locomotive boiler, having all the essential elements; its principal difference was that the firebox was outside the barrel, and connected to it by pipes. However, it was moved inside the barrel on engines built the following year. Later engines built for the Liverpool & Manchester by Robert Stephenson in 1830 and 1831 developed features which have been conventional ever since; cylinders horizontal (more or less), in line with the wheels and placed ahead of the boiler,

smokeboxes, and strong independent frames. The year 1830 was really the steam locomotive's *annus mirabilis*.

Although Britain was in the forefront of locomotive development at this time, other countries were watching with interest. Two Blenkinsop-type engines were built in Berlin for experimental purposes in 1816 and 1818; Marc Séguin in France built a number of interesting machines in the late 1820s for the Lyon–St Etienne railway, which used multi-tubular boilers (which he developed about the same time as Robert Stephenson) in combination with a furnace beneath the boiler barrel, a remarkable drive arrangement using vertical cylinders, and draught induced by a pair of large fans driven by the wheels (which unfortunately tended to blow the fire into greater fury

A model of John Stevens's experimental engine, demonstrated in New York in 1824; this had a single cylinder, rack drive, a watertube boiler capable of working at 500 psi, and ran on flanged rails.
Association of American Railroads

The first locomotive to operate on a public railway in America; the Delaware & Hudson's 'Stourbridge Lion' (1829). The painting, by Sheldon Pennoyer, was for the railway's centenary. Science Museum, London

going downhill than up). Several American engineers also experimented; John Stevens built a small engine, demonstrated on a circular line in New York in 1824, noteworthy for having a watertube boiler capable of working at the astonishingly high pressure of 500 lb. per square inch. The Delaware & Hudson Canal Co. imported two locomotives from England to work on a 16-mile feeder railway they had built at Honesdale, Pa., in 1829; only one of them ever ran, and proved too heavy for the track, but the *Stourbridge Lion*, built by Foster & Rastrick of that town, though a very conservative design for its date, achieved the distinction of being the first locomotive to operate on a public railway in the American continent (9th August 1829).

The first real main-line railway to be opened in America was the first section of the Baltimore & Ohio, in 1829. At first they used horses, but Peter Cooper of New York built a small vertical-boilered engine, the *Tom Thumb*,

A replica of Peter Cooper's vertical-boilered 'Tom Thumb', the first locomotive to operate on the Baltimore & Ohio Railroad in 1829. Baltimore & Ohio Railroad

Having won the B and O contest in 1830 with an enlarged and improved version of Cooper's engine, Phineas Davis built several more for the company. His 'Atlantic' was the first locomotive to enter Washington, in 1832.
Gulf Oil Co.

The Mohawk & Hudson's 'De Witt Clinton', built at West Point in 1831, steaming again for the B & O centenary. Lack of boiler lagging must have made her sluggish in winter! Association of American Railroads

to prove to the company that the new power was practical; and in 1831 the B & O organized a contest on the lines of the Rainhill event, except that the terms included a thirty days' trial in service. Five engines competed; the winner was a vertical-boilered 0-4-0 by Phineas Davis, which combined vertical cylinders with an indirect drive through beams and a jackshaft, so that proper springing was possible; unlike Timothy Hackworth on the Stockton & Darlington, who also continued to use vertical cylinders long after other engineers had abandoned them, Davis contained his within the wheelbase, so that much greater stability resulted and a reasonable speed could be reached. No fewer than eighteen engines were subsequently built to this design, known as 'grasshoppers' from the elbowing action of the beams, and the last was not taken out of service till 1893. By then it was considerably the oldest locomotive at work anywhere in the world, except for one of George Stephenson's earlier ones which remained active (though somewhat rebuilt) at Hetton colliery until 1908.

3
Building the Networks

The technical and financial success of the first locomotive-worked main-line railways in the early 1830s generated a world-wide interest in the new means of transport: the shortcomings of canals were by that time well known, and there was an urgent need for something better. However, railways were unquestionably vast undertakings; they would cut ruthlessly across the land, and would inevitably have to be given authority which could outweigh the rights of private landowners. The Englishman's home might be his castle, but a railway company could often be empowered to knock it down if it was in the way. Apart from this question of judging private rights, the national interest also had to be considered. Nothing so vast had been built since the times of the Pharaohs; a very large proportion of a country's capital would need to be devoted to building its railway network; what would be the effect of all this on the balance of industry, and other business as a whole? And above all, what railways were needed, and how could the merits of rival schemes be judged?

In Britain, it was the age of laissez-faire; government interfered as little as possible. Hence, there was little question of drawing up any national plan of railway construction—that sort of thing, it was believed, was not the government's business. As a result, Britain's railway system grew up piecemeal; lines were promoted from A to B, or E to F. The largest single scheme ever authorized at once was the Great Northern main line from London to Doncaster, in 1846; perhaps this can be regarded as running from A to about D. Later on, of course, large systems were brought about by amalgamations, but the lines were built as a patchwork. The major effort of the British legislature went into settling disputes between private interests—the terms on which the companies should be allowed to buy the land of those unwilling proprietors who could afford to argue their case for something over a market price before Parliament, or the decision whether one company or another should be allowed to proceed with conflicting schemes. More often than not the answer given to this last conundrum was

Both, but One after the Other. Writing in 1852, Robert Stephenson lamented that even by then £60 million had been wasted on the construction of railways 'which would never have been built had a directing genius presided over the chartering of them'. All this went on against an occasional background of more or less interesting skullduggery, with hired gangs of toughs sent out either to beat up or protect railway surveyors, obstructionism and midnight evasions in the field, and occasional pitched battles for possession of the works between armies loyal to the company or the contractor. It was a robust age. The dreams of wealth fuelling it all were reflected in the stock market, and during the 'Railway Mania' of 1845–6 fortunes were won and (just as often) lost on a scale that had not been seen since the South Sea Bubble, with outcry and complaints to match.

In Europe progress was considerably more decorous, though also considerably slower. France and, to some extent, Belgium stood at the opposite pole of policy to Great Britain. In France very few railways were built during the 1830s, and those were admittedly planned on

Robert Stephenson's 'Planet' of 1830: a remarkable advance in the twelve months or so since the 'Rocket', with cylinders finding their place at last, horizontal and at the front. Science Museum, London

A selection of carriages 'employed for the conveyance of passengers and cattle' on the Liverpool & Manchester, 1830. Science Museum, London

'Old Ironsides', the first locomotive built by Matthias Baldwin, the founder of the famous Philadelphia works, in 1832. It followed Stephenson's 'Planet' design very closely. Reading Railroad Co.

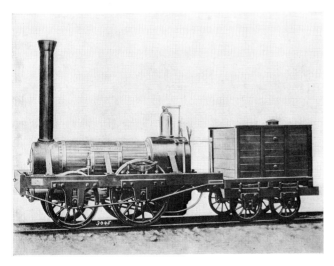

a piecemeal basis. But a great deal of thought went into the shaping of a railway policy, aimed at the construction of a network planned as a national whole, and in 1842 a Fundamental Law of railway development was promulgated. This laid down the main-line routes that were to be built, in fair detail; the state was to have the responsibility of building them, and they would be let out on lease at the best commercial terms obtainable to private companies, who would operate them. What the terms were finally varied somewhat according to the likely amount of traffic; in the industrial north the company repaid the construction cost *in toto*, over most of the country the company provided track, locomotives and rolling stock out of its own pocket; in some rural parts the government had not only to build but also to equip and operate the lines before a bidder could be found. Naturally, additional railways were authorized later, under arrangements which differed in detail but not in principle. One of the factors leading to the nationalization of the French railway system in 1938 was that the leases, all for 99-year terms, were running out and the companies had become unwilling to spend capital sums while unsure of their renewal. In Germany and Austria, and most other countries, the initiative in the planning of routes always lay with the government. Throughout continental Europe, therefore, it is relatively uncommon to find competing railways running parallel over any distance (except where one country's railways competed with

The 'Lafayette', a 4-2-0 with a leading bogie, built for the B & O in 1837, demonstrating the evolution from the 'Planet' type to the standard American 4-4-0 of later years.
Baltimore & Ohio Railroad

Assembling the great tubes for Robert Stephenson's Britannia Bridge across the Menai Strait; the contractor's staging in 1849, with travelling crane and riveters' furnaces. John Snell Collection

another's, as for example the Swiss or Austrian trans-alpine routes).

In America matters were even freer and easier than in Britain, with the major difference that it was government policy to encourage the construction of railways to open up the unsettled parts of the nation. The West was won—or at any rate the winning of it became useful for the first time—through the advance of the steam engine. The typical gaudy 4-4-0, with flaring chimney and long cow-catcher, hauled in civilization with all its mixed blessings. Buffalo herds might impede its progress for hours as they wandered slowly across the new-laid rails; but their decimation, quite often by idle sharpshooters pointing rifles out of the carriage windows as the train clattered past the herds, was symbolic of the victory of the machine. The way in which the building of these lines was encouraged was, in the remoter areas, for the state to grant the company the ownership of so many acres of

land per mile of track laid; this was a very fair arrangement at first, since it provided useful collateral. The land was worth only so many cents per acre, but there were a lot of acres. But later on, when the first transcontinental lines were well established, there were some pretty villainous goings-on, and some quite ruthless business methods were used to attack some other railway's route or traffic, or in defence against such attacks. They were not always confined to business methods either; there were one or two famous cases where company A hired gunmen to snipe at company B's construction crews, so that company A could lay iron first through some narrow canyon and so block the other's passage.

So much for railway politics; in microcosm, even at their worst, no different in principle from the stratagems of Macchiavelli or Metternich. But in the rather staider world of the engineers, there were also many different ways of building railroads.

The predominant British school in the early days, led by George Stephenson, believed in going to great trouble and expense to build a line as perfect as possible right from the start. In this he followed the spirit of the instruction given to him by Edward Pease, the principal moving force behind the Stockton & Darlington, when he wrote in 1821: 'it must be borne in mind that this is for a great public way and to remain as long as any Coal in the district remains.' Hence the earliest main lines in Britain were extremely well built, with generous curves and easy gradients (seldom steeper than 1 in 200), even though this involved very large earthworks, tunnels and viaducts. As a result, they are still capable of carrying today's trains, running at speeds far beyond the reach of their builders (but not beyond their foretelling), with no significant alterations to line or level and usually with no rebuilding of the original structures. During the 1840s the doctrine was modified to some extent by the followers of Joseph

The bridge over the Recco River, Turin & Genoa Railway (1853); one of the early mountain main lines in Europe.
British Railways

The first train arriving at Venice (*1846*).

Italian State Railways

Another American vertical-boiler engine: the South Caro-lina Railroad's 'Best Friend of Charleston', complete with conspicuous safety-valve lever which was held down once too often by the fireman. John Snell Collection

Locke, who was prepared to accept steeper gradients (up to the 1 in 75 over Shap Fell) if necessary in order to avoid earthworks and particularly tunnels. But even then, Locke minimized gradients and would not countenance rapid changes; he kept curves easy, and built as solidly as Stephenson, so that his lines are in general just as suitable for today's speeds. In fact, the whole British approach shunned the idea of depending on deviations and improvements at a later date, and aimed at building to last right from the start. This was the normal method of approach on the Continent also, though less and less rigorously applied, perhaps, as one moves east.

The American school of engineers, however, had no patience with this perfectionism. They stressed the importance of getting trains through as soon as possible;

there was plenty of traffic waiting, and in any case it was necessary to keep ahead of the competition. There was also the point that the land grants were generally made over only when the line was opened. As a result, construction works were kept to a minimum. Sooner than tunnel through a hill, go over it—even on ridiculous grades of about 1 in 20 if necessary—provide enough engines, and any train could be got over. Sooner than build a stone viaduct or a large embankment, run up a timber trestle. Never build a mile of straight track if two miles of bends would be quicker to open. Nobody disputed that this made a pretty rough railroad, but it made it in a hurry. As the money came in from receipts, so bit by bit the kinks (horizontal and vertical) could be taken out. And this was done fairly energetically. However, it is a continuing process; for the standards were improved

A centenary replica of the first train in Switzerland, on the Zürich–Baden line in 1847. The engine is a long-boiler 4-2-0. Swiss Federal Railways

89

*Opening day of the railway from Paris to Chartres, in
1849; two locomotives, but not their presumably
unworthy tenders, receive the sacramental rites.*

La Vie du Rail

only up to what was necessary at any one time (except for
a few lines, most of them built considerably later, that
were well funded from the start and engineered more in
accordance with European ideas). So the process of
line changing and diverting tracks is still going on, and
although American main lines have for many years been
quite capable of carrying extremely *heavy* trains, few of
them are well laid out for extremely *fast* ones, both
because of sharp curves and because of an abundance
of level crossings.

A similar pattern was found in the various types of
permanent way. The very phrase 'permanent way'
reflects the approach of the first railway builders, who
hoped to lay a track that would stay there—well perhaps
not for ever, but certainly for a very long time, without
attention. The cast-iron rails used on horse tramways
and the first locomotive lines had begun to be superseded,
by the time of the Stockton & Darlington, by wrought-

iron rails, rolled in lengths of 15 to 20 feet. Wrought iron
was tougher than cast, and certainly no more quickly
worn away by the wheels; it was considerably more
expensive at first per ton, but its greater strength and
almost complete freedom from rail breakages (if it was
made with care) meant that for public railways it was the
only possible material, until it was gradually superseded
in turn by mild steel after the 1860s.

George Stephenson at first hoped, on the Liverpool &
Manchester, to build a permanent way by fixing wrought-
iron rails onto heavy stone blocks. The blocks were carefully tamped and consolidated into place, exact in line
and level, one by one, and the rails carefully laid on top.
Then the trains started running, and in a short time line
and level had vanished and the coaches—and above all
the locomotives—began to bounce and sway. Discon-
certingly, the rails laid on wooden sleepers on what had
been intended to be a temporary way across the as yet

unconsolidated bank over Chat Moss stood the strain noticeably better. At first engineers believed that it was just a matter that had to be persevered with; Robert Stephenson used stone blocks on parts of the London & Birmingham; I. K. Brunel, original as ever, devised a permanent way laid on continuous wooden beams under the rails, held firmly down (in theory, but in practice up) by piles hammered into the formation. Finally, by the early 1840s, it was accepted that the sought-for degree of permanence could not be attained. Perhaps the clincher was an experiment in a cutting on the Manchester & Leeds line, where the rails were secured directly to the solid rock, accurately levelled indeed, but the riding was so appallingly rough and noisy that the length had to be replaced at once. In fact what was needed was a resilient way, best provided by using wooden sleepers packed into a bed of ballast, which could be any available sufficiently hard material, though crushed rock was much the best. Constant petty repair would be needed as the track was distorted by the weight of trains, but small gangs of men coming round at intervals with jacks, bars and shovels could restore matters.

The Liverpool & Manchester was opened in 1830; the first American transcontinental rail link was completed in 1869. The growth of the industry in the short space of half a lifetime was enormous; yet during the following half-century it continued at the same pace, filling in the gaps in the earlier network in advanced countries, and establishing systems for the first time on wilder shores. Writing in 1857, the mathematician Thomas Baker broke rather oddly into verse in the form of a twelve-canto Byronian poem entitled 'The Steam Engine, or the Powers of Flame'. Writing with satirical intent of the brief period of commercial hysteria of the late 1840s, he said:

'Nor was this MANIA, this eccentric roar
Confined alone within Britannia's shore.
It made its way at that eventful time
To every land without respect to clime!
Vast were the schemes that now came forth in France
(Tho' not so wont in Britain's wake t'advance).
Europe was smitten to the very core
And thence the MANIA rag'd from shore to shore.
East and West Indies groaned 'neath the disease
Its virulence uncheck'd by rolling seas.
Nay, e'en Van Diemen's Land and New South Wales
Determined, like the rest, to have their rails.'

And inside ten years they got them too: a nice example of the poet's fancy not winging quite so far as the imagination of staid financiers.

An American standard 4-4-0 of 1874, from the Baldwin catalogue. British Museum

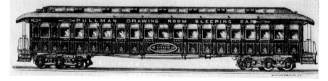

The Pennsylvania Railroad as early as 1875 had a claim to the title of best and most prosperous railway in the USA. Here is a selection of typical passenger equipment; the engine, being a coal-burner, has a parallel chimney.

British Museum

*Two Baltimore & Ohio engines, each representing a major
advance for its time: the 0-8-0 'Memnon' of 1848, and the
4-6-0 'Thatcher Perkins' of 1863. Both are still preserved
at Baltimore.* Baltimore & Ohio Railroad

4

Mechanical Development in the Nineteenth Century

The one constant movement in locomotive development after 1830 was towards increasing power, size and constructional strength. Just as the Stockton & Darlington had shown up the weaknesses in locomotives which had never had to do anything more strenuous than trundle up and down the few miles between colliery and waterside, so the Liverpool & Manchester proved how many improvements were needed to be able to handle a heavy inter-city passenger and general merchandise traffic with speed and dependability.

At first there was only one school of locomotive design —the British, led by Robert Stephenson (though several other builders rivalled him, notably Edward Bury of Liverpool). The main line of development for the first five years (after which there was something of a pause until the 1840s) lay from the 4½-ton *Rocket*, through the later engines of the same type built only a few months after but which included such important improvements as separate frames and smokeboxes and which practically doubled in size, to the 'Planet'-type of four-wheeler of late 1830, which had for the first time horizontal cylinders at the front of the engine and a crank axle, and which came in two forms, with a single driving wheel for passenger or coupled wheels for freight traffic; to the six-wheeled *Patentee* of 1833, which was in essence an enlarged version of the *Planet* with an additional axle to improve riding and lessen damage to the track, and which came in four separate varieties: 2-2-2 for ordinary passenger trains, 0-4-2 or sometimes 2-4-0 for ordinary

Apart from the rather rudimentary cab, a very typical British 2-2-2 of 1863; but this example was built for New South Wales. NSW Govt Railways

Perhaps the nearest thing to an American 4-4-0, and the first engines to have full cabs, to run in Britain; Bouch's 'Brougham', built in 1860 for the Stockton & Darlington.
Science Museum, London

freight and 0-6-0 for especially heavy duty. As early as 1834 an 0-6-0 was delivered to the Leicester & Swannington which weighed 17 tons, without tender, and was both much the largest locomotive yet built and the ancestor of the standard British goods engine for the next 120 years. The advance in the five years since Rainhill was truly remarkable.

Early locomotives in other countries were much influenced by British design, not surprisingly since most

The Semmering Trial contestants of 1851: the 'Wiener Neustadt', 'Seraing', 'Bavaria' and 'Vindobona'.
John Snell Collection

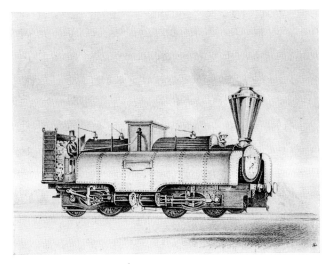

early examples were in fact imported from Britain. Séguin in France had been an original, but the first important lines in that country, notably the Paris & Versailles, used machines built by Stephenson. The first locomotive to run on a public railway in Germany, the *Adler*, was a 2-2-2 'Patentee' also by Stephenson, as was the first in Russia, which reached a speed of $62\frac{1}{2}$ mph on the 6-foot-gauge line from St Petersburg to Tsarskoe Seloe in 1837. It was some time before any of these countries established their own distinctive practice.

In America, however, matters were different, principally as a result of the consequences of railway-building policy in that country. The emphasis on rapid construction, together with the use of light rail for financial reasons, meant that the tracks on which the engines had to run tended to be much rougher than the carefully laid 'permanent ways' of Europe, while they also had to be able to climb some fairly unreasonable gradients with useful loads. These things put a premium on flexibility of wheelbase and increased power. European engineers were seeking principally for economy, both in fuel consumption and in repairs; brute power was not so important, and the simpler rigid-wheelbase locomotive with all wheels directly attached to the frame was greatly preferred.

The first British engines in America therefore did not do particularly well. One interesting case in point was the *John Bull*, an 0-4-0 'Planet' built by Stephenson in 1831 for the Camden & Amboy line, which kept on leaving the road. In an effort to guide her round the dog-legs she encountered, an additional pair of wheels was therefore mounted on a separate frame consisting of a pair of wooden beams mounted fairly flexibly on the front of the engine; the device succeeded, and was the origin of the

two-wheeled sub-frame or 'pony truck' providing support and guidance at front or rear of many steam locomotives from that day on. The next step was to go further and have a four-wheeled sub-frame, capable of carrying greater weight and with even better tracking ability. The 4-2-0 type built, among others, by Norris of Philadelphia during the late 1830s thus evolved fairly naturally out of the 2-2-0 'Planet', though it generally used outside instead of inside cylinders, which were always rare in American practice and unknown after about 1880. From the 4-2-0 it was an easy and obvious step to the 4-4-0, and by 1836 this type had appeared.

Robert Stephenson was responsible for two further technical improvements in 1841 and 1842. The first was the 'long-boiler' engine. It was noticeable that locomotives of the 1830s, when working hard, tended to get very hot at the front end; smokeboxes and chimneys glowed red. This could only mean that a great deal of heat was being wasted; hot gases were being whirled through the tubes so rapidly that they did not have time to heat the water adequately. The answer was clearly to make the tubes, and therefore the boiler, longer. This first step in the study of the ideal proportions of a boiler to maximize thermal efficiency reached its final climax in the work of Wagner in Germany in the 1920s; but like most changes and developments in steam locomotive design, especially in Britain and America, it was worked out on an entirely rule-of-thumb and unscientific basis. (Academics and theoreticians always seem to have been held in especial scorn on the railways of these countries; the resulting loss is now becoming painfully clear.) However, the long-boiler engine succeeded in its purpose, though at the price of another disadvantage. Stephenson's patent prescribed a six-wheeled engine with all axles in front of

One of the first mountain rack railways was the Arth-Rigi-Bahn, in Switzerland; the Rothenfluhbach viaduct in 1883. John Snell Collection

the firebox; as a result, its wheelbase was short and it was unsteady at speed. Long-boiler express engines thus had a short and rather unhappy career; the type, however, did very well in slow freight service, where its economy in large power output at low speeds told, and the typical European freight engine of the nineteenth century was an outside-cylinder long-boiler 0-6-0 (or an enlarged 0-8-0 version).

The other and even more important improvement was the evolution of the first mechanically satisfactory valve gear which both allowed easy reversing of the engine by the movement of a single lever, and also made it possible to adjust, while running, the point of piston stroke at which the admission of steam to the cylinder was cut off. Previously, with a fixed and invariable cut-off, it was necessary to have steam admitted to the cylinder for at least half its stroke, otherwise in many positions of the cranks the engine would be unable to start; but in running this meant that the steam could only be expanded to about half its original pressure and still contained a great deal of energy when it had to be exhausted. It was now possible to alter the cut-off as speed and load dictated to

Portage viaduct, on the Erie Railroad, in 1875; this spindly steel trestle, now replaced by something stronger, itself replaced a timber trestle which burned down.

British Railways

obtain the most economical rate of expansion. Stephenson's valve-gear was the most common in nineteenth-century practice throughout the world, and is still largely favoured; during the twentieth century the alternative gear invented by the Belgian, Eugene Walschaerts, at about the same time came into greater favour since it gave better valve performance at the very short cut-offs which had by then become feasible.

With these developments, no really fundamentally new steps in design were taken for the remainder of the century; progress consisted rather in building bigger and better, and after 1870 or so gradually changing over from wrought iron to steel. One noteworthy landmark, however, was a third set of competitive trials, this time held in Austria in 1851. The object this time was to produce a locomotive capable of economical work on mountainous main lines, and in particular to draw 140 tons up the 1 in 40 grades of the newly built line over the Semmering Pass, between Vienna and Trieste. Four entrants competed, and each in its different way was unprecedented; for they all had in common the fact that they had powered wheels which were not rigidly connected to the frame. Before

Building several miles of track a day across the open prairie needed a considerable supporting organization; trains like this acted as stores and living accommodation.

John Snell Collection

A very typical British passenger train of the 1860 era, complete with four-wheeled coaches; as delivered to the first railway in New South Wales.

NSW Govt Railways

Latterday long-boiler 0-6-0s: built by Beyer Peacock between 1877 and 1889, two New South Wales veterans on a special train to celebrate the end of their reign on the Oberon branch, in March 1963. I. K. Winney

them, only a few oddities like the 'Puffing Billies' in their eight-wheeled form had had this feature. Two of the entrants, depending on chains or rods and jackshafts to give motion to all the wheels (including those of the tender) looked back rather than forward for their inspiration; the other two were the founders of two of the three main families of articulated locomotive. The *Seraing* was (except for an unsuccessful American experiment of 1831) the ancestral Fairlie, with a double boiler having central firebox and chimney at each end, the cylinders and motion mounted on two separate bogies connected to the frame with swivelling joints and flexible steampipes. The *Wiener Neustadt* had a conventional boiler, but the frame was again carried on two power bogies of the same sort; it was therefore the ancestral 'Mallet', and the forerunner of the largest and most powerful type of steam locomotive ever built.

Apart from specialized machines of this kind, the main

King of the Broad Gauge: Gooch 4-2-2 'Timour' at Newton Abbot in 1886, with Driver Greenaway and Fireman Crabb. British Railways

line of development in Europe ran from the early 2-2-2s and other types of six-wheeler to the 4-6-0s and 0-8-0s becoming standard types at the end of the century. Especially in Britain and France, but also elsewhere, the single-driving-wheel engine was at first favoured for the fastest trains for a sound practical reason. These trains were still quite light and could be handled by an engine with a limited amount of adhesive weight; the frictional and other losses due to having to drive more than a single pair of large wheels could be avoided; and especially while tires were still made of wrought iron, relatively soft and inconsistent, it was hardly possible to keep two pairs of wheels exactly the same diameter for long due to inequality of wear—this strained the rods and led to a considerable danger of their bending or breaking at high speed. Where expresses were hauled by engines with coupled wheels before steel tires became common in the late 1860s, it was a sure sign that they did not go very fast. With steel tires, of course, the picture changed.

In America between the 1850s and 1880s the 4-4-0 was almost universal, though there were plenty of other types in special circumstances, including 4-6-0s and 0-8-0s even during the 1850s. Of course trains were not especially fast. The emphasis on power output led to ever larger boilers and particularly fireboxes, though in fact

no really large engines were practicable in America until the late 1880s, when the primitive link-and-pin coupling standard till then was replaced by the present Janney central coupling, whose vastly greater strength allowed train weights to increase. It was at about that time also that the process of track and route improvement began to produce some main lines on which reasonably high speeds became feasible. The dry nature of much of the country, with its enormous and highly inflammable forests, coupled with the use on many lines of wood fuel, meant that the enormous diamond-shaped spark-arresting chimney fitted to the great majority of American engines at this period, especially in the West, was a very necessary addition. It did not arrest all the sparks by any means, but it intercepted most of the bigger ones. But the main contribution of American locomotive designers during this period was the bogie, at first disliked in Europe, but from about 1870 onwards increasingly appreciated as a useful aid to stability and tracking on curves even on well-maintained lines.

Passenger rolling stock, in Europe and in America, originated with vehicles based on the stage-coach, with a small single-compartment body with side doors and roof seats, carried on a four-wheeled frame. In Europe, economics soon dictated that three-compartment bodies

On the last day but one of operation on Brunel's 7-foot gauge, 'Iron Duke' (broad-gauge engines had no numbers) near Uphill, Somerset, with the Plymouth–Paddington 'Jubilee'. British Railways

Elegance of the 1860s—I. Norwegian State Railways 2-4-0 No. 17, 'Caroline', built by Robert Stephenson & Co. in 1861, at Oslo in 1954. Dr P. Ransome-Wallis

Elegance of the 1860s—II. Pope Pius IX's special saloon. Italian State Railways

be carried on the same frame and pair of wheels, and by the time of the Liverpool & Manchester this was the standard type of passenger coach (in the superior classes; third-class passengers had to put up with an open box, with or without seats). In Britain development proceeded from that point; there was a slow tendency to improve standards of comfort for the lower orders (the best first-class stock even in the early days was pretty good), especially after Gladstone's Act in 1844 had enjoined the running of at least one daily train for third-class passengers travelling in coaches both ventilated and protected from the weather. By the 1860s there was a tendency to build longer—there were some four-wheeled coaches with five compartments or even more—but this soon led to the point where six-wheeled coaches, known since the 1840s, became the standard type. Bogie stock began to be used during the 1870s, at first only on particularly important trains, but during the 1880s and 1890s passenger carriages were being built which in size and comfort, apart from such matters as air-conditioning, were the equal of anything running today. The change from wood to steel construction during the first part of the twentieth century was not for reasons of amenity so much as for protection in accidents.

American passenger coach design followed a different course. Just as with locomotives, rigid four-wheelers were found prone to derailment, and by the end of the 1830s the typical American coach was already a long eight-wheeler carried on two bogies. (For the same reason the same thing applied to freight stock.) The

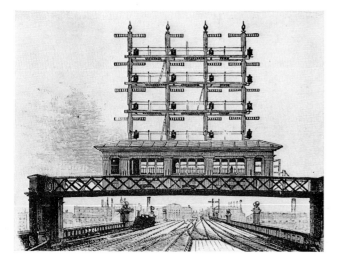

The array of signals above the signal-box at Cannon Street, London, when the line opened in 1864.

John Snell Collection

Early streamliner: C class compound 4-4-0 no. 55 of the Paris–Lyon–Méditerranée, built in 1895.

La Vie du Rail

101

The Austrian State Railways Golsdorf express passenger 2-6-2 compound, class 10, of 1905; a painting by H. M. le Fleming. (Mrs) H. M. le Fleming

Sleek Briton: London Brighton & South Coast K class 2-6-0 of 1913. John Snell Collection

There was a time, long ago, before all the Swiss main lines were electrified: a Simplon-line express at Geneva in 1906, the year the tunnel was opened, with an A3/5 4-6-0.
Swiss Federal Railways

greater length of the car was taken advantage of by adopting a radically different and much cheaper form of body construction, with doors giving onto open platforms at each end of the car, and a single space inside with seats on either side of a central corridor. This could be more or less effectively heated by a stove at each end of the car, so that travellers in winter suffered proportionately less than they might in the freezing privacy of a European compartment; the robuster and more egalitarian atmosphere in the States meant that passengers put up with the communal character of life in a single coach carrying fifty or sixty all together. Continental designers tended to follow the British style, though not without some leaning towards American practice, particularly in Germany and Austria (where of course the winters tended to be harder). The Russians, with harder winters still, followed American practice in general, but for the superior classes very early developed a heating system depending on hot water circulated from individual

furnaces in each car, a method still used on modern stock. Compartments remained chilly places (though one could usually hire hot-water bottles) until steam heating supplied from the locomotive came to the rescue after about 1890.

One final question of considerable technical interest occupied a great deal of attention during the nineteenth century; the matter of track gauge. As we have seen, Stephenson followed a very old tradition indeed in fixing on 4 ft 8½ in., though the additional half-inch was added as a result of experience on the Liverpool & Manchester, which revealed that some freedom between rail and flange was desirable. But there were many engineers who felt that this standard gauge was far too narrow. There was great fear of overturning in derailments (possibly as a result of stage-coach experience, when capsizes killed and injured a remarkable number of people; the toll of the road is nothing new), and as a result it was desired to keep the centre of gravity as low

103

Holiday traffic at Shasta Springs, California, about 1900.
Southern Pacific

A happy band of travellers (or publicity girls) in a Santa Fe Pullman about the turn of the century. The boxes above the seats let down to form beds, and the seats below were similarly convertible. A.T. & S.F. Railroad Co.

as possible. A 6-foot gauge, which allowed reasonable width of a carriage body slung between the wheels, was favoured somewhat, though illogical compromise in Ireland determined the Irish standard of 5 ft 3 in. In Spain and India 5 ft 6 in. was adopted; 5 ft in Russia, mainly out of a desire to be different on principle. The widest gauge of all was 7 ft on Brunel's Great Western Railway in England, whose original justification was that it would allow larger wheels (and hence less friction) while carriage bodies of ample size could be slung between them—but the main reason was a rather bold grandeur of imagination coupled with a very decided opinion that speeds of 100 mph ought to be contemplated. Full advantage was never taken of the technical possibilities of the broad gauge on the GWR, since it was soon vitiated commercially by the break-of-gauge problem regarding communication with the rest of the country, but the system survived in Devon and Cornwall until 1892. It may in fact be argued now that the benefits of the broad gauge were illusory; the only certain thing about it is that it brings about an inescapable increase of cost in all departments—track, rolling stock, motive power—at once, while the benefit of high speed can only be obtained where the considerable further expense of high accuracy of maintenance is commercially justified. But where it is justified, high speeds can also be attained on the standard gauge. Certainly, one can point at the generally sluggish running in the broad-gauge nations remaining, all (as it happens) relatively poor: Spain, India, Brazil, Argentina and even Ireland and southern Australia, where trains are no faster than in countries with similar standards of living but narrower gauges.

By the 1860s the gauge question had come to mean something else; the wisdom of using a gauge narrower than standard. Here the arguments were reversed; narrow-gauge tracks and trains were much cheaper to build, while if sufficiently developed could carry heavy traffic at fair speed. Two sorts of narrow-gauge railway then developed. There were light secondary feeder lines in remote districts, connecting with the national standard network; they served an essential purpose once, but with the growth of road transport railways of this kind are now rapidly disappearing, apart from some special cases. On the other hand, somewhat broader gauges, from 3 ft to 3 ft 6 in., became the basis of heavy-duty national networks. The African standard gauge south of the Sahara is 3 ft 6 in. (or 1 metre in the east), and similarly in Japan, parts of Australia, New Zealand and elsewhere. The highest practical speeds on these lines are generally about 70 mph; but in other respects performance is fully equal to European standards.

5

The Age of Steam

For most of the first half of the twentieth century the world's trade goods moved on land behind steam locomotives, and most land passenger journeys, especially over long distances, were by steam train. For short-distance urban and suburban passenger traffic the horse bus had never been displaced and in many cities it worked alongside horse trams; when electrified from about 1890 onwards urban tramway networks proved formidable competitors to the railway and by 1914 had already forced the start of the process of station and line closures. One of the two most compelling arguments in favour of railway electrification was then the menace of the tram (the other was the smoke nuisance, especially in long tunnels). In its turn, of course, the electric tram has now nearly everywhere given place to the cheaper, faster and more flexible motor bus, which has extended very greatly the area in which railways have become liable to competition for their passenger business.

The other type of railway on which electrification was already predominant during the first years of the twentieth century was the purely urban passenger line, running (unlike trams) on its own right-of-way in tunnel or on viaduct right into the central areas of the city. This is a very specialized type of railway, although one of the early ones, the Metropolitan in London, was originally promoted as a feeder to and extension of the Great Western Railway, whose main-line terminus at Paddington was remote from the business quarters. Soon after it opened in 1863, it was found that its 4-mile route generated a great deal of short-distance business of its own, and the original service of one train every 15 minutes soon proved insufficient. Other lines followed as the years passed, in spite of the very high costs of construction through the congested and built-up urban areas; the driving motive was the impossibility even then of road traffic conditions. The earliest urban railways were built on the 'cut and cover' principle, with a large trench excavated along the route, following main roads wherever possible, and then after completion roofed in and the surface status quo more or less restored. In fact, this method of construction is perhaps the commonest, being

Three early twentieth-century Pacifics. Missouri Pacific no. 1118 was one of the first class of the type in America, built in 1902. Hungarian State Railways 301 class, built in 1911; a relatively lightweight but powerful example. S.N.C.F. 231K class at Boulogne-Maritime in 1964; these engines were originally built for the Paris–Lyon–Méditerranée in 1909, but comprehensively modernized in the 1930s.

Missouri Pacific, A. E. Durrant Collection, Brian Stephenson

used not only in London but in Paris, Berlin, New York and other cities, not to mention in current construction in San Francisco.

The urban railway developed in two ways. First of all, by replacement of steam power. All or nearly all the lines built before about 1890 originally depended on steam traction, including such affairs as the Elevated lines in New York and other American cities. Steam engines were never happy in such constricted surroundings; put them in tunnels and they exhale steam and smoke in such quantity that life is soon made pretty appalling for the customers (though a steam-worked underground line survived in Glasgow until the mid 1950s); put them on viaducts running along the middle of roads, and they blow smoke in at people's windows and drop hot coals down people's collars. Neither is popular, so by 1900

electrification of all these lines was well advanced (though the first urban underground electric railway was actually not one of the main ones, but in Budapest in 1889).

The other development was a change in the method of construction from cut-and-cover to deep-level tunnelling. This was normally combined with a reduction in the cross section of the tunnel and the loading gauge of the trains for economy's sake. Only a minority of metropolitan railway systems include lines built on this principle; in fact the only true 'tube' lines are in London, Berlin and New York (Hudson & Manhattan). Although a couple of tube-gauge steam locomotives were built for London's second tube (the Central Line) opened in 1900, they were short-lived and never used for public trains. The first of these railways, the City & South London,

Two restored British veterans show their paces near Carlisle in 1964: ex-Great North of Scotland 4-4-0 no. 49, built in 1893, leading ex-Caledonian 4-2-2 no. 123 built in 1885, and the last single-wheeler to run in Britain. Derek Cross

Francis Webb's 'Eighteen Inch Goods' 0-6-0s, otherwise known as 'Cauliflowers', built for the London & North Western from 1885, lasted well; no. 8367 on a Bletchley–Cambridge train in the late 1940s. C. R. L. Coles

opened in 1890, had originally been intended for cable haulage, but was in fact worked by electric traction right from the start.

Urban railways of this kind have little in common with main-line railways; they share some of the basic technology, but their purpose in life, and economic problems, are fundamentally different. They are part of the armoury of urban amenity, and their early adoption of electricity, for non-economic reasons, signalled this. On the main lines during the first half of the twentieth century, steam reigned supreme and reached the peak of its development. Two main factors, operating by 1900, provided the motives for fresh advance. One was the increase in the use of steel for locomotive and rolling stock construction, together with a movement which gained impetus during the 1890s (very largely for reasons of competitiveness between rival lines) towards greatly improving passenger comforts and amenities. At the same time, there was improvement of couplings and brakes. As a result of all these things trains became very much heavier; thus

considerably larger and more powerful locomotives began to be required. The other principal factor was a design improvement; the invention of a workable superheater. The trouble about using steam taken directly from the boiler is that it is 'saturated', containing a great deal of water in the form of droplets, and as it expands condensation rapidly takes place so that its capacity to propel the piston falls off quickly. Passing hot water through the cylinders in this way is also wasteful of fuel. If the steam can be heated after it has left the boiler, the suspended water is removed and the amount of useful work that can be obtained is much increased; it becomes possible to reduce cut-off points from around 40 per cent to 20 per cent or even less. The question was how to find a workable method for this reheating, and success was achieved by Schmidt in Germany and Flamme in Belgium during the first few years of the twentieth century. The Schmidt superheater rapidly ousted other experimental types, and by 1914 was pretty well universal on locomotives intended for main-line duty. In turn, the

108

*Southern monsters; two of the Virginian Railway's
2-10-10-2 'Mallets' of 1918.* H. M. le Fleming

short cut-off points which it made possible showed up shortcomings in cylinder and valve designs; it was not only necessary to get the steam into the cylinder, but it had to come out again. Increasingly careful attention to steam passages and valve behaviour meant that by the late 1920s locomotives capable of 100-mph speeds in regular service were at last a possibility. (There had been legendary speed exploits in earlier years, most of them quite unsubstantiated; there is in fact no record of a speed of 100 mph attained by a steam locomotive anywhere in the world before 1920 which is authenticated beyond dispute.)

Heavy loads and high speeds meant that as well as subtle design, brute power was also needed; the boiler had to be able to deliver the horsepower required. This really hinged in most cases on getting a large enough firebox, with a good big grate. Except for tank locomotives (carrying their coal and water supplies on one frame) it had been rare to have the rear of an engine supported by a carrying wheel; the last pair of wheels were drivers. But

their large diameter tended to inhibit much increase in firebox size (except in some countries with very large loading gauges where it was possible to lift the whole boiler upwards); thus a firebox of the size that had begun to be needed usually had to be supported on at least one pair of trailing wheels. So the 4-4-0 gave way to the 4-4-2 or 'Atlantic' (so called because some of the first were used on the high-speed trains between Philadelphia and Atlantic City), and the 4-6-0 to the 4-6-2 or 'Pacific' (so called either because the Pacific was the larger ocean or because the first series of such engines were built in America for service in New Zealand). The 'Pacific' type really became the twentieth-century classic express engine; occasionally a 4-6-4 variant with an even larger firebox was used; much more often it was eclipsed in size by 4-8-2s or 'Mountains' and 4-8-4s, which were more suitable for really heavy work and freight duty. The absolute speed record for steam power was attained by a streamlined 'Pacific' of the London & North Eastern Railway, the famous *Mallard*, in July 1938, when it reached 126 mph on a 1 in 200 downgrade with a 240-ton train; though in fact the achievement of a German 4-6-4 in May 1936 in reaching 124·6 mph on a near level with 197 tons was really marginally more impressive.

For freight work, the important thing was not only horsepower; it was the ability to pull heavy loads (at lower speeds). Thus the question of adhesive weight was uppermost; and since the maximum weight that can be put on an axle is limited by the strength of the track, adhesion can be increased only by increasing the number of coupled wheels. Freight engines with eight coupled wheels were quite common by the 1880s, either 0-8-0s or 2-8-0s; by the turn of the century the 0-10-0 was becoming popular in some countries (including Germany and Russia). American practice still favoured using a leading pony wheel or bogie, and so the 2-10-0 or 2-10-2 was a common heavy freight engine by about 1910. Beyond this point matters began to be difficult, since it was increasingly awkward to get round curves. Engines with twelve coupled wheels were used to some extent in Germany,

Austria, America, Bulgaria and Indonesia, but the Russian attempt to go one better and build a 4-14-4 was a fiasco. Further progress was possible only by taking up the ideas demonstrated in the Semmering trials, and using articulated locomotives with two (or rarely three) independent sets of driving wheels mounted on bogies. Initial progress was due to the engineers of light and narrow-gauge railways, where the curve problem was worst, and the first engines of 'Mallet' type (due to the Frenchman Anatole Mallet, with a conventional outline above the frames) were used on lines of this sort. However, the main-line potentialities of the design were recognized quite soon, especially in America, where really large 'Mallets' were quite common on some lines by 1914, and where they finally developed into the largest steam engines ever built (the Union Pacific 'Big Boy' 4-8-8-4s of 1941, 340-ton monsters capable of developing some 9,000 hp and also of running at 80 mph). The other main type of articulated engine was the 'Garratt', in essence two entirely separate conventional locomotive frames,

Off to the sea at Skegness: Ivatt D2 class 4-4-0 of 1897 on a London & North Eastern excursion in the 1930s.

Real Photo Co.

A study in German front ends; the 38 class 4-6-0 on the right is a survivor of the Prussian standard class of 1906, the first numerous and wholly successful modernized and superheated type in Europe. The 64 class on the left is a lightweight 2-6-2T dating from the 1920s. A. E. Durrant

cylinders and wheels with a large boiler slung between them, and coal and water tanks at either end; these were due to H. W. Garratt and mostly used by railways under British influence. They were also entirely successful, and approached the largest 'Mallets' in size; many are still running in southern Africa.

To be able to haul a heavy train at high speed is important; but it is no less important to be able to stop it.

Twelve-coupled: Union Pacific 3-cylinder 9000-class 4-12-2 of 1926. Kalmbach Publishing Co.

The question of train brakes was a vexed one during the nineteenth century; normal practice was to depend on men spaced along the train operating handbrakes by pre-arrangement or on emergency whistle signals. But the need remained to have all the brakes under the direct control of the driver, and working on every wheel. Various mechanical devices were tried, using chains or ropes slung along the length of the train, but friction and the inconvenience of making couplings defeated them. The answer was an air-powered system of some kind. Several were tried; some worked quite well except when a coupling parted (most often at the start of a derailment), when it was desirable to have every brake applied fully and automatically to reduce resulting damage. Two methods finally emerged as more or less satisfactory. The vacuum brake, used in Britain and a number of countries under British influence, is satisfactory on trains of moderate length, but hampered beyond that by the fact that it is a low-pressure system and thus somewhat sluggish (working 'pressures' are usually 15–18 lb. per square inch). The principal rival to the vacuum brake, tested against it during the 1880s, was George Westing-house's compressed air brake, working at much higher pressures (100 lb. per square inch or more), and preferred by nearly every railway in the world (including a large minority of British lines until standardization swept it away). The ordinary type of Westinghouse brake, as used in America, has the disadvantage that when the brake has been applied, it can either be applied harder or released completely, but not partially released; it is thus inconvenient in mountain country and needs careful handling. The Oerlikon pattern of Westinghouse brake used in Europe has valve modifications which overcome this drawback.

The need to have some form of signalling was recognized in the very early days, but at first hand signals given by men at stations, who had the task of maintaining a standard time interval between trains moving in the same direction, sufficed. As junctions became more common and speeds increased, the need for large fixed signals easily visible at a distance became greater, and by the 1850s these were normal on main lines in advanced countries; the desirability of mechanically interlocking these signals with the points so that the indications given

One kind of steam locomotive oddity was the 'camelback', a type confined to the U.S.A. The driver travelled in a second cab atop the boiler, since the wide firebox would otherwise obstruct his view. This one is a Jersey Central 4-6-0, which survived into the 1950s.

Dr P. Ransome-Wallis

to the driver were forced to agree with the route actually set up was demonstrated by some fairly harsh experience, and in Britain interlocking of this kind began in the 1850s as well. Other countries followed according to the amount of traffic they had to deal with. Finally, the use of the electric telegraph enabled a positive check that the preceding train had actually cleared the other end of a section of line before another was admitted, which was a useful improvement on the time-interval system. So by 1900 there was a well-established tradition of signalling depending on a chain of signalboxes linked by telegraph; perfectly satisfactory from the point of view of safe working, though in more recent years considerable savings in manpower, coupled with a certain improvement due to being able to control longer lengths of line from one point, have brought about an increasing amount of colour-light signalling, wholly electrical and often considerably centralized and automated.

The question of travellers' comforts has already been mentioned. The first carriages with accommodation for sleeping (or at any rate facilities for passengers to lie down) were very early, and it was possible to occupy a horizontal position on a couch while travelling by night from London to Manchester, as soon as the line was completed, in 1838. More or less makeshift arrangements in ordinary first-class compartments were always possible. A greater need was felt in America, where journeys more often took a matter of days, and during the 1850s George Pullman was the principal mover in establishing an organization which operated coaches convertible from day to night use, with let-down beds and seats; American practice was for the coaches to be owned and staffed not by the railway but by a separate company, which facilitated through running over different lines. By the turn of the century Pullman cars reached a high standard of elegance and comfort, though the latter was still further improved stage by stage until the economic collapse of American passenger trains commenced about 1950. In Europe progress was a little slower at first, but by the 1870s a network of sleeping-car services was becoming established. However, it was on a different basis; convertibility for day or night use was not sought, and the Compagnie Internationale des Wagon-Lits (and the separate British railways) built specialized sleeping-cars

used only on night runs. In very recent years, since the 1950s, there has been some modification of this in Europe, though not in Britain, by introducing 'couchette' coaches which are in fact convertible, more or less standard compartment stock by day but with let-down beds for night use. This type of passenger accommodation has always been standard on long-distance trains in most of Africa and certain other countries.

Dining accommodation on trains also began to be provided during the 1870s and 1880s, while railways were competing among themselves by improving their accommodation and amenities. Again, American practice with its long-distance runs was somewhat ahead of European, although the older custom of providing large refreshment rooms at intervals and making a long halt at them took many years to vanish. But dining-cars connected to the whole of the rest of the train by a continuous gangway and available for use by all comers were rather later—the first British diner was a self-contained affair in which passengers remained in the same seat throughout the run —and were not at all common before 1900. Their spread to practically all long-distance trains of any importance in practically every country of the world mainly took place after about 1920.

6
Diesels, Electrics and a Changing World

During the last fifty years the railway's predominance in long-distance inland transport has been steadily eroded by the competition of the bus, the aeroplane and the passenger car for passenger traffic and by the road haulier and the trader's private lorry for freight. The process perhaps began with the motor bus, which was much cheaper and more flexible than the local train for handling small flows of passengers in rural areas and on branch lines; by 1930 the process of closing lines to passenger traffic had already begun in many countries, and it has continued since. Some railway administrations attempted to compete with the bus by replacing steam trains with light petrol- or diesel-engined railcars, at a fairly considerable saving; but nowhere has this form of vehicle done more than slow the trend, since it is still a heavier and more expensive machine than a road bus, inconveniently tied to a fixed route which has to be paid for and which often has stopping-places less well sited. A bus is of course often a less comfortable thing to ride in, which has meant that it competed much less well with the long-distance train; though in the last twenty years or so the construction of motorways has considerably reduced or even abolished the train's lead in this sector of the business. The development of air transport, especially during the 1960s, has attacked rail passenger trade from the other end, so that in advanced countries few people now consider a journey of more than five or six hours by train.

In most countries road transport was hardly a serious competitor for freight before 1939; in some, where the railways are protected (and the cost of track maintenance and improvement kept down) by legislation, it is still not an important competitor. But by about 1950 the road haulier was well able to hold his own against rail for high-value, low-bulk types of freight; he might have to charge more, but his customer paid willingly because the railway, tied to bulk traffics and too large to care greatly about the troubles of a single consignor, did not offer him the speed and reliability that tailor-made road transport provided. Since that time the growth of motorway networks and the considerable increases in permitted weights and sizes of big trucks have improved the road haulier's position still further.

Private road transport has done a great deal more to wear down the prosperity of all kinds of public transport; the passenger car, despite its heavy cost, is so nearly ideally flexible and convenient that it carries a large share of total passenger movement, by providing a service that train, bus or plane cannot hope to match. As a result, the rural bus (as opposed to the long-distance bus) is slowly going the way of the rural local train—though it will be longer dying in most countries, it is already effectively dead in some places, notably the United States. Similarly, the increasing numbers of trucks operated by the owners or distributors of the freight they carry undermine both the railway and the general road haulier.

The railways are fighting these unfavourable factors with a great deal of improved machinery, first among which are new and improved locomotives. Except in a few countries, the steam locomotive has more or less ceased to exist as an important source of traction power. Before 1939 its position was already under attack here and there, mainly through electrification; certain long-distance main-line electrifications were already in existence before 1914, and in several countries (Switzerland, Austria, Italy, Germany, France, Sweden and Japan notably) a great deal of mileage was converted between the wars. However, the economics of electrification were not all that promising; a very large capital expenditure was necessary, and although there was a reasonable economy in the actual cost of train haulage on a converted line, the business would not be worth while unless either there was a heavy traffic, or some non-financial consideration operated. This could be, as with the Alpine lines, a desire to convert simply because more powerful electric locomotives could climb the grades more quickly and without producing smoke.

Electrification has proceeded apace since 1945, especially in Europe, for much the same reasons as before. But the force which finished off steam was the diesel locomotive. As between the diesel and the electric, it was the old argument of Rainhill and the Liverpool & Manchester all over again, power supply from fixed or moving sources, only this time, with a vastly better system of transmission, the scales have been more evenly balanced. But as between steam and diesel, the machine which did more than any other work of man to spread civilization over the face of the earth has been outclassed by its successor. It was an honourable defeat, and sometimes a very narrow one; complex causes have operated, and even now many thousands of steam locomotives are still at work throughout the world. It would be a nice point to determine whether or not diesels yet outnumber them! But in most countries diesels are sweeping the board, and most remaining steam power is living on borrowed time, since its owners refuse to discard a machine still capable of performing its task as competently as its rival and not yet worn out.

Some of the reasons why diesels have succeeded are technical; others are not. In an internal combustion engine, as its name indicates, fuel is burnt inside the cylinder and the resulting explosion drives the piston directly; the economy, compared with the indirect method of heating water to produce steam which then expands elsewhere, is more than sufficient to outweigh the cost of the resulting complications—a steam engine is basically a simple, rugged and reliable machine, but the complicated, delicate and sometimes only adequately reliable diesel is cheaper. Again, steam engines (especially when they burn coal) tend to be dirty, although the force of this argument is less than seems apparent, since much of the dirt was because they were maintained and serviced in old, broken-down premises and the money for cleanliness was not forthcoming; we have all seen plenty of dirty diesels, showing that the machine can be no better than its surroundings and management allow. It is sometimes said that diesels are more powerful; this is a half truth, though sufficiently true in practice to explain some of the reasons in their favour. No diesel yet built has

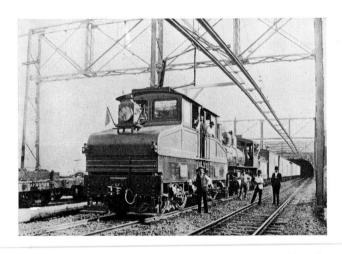

The world's first main-line railway electrification; 3½ miles through Baltimore on the Baltimore & Ohio, in 1895. The 1,440-hp locomotives hauled trains, complete with steam engine, through some tunnels.

John Snell Collection

Early Italian electric: a scene on the Valtellina line, about 1910. Italian State Railways

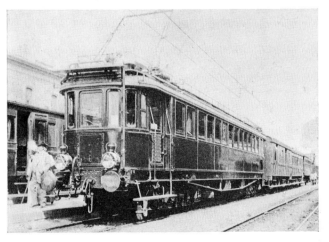

developed the power of some of the big steam engines; on the other hand, electrically operated control gear allows any number of locomotives coupled together to respond to the control of a single driver, so that all that is necessary to increase power is to add another unit. Combinations of over 10,000 hp are common on certain American lines. It is even possible, by radio or by devices responding to coupler stresses, to have locomotives spaced along the length of a very heavy train but still operated by only one man. In certain cases it has also been possible to design diesels to fit tight loading-gauge or weight restrictions that were unduly restrictive in steam days; and finally in certain districts where water was in short supply or contained corrosive salts, steam power was always at a disadvantage (though even this drawback can be got round, as can still be seen in South Africa, where large modern 4-8-4s with enormous condensing tenders haul heavy trains across the Karroo desert, using no more than four or five gallons a mile). All these things, however, have meant that operating a dieselized railway has

become a much simpler business than operating a steam one, while transits have tended to become faster.

New locomotives are not the only improvements in recent years. There has been considerable progress towards making railways less labour-intensive (though at the price of making them even more capital-intensive). Mechanization of track maintenance, combined with the use of long welded rails, has been a notable saving of labour, and so have modernized marshalling yards. But the biggest savings of all have been made by abandoning short-haul traffic to the roads, and in many countries (notably America) the savings due to modernization have been largely diverted by trade unions into quite unjustifiable featherbedding. Containerization, packing goods into strong boxes the size of a car body, which can be transferred easily from road to rail or sea by standardized handling equipment and carrying vehicles, is an important current move; clearly this offers great scope for savings to the consignor of the freight, since handling costs are reduced and pilferage made practically im-

(LEFT) *The end of an era; one of the last Swiss Federal steam locomotives bids farewell to a station festooned with overhead wires.* Swiss Federal Railways

(ABOVE) *Modern elegance: the Paris–Milan 'Cisalpin' Trans-Europ-Express, electrically powered, runs beside Lake Geneva with the Château de Chillon in the background.* Swiss Federal Railways

possible, but the real impact of the system seems likely eventually to be felt most in the docks. It is unlikely to be of much benefit to railways in the long run, since (except for rail hauls of many hundreds of miles) the maintenance of a fleet of road vehicles to carry out the short-distance shuttling of containers from starting point to railhead and from railhead to destination is very expensive and the vehicles cannot normally be used economically; the

117

economics of using road haulage throughout are very competitive over short and medium distances, up to about 200–400 miles.

It is not easy nowadays to be optimistic about the future of railways; even if they find a secure niche, it will be a much smaller one than they occupied in the past, and they are handicapped by their history. One aspect of this is that in many countries, including Britain and the United States, they have been in a depressed and declining state for so long that it is fifty years since they were able to pay competitive salaries for brainpower. The quality of management has suffered accordingly. It has always been fashionable to fling rude comments at railway managers, if only because they are seldom in sight when anything goes wrong; but in general, and especially in these two countries, so many catches have been missed in the last twenty years that one is bound to start wondering whether perhaps railways, like wars, are too important to be left to the professionals. During the last ten years in both countries, in fact, there has been a certain infusion of new blood at the top of the industry; in Britain, it has made an honest and energetic search for a viable new role, though the ruthless pruning of lines and services that went with it took most of the public attention. In America, there has been comparatively little cutback of routes so far (for freight traffic); instead, all the signs are that the more competent railway administrators are doing all they can to get out of the business altogether in due course, with the major effort going into diversification into the property and general industrial fields while the rail side becomes semi-moribund. As a way to salvage as much as possible of the shareholders' investment in these privately owned undertakings, this seems wise. In other countries, and especially in continental Europe, no such serious crisis yet exists; and since railway management has remained in good standing in these lands, perhaps it can yet be avoided.

It may be that in the history books of the future the story of the railway industry will be told in terms of the story of the steam age; that 120 years of steam haulage will outweigh n more recent years of other traction. Certainly it is the steam locomotive that has passed into folklore, and had a hold on the public imagination that its rivals never have approached. Countless American (and now European) infants are still puzzled by their parents saying 'look, there's a choo-choo train' as a diesel rumbles past; and the few surviving examples which have been preserved as operating tourist attractions here and there draw considerable crowds. But against much of the evidence one still hopes that the technical possibilities offered by the steel wheel on the steel rail will continue to prove saleable; it is the growth of road transport that is threatening to strangle our cities and dissect our countryside, and railways could do much more to reduce this pressure. Ruskin fulminated against the desecration of a railway (now abandoned) through Monsal Dale; what would he have said about a super-highway?

Modern elegance again: the comfortable, if austere, interior of the 'Cisalpin' T.E.E.

Swiss Federal Railways

118

PART FOUR
Ships
by Captain Donald Macintyre, D.S.O., D.S.C., R.N.

1

Paddles and Oars

The date when primitive man first ventured on to water—to cross a river or lake no doubt—is lost in the mists of antiquity. From such evidence as we have in the form of illustrations in tombs, on monuments or on remnants of decorated pots, and of ancient craft of the 'dug-out' type, which have been found preserved, it can be assumed that, where the land was well timbered, floating logs were the first inspiration, with improvements developing first from shaping the logs and later from hollowing them out. The latter process in the stone age of primitive, inefficient tools, was largely achieved by the use of fire. Craft made from hollowed-out tree trunks are still to be found in use in Africa, South America and elsewhere.

Perhaps the most remarkable voyages made in them were those by means of which the Polynesian race peopled the myriad scattered island groups of the South Pacific, including New Zealand, the Society Islands, the Marquesas and the Tuamotus, migrating eventually northwards also to populate the Hawaiian Islands. Where this attractive, laughing race came from originally is uncertain. The 'Kon Tiki' expedition under Thor Heyerdahl sought to prove that they came from South America on rafts of the feather-light balsa wood wafted by the prevailing south-easterly trade wind. Though this may be true, it is certain that it was hollowed-out trees the Polynesians made use of for subsequent voyages and for war canoes. Large, double-hulled craft of this type were in regular use when Tahiti was first visited by Captain Wallis in 1767 and by Bougainville and Cook soon afterwards.

Where suitable timber was not available—in Egypt, for example—papyrus reeds were bound together to make

Egyptian sea-going boat, c. *2600* B.C. *This is a model of the earliest known sea-going sailing ship, from an Egyptian bas-relief.*

Crown Copyright. Science Museum, London

Model of Egyptian ship, c. *1300* B.C.
Crown Copyright. Science Museum, London

spool-shaped craft, pointed and curved upwards in the bow to facilitate beaching. Such boats are still to be seen on the White Nile. Elsewhere bamboo poles or inflated animal skins were used to make rafts; or hides stretched over wooden ribs to make such simple boats as the Greenland 'kayak' or the ancient British coracle.

All these latter craft were essentially for use in inland or sheltered waters. So, too, were the first boats of which pictorial evidence exists, Egyptian craft dating from about 6000 B.C. No evidence remains of how they were constructed, but it is likely that the method was similar to that used *c.* 2700 B.C. revealed in pictures from that period. Forced to rely upon the native acacia or sycamore trees from which only short planks or blocks of wood could be obtained, the Egyptians joined these together with wooden pegs and with hour-glass-shaped or double fish-tail pieces of wood to make up the hull. On the up-

standing stem piece was painted the hawk-eye of the god Horus, a standard feature which in time to come was to spread to ships in many parts of the world, but more especially eastwards to India and China, where they are to be seen to this day. The boats were propelled at first by paddles with two or three paddlers standing in the stern to steer. The development of oars made it possible to employ larger boats.

Such boats were inherently of flimsy construction; when, eventually, the Egyptians put to sea in them, they strengthened them fore and aft by means of a double rope stretched from bow to stern over wooden 'horses' and twisted taut by a batten inserted between the two ropes. Having no deck beams to hold the sides together, their craft were given added athwartships strength by two ropes bound round the upper planking and kept taut by another rope zig-zagging between them. These details

122

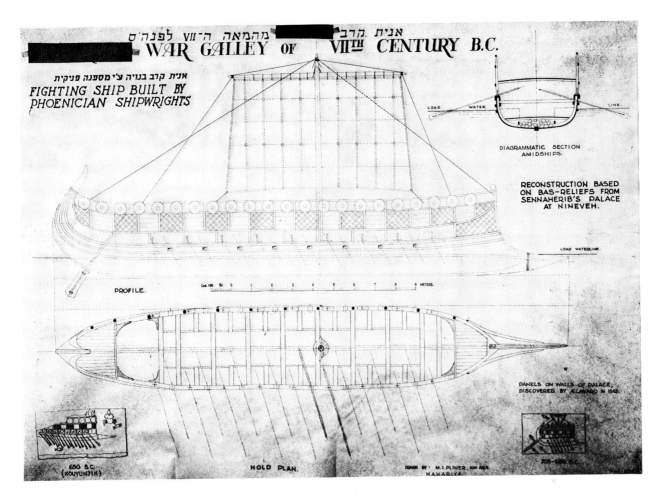

אנית הרב מהמאה ה־ז״ץ לפנה״ס
WAR GALLEY OF VIITH CENTURY B.C.

אנית קרב בנויה ע׳׳י מסמנה פניקית
FIGHTING SHIP BUILT BY PHOENICIAN SHIPWRIGHTS

DIAGRAMMATIC SECTION AMIDSHIPS.

RECONSTRUCTION BASED ON BAS-RELIEFS FROM SENNAHERIB'S PALACE AT NINEVEH.

PROFILE.

PANELS ON WALLS OF PALACE, DISCOVERED BY A.LAYARD IN 1845.

HOLD PLAN.

General arrangement of Phoenician war galley, seventh century B.C. *A reconstruction based on bas-reliefs from Sennacherib's Palace at Nineveh.*
Photo: Science Museum, London, by courtesy of the Maritime Museum, Haifa

can be seen in carvings in a temple near Thebes illustrating a famous sea-borne expedition to the land of Punt (Somaliland?) by the order of Queen Hatshepsut in about 1500 B.C. The boats illustrated were apparently about 100 feet long and were propelled by fifteen rowers on each side, though they could also hoist a huge square sail spread on a yard as long as the boats themselves, made up of two spars spliced together in the middle.

The next evidence of Egyptian naval activity is again in the form of inscriptions in the Temple of Victory at Thebes, celebrating a great sea victory by Rameses III (1200 B.C.) over invaders from the north. The vessels were, of course, war galleys; details of their hull construction are not shown, but it is likely that by this time dug-out hulls, using imported timber, would have been substituted in sea-going ships for the built-up craft of acacia and sycamore described above, though the latter method

was still in use for Nile boats in the fifth century B.C., when the historian Herodotus described it. Rameses' warships are depicted with a ram's head in the prow, a mast carrying a large square sail and a crow's-nest on the top. The oarsmen were protected by bulwarks.

The supremacy of Ancient Egypt in the field of shipbuilding came to an end with the rise of the Phoenicians and the Greeks, both of whom had easy access to good timber and used the dug-out for the main hull, with outriggers or extensions to provide the point of balance for oars. The forward portion of a Phoenician war galley can be seen in a fragment of inscription discovered in the ruins of Nineveh, dating from about 700 B.C., from which it appears that a sharpened ram formed an integral part of the hull. It was a bireme: oarsmen, sitting within the hull, worked a lower tier of oars, while others, on benches fixed on the side extensions, pulled an upper tier.

123

Greek galley, c. *480* B.C. Science Museum, London

Model showing probable arrangement of rowers in the plate above.

Crown Copyright, Science Museum, London

Down the centre-line, above the inner oarsmen, ran a narrow, protected fighting deck.

The Phoenicians were the most enterprising sea traders of that age, voyaging to Cornwall in search of tin and to West Africa. Some of their ships are even said to have circumnavigated Africa between the years 610 and 594 B.C., setting out from the Persian Gulf and returning home through the Straits of Gibraltar. The only representation of a Phoenician merchant ship shows an oar-propelled, (probably) dug-out hull with a fencing running fore and aft to contain the cargo. For their ocean voyages, however, they must have built hulls of planking held together by ribs in the fashion first contrived by the Corinthians during the sixth century B.C.

The Greeks, too, engaged widely in trading by sea and relied on ships for the import of grain from Egypt. From the few pictures of such ships that remain, it appears that they were short, tubby craft relying mainly on sail for propulsion. More evidence exists about Greek fighting galleys which were produced in great numbers to oppose the Persian fleets where the majority were Phoenician galleys. Uniremes, biremes and triremes were common; quadriremes and quinqueremes also existed; but contrary to the general belief until fairly recent times, these terms did not mean tiers of rowers on four and five levels, an arrangement which would have made the uppermost oars of too great a length to be efficiently wielded. No certain evidence remains of how, in fact, the rowers were stationed, but the following is the generally accepted belief.

In the triremes, which were first designed by the Corinthians, two tiers of thwarts were arranged slanting forward and outward from the centre line. On each upper thwart sat two rowers on each side, their oars of different length supported on outriggers; on the lower thwart a single oarsman, positioned so that his arms and the

Model of Viking ship found at Gokstad.
Crown Copyright. Science Museum, London

The actual Gokstad ship, ninth century A.D.
Science Museum, London

loom of his oar on the forward swing would pass between the backs of the two upper rowers, wielded an oar which passed through a hole in the side. In the quadriremes and quinqueremes there were similarly oars on only two or three levels respectively but with more than one man on some of the oars.

Greek galleys were at first open boats but, as time went on, came first to have a fore and aft flying deck as in the Phoenician galleys and eventually to be completely decked in. The main offensive weapon, however, was not the force of soldiers armed with spears and bows, but the ram of hard wood projecting from the bow, originally above the water-line, when it was carved as the head of a ram or other animal. Later it was realized that it was more effective if below the surface.

Following the decline of the Greek city states, the Phoenician state of Carthage became for a time the principal naval power in the Mediterranean. The design of their galleys did not change noticeably and, when the struggle for power began between Carthaginians and Romans, the latter, who up to that time had maintained no navy, simply copied the vessels of their opponents.

The Mediterranean, as the cradle of European civilization, had thus more than two thousand years of ship-building history before anything at all comparable to the galleys emerged in northern waters. It was to retain the supremacy in that type of craft until the end of its era. Before we return to look at the development of the great galleys of the Italian city states, however, we should perhaps note what developments had taken place elsewhere in European waters. That the Scandinavians used small dug-outs in sheltered waters from a very early date can be inferred from the great many that have been found embedded in marshlands. There is evidence, too, that they made use of hide-covered boats similar to Greenland 'kayaks'; and the design of the earliest wooden boat discovered, found at Hjørtspring in Denmark and dating from about 200 B.C., seems to derive from them, its overlapping planks being stitched together, the hull held together by ribs attached to them with bass binding (a wood fibre string which preceded hemp in early times in the north, and is still used in a flimsy form by gardeners).

The ultimate design in early northern oar-propelled ships was the Viking 'longship'. Though little direct evidence of details of these famous ships exists, it can be assumed that they were enlarged examples of the ship uncovered at Gokstad, near the entrance to Oslo fiord, which dates from the ninth century. Like all northern boats, this is built of overlapping oak planks—clinker-built—as opposed to the Mediterranean custom of carvel building or placing the planks edge to edge. There are

sixteen of these planks riveted together, the average breadth of which amidships is $9\frac{1}{2}$ in. and the thickness 1 inch, except for the tenth plank from the keel which is $1\frac{3}{4}$ in. to form a shelf for the beam-ends and the fourteenth plank which is $1\frac{3}{4}$ in. thick and pierced with holes for the sixteen oars on each side. The boat is nearly 78 ft in length, the stem- and stern-posts tapering and curving gently up from the 57-foot oak keel to which they are connected by vertical scarves and a double row of iron rivets. On a single mast amidships a square sail, spread between a yard and a boom, could be used for proceeding down-wind. Steering was by means of a short rudder or steering board on the starboard (steer-board) counter.

Such expertly built longships, admirably combining strength with lightness, enabling them to be pulled up on land when required and to travel at high speed through the water, were the standard passenger or war galley in northern waters throughout the Viking era. That there were also beamier trading vessels propelled primarily by sail is evident from the illustrations of William the Conqueror's transports in the Bayeux tapestry, but few details of these survive. As in the longships, stem and stern were shaped alike.

Though the Swedes and Russians made use of oar-propelled galleys for warlike purposes for several centuries longer in the Baltic, achieving some ingenious designs to enable broadside guns to be mounted, the wind in the sail soon displaced the oar as motive power for merchant and passenger ships in the stormy waters of the north. In the Mediterranean, galleys were used both as fighting and cargo ships, though from the time of the Phoenicians there had been 'round' ships for cargo-carrying as well as the oar-propelled 'long' ships.

The foremost maritime power in the Mediterranean in the Middle Ages was Venice. She was fiercely rivalled by Genoa and later by Turkey; but Venetian ship-building and design generally set the fashion until the sixteenth century. In the thirteenth century, though galleys were often used to carry cargo, especially valuable, light merchandise, they were primarily for fighting and to escort the convoys of round ships in which the more bulky cargo was carried.

The standard Venetian galley was a trireme with twenty-five to thirty benches on each side, slanted as in the ancient Greek triremes but with three oarsmen on each bench, each pulling a separate oar pivoted on the outrigger frame overhanging the side of the hull and supported by brackets rising from the beam-ends. Prior to the sixteenth century the rowers in Venetian galleys were not slaves but free men and volunteers. Soldiers, called 'bowmen' long after the bow had been replaced by

Venetian galleys, c. 1560. These vessels employed several men to each oar, and were used for cargo carrying as well as for fighting. Science Museum, London

firearms, were stationed in action in a fighting platform in the bow, on the fore and aft deck which ran down the centre-line between the banks of rowers and in the stern-castle. When cruising, they sat along the sides between the benches.

The steering was by means of three rudders, one on the centre-line, an innovation copied from northern ships about 1300, and two mounted on the quarters for additional use when turning sharply. Smaller longships of various types known as *fuste, galeotte, brigantini* or *fregate,* either biremes or uniremes, were used as dispatch vessels or to patrol the coasts.

About 1300 the Venetians brought out a new type of major vessel, the Great Galley, which was designed to combine some of the cargo-carrying and sailing capacity of the round ship with the fighting capacity and independence of the wind of the galley. Various types were built at first according to the trade in which they were

engaged. The most numerous and largest were the 'Flemish' galleys which could carry some 200 tons below deck. By the fifteenth century, however, the great galley had become more or less standardized, carrying 250 tons of cargo and rigged for sailing with lateen sails on a tall mainmast with a smaller mast fore and aft.

The era of the merchant galley finally came to an end early in the sixteenth century when the development of the square-rigged sailing ship, the shift of trade from the overland routes from the Orient to the ocean routes pioneered by the Portuguese, and the introduction of artillery all combined to deprive the Great Galleys of their advantages.

War galleys persisted longer in spite of numerous demonstrations of the superiority of the galleon as in battles with the Turkish galley fleets at Zonchio in 1499 and Prevesa in 1538, and in Drake's attack on Cadiz in 1587. The last great fight in which war galleys played the major part was that of Lepanto in 1571, when a combined European fleet under Don John of Austria defeated the Turks. Included in Don John's fleet were fighting versions of the Great Galley, known as 'galleasses', hybrid ships with which Mediterranean seamen prolonged the age of oar propulsion for some time after the introduction of the sailing galleon had proved it to be the queen of the seas in the sixteenth century.

2

Sail

From Galley to Carrack

The erection of a simple pole mast and the hoisting on it of a square of reed matting to make use of a fair wind must have been a very early development of man's waterborne ventures.

As early as 6000 B.C., it is conjectured from the evidence of crude representations on vases and walls, Egyptian craft hoisted a square matting sail on a mast made from a palm tree which may have been supported by stays from the lofty stern post made from another palm. By 4700 B.C., a period of great ship-building activity in ancient Egypt, the palm-tree mast and stern post had been replaced by a tripod mast amidships supported by fore- and backstays. The rectangular sail of rough cloth, now longer than it was wide, was spread on a yard, the braces of which were controlled by a man seated on a superstructure in the stern erected over the three steering paddlers. The sheets were led to the waist of the ship.

When the Phoenicians, Greeks and Romans became in their turn the leading ship-builders of the Mediterranean they continued, like the Egyptians, to depend primarily on oars for propulsion, but with, usually, a single mast hoisting a square sail for use with a fair wind. By the heyday of the Romans, however, merchant ships relying chiefly on sails had been developed, in many of which a foremast slanted sharply forward to resemble a later development, the bowsprit, carrying another small square sail.

There was little advance in design or rig of ships in the Mediterranean for several hundred years more. A new inspiration was needed: it came during the eighth century from the Arabs with whom a rich trade in the silks and spices of the Orient was carried on by the rival city-states of Venice and Genoa. At some time in their history Arab sailors had no doubt discovered that by shifting the point of suspension of the yard of a square sail, and tilting it with the shorter part downwards, the resultant 'lug' sail enabled them to sail much better with a beam wind or even to beat to windward. Then, by making the sail triangular, they produced the lateen which to this day is to be seen in Arab 'dhows' in the Indian Ocean.

Such, at least, is one theory of the origin of the lateen sail. Some authorities on the other hand believe it may have come to the Arabs across the Indian Ocean from the Malays who rigged their 'praus' in the same way. Be that as it may, the one thing certain is that it was the Arabs who introduced it into the Mediterranean where it soon displaced the square sail everywhere.

A limiting factor in the use of the lateen sail is its very long yard. This became increasingly unwieldy as ships, and consequently sail area, grew larger. The next step therefore was to divide the sail area between two masts, the taller of which was forward, a rig still to be seen in the Mediterranean today. By the end of the fourteenth century lateen-rigged, two- and three-masted ships were common in that sea, some retaining the oar arrangement of the galley as an auxiliary means of propulsion; these were basically 'long' ships as described in the chapter on 'Paddle and Oar'; others, though they retained the ability to make use of long sweeps when becalmed, were essentially round sailing ships which become known as 'caravels', a name of uncertain origin.

It was with this type of ship that the Portuguese made their earliest, tentative voyages of discovery which, by 1448, had taken them as far as the Azores, under the encouragement of Prince Henry the Navigator who had established an observatory and navigation school at Sagres near Cape St Vincent. Such ships were too light and too small for more distant voyages, however. The great age of discovery which was about to dawn came about through the development of the square-rigged ships out of a combination of the best features of the caravel and of the northern ships such as the single-masted 'cogs' of the Hansa ports, which had retained the square sail from the earliest times and by this time were voyaging increasingly to the Mediterranean.

The system of 'clinker' building favoured by the Vikings had persisted in the north with the fore-and-aft side planking of strakes each overlapping the one below it. Northern seamen now saw carvel-built ships in Mediterranean ports and, appreciating the reduced resistance to movement through the water of the resultant smooth-sided hulls, they copied them. The southern ship-wrights, in their turn, adopted the round stern and centre-line rudder, so much more efficient and easy to handle than the old side rudder, developed from the steering oar.

In regard to rigging, too, each borrowed from the other, the southerners hoisting square sails on the fore- and mainmast, the northerners adding a square-rigged foremast and a mizzenmast with a lateen sail. In pursuit of greater sail area, topsails spread on topmasts were soon added to the fore and main, the controls for which were led at first into the 'tops'—platforms built at the top of the fore- and mainmasts. The new rig called for stronger standing rigging and in particular for stout forestays on the square-rigged masts to take the strain when taken aback. That on the foremast brought about the addition of the bowsprit to which it could be efficiently led.

Other features of the new type of ship were the fore- and after-castles which originated as open platforms built on to the hull, but as time went by became integral parts of the hull structure. The forecastle was only a single-decked structure projecting out forward of the bow. The after-castle might comprise several decks. The

Roman merchant ship, second century A.D. *St Paul travelled in a ship similar to this.*
Crown Copyright. Science Museum, London

Ship of the Cinque Ports, thirteenth century.
Crown Copyright. Science Museum, London

first one, above the upper deck of the hull, stretched from the stern to the mainmast, and was the 'quarter-deck'. The next deck, which did not extend so far forward, was the 'half-deck' with, above it, the poop. Between quarter-deck and forecastle was the waist with the hatches of the hold amidships and fore and aft connecting gangways running down each side.

The square-rigged ships known in the fifteenth and sixteenth centuries as 'carracks' or, less professionally, as 'argosies', could be much bigger than either of the two types from which they developed. They could not beat against the wind so efficiently as the caravels with their lateen sails—indeed they could, in early times, hardly do so at all, some 80 degrees off the wind being as close as could be steered; but for voyages in the great oceans this was not of vital importance since they could always reach

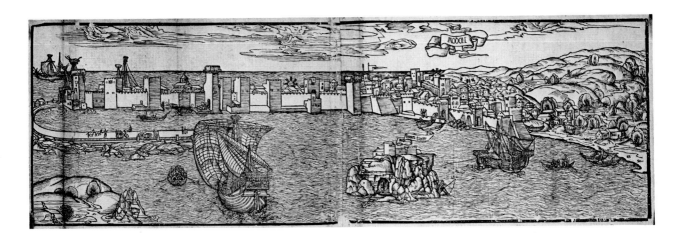

*Typical commercial ships of the Mediterranean at the end
of the fifteenth century, at Modon, and at Corfu.*
National Maritime Museum, Greenwich

their destination by taking advantage of the various constant winds such as the trade winds and the monsoons.

At the same time other developments had occurred to make ocean voyages feasible. From China, through the hands of the Arabs, had come the mariner's compass with which by 1400 every Mediterranean ship of any size was equipped. Mathematics and astronomy, too, with their application to navigation, had been learned from the Jews and the Arabs. Simple devices for measuring the altitude of the sun, the backstaff and the astrolabe, enabled the calculation of latitude to be made.

And all the while a ferment was stirring to discover an easier and more economical route whereby the spices, so vital to the European diet of that era, and the pain-killing drugs, obtainable only in the Orient, could be transported. The old caravan routes, terminating in the

Flemish carrack, c. 1480. A typical northern craft of the period. Crown Copyright. Science Museum, London

sea passage to Venice in the great galleys, were being barred by the rise of the Ottoman Empire. There was thus an overpowering incentive to reach the Spice Islands and Cathay by sea.

Expeditions setting out from Lisbon probed ever farther south down the coast of Africa, and in 1488 Bartholomew Diaz rounded the Cape of Good Hope in the *São Pantaleo*. Four years later the Genoese Christopher Columbus under the patronage of Ferdinand and Isabella of Spain set out in the square-rigged *Santa Maria*, accompanied by two little caravels *Pinta* and *Nina* to seek a westward route to Cathay. After discovering the Bahamas, Haiti and Cuba on this first voyage, he repeated the Atlantic crossing three times more to reach the mainland of South America, henceforth the 'Spanish Main', and to bring the New World into existence.

Before this, however, an event which was to lead to a transformation of the whole pattern of world trade had taken place in 1498 when a Portuguese flotilla of four ships led by Vasco da Gama in the *St Raphael*, having rounded the Cape of Good Hope, arrived at Calicut on the west coast of India. Their return, with their holds laden with silks and spices to make a profit of 600 per cent, marked the final eclipse of Venice as the foremost maritime power. The bold, wide-reaching ocean passages made by the square-rigged carracks as they made use of the prevailing winds is illustrated by the voyage of Pedro Alvares Cabral with a squadron of twelve ships in 1500. In the latitudes of the south-east trade wind, he reached clear across the South Atlantic to discover the coast of Brazil, of which he took possession in the name of the King before tacking back to the Cape of Good Hope and on across the Indian Ocean to claim Portuguese sovereignty there also.

The Spaniards were similarly laying claim to and colonizing their discoveries in the New World; both nations claimed also a monopoly of trade with their own areas, a monopoly encouraged by the decree of Pope Alexander VI who assigned all discoveries west of a line from pole to pole 370 leagues to the west of the Cape Verde Islands to Spain, all east of the line to Portugal. In defence of their claims, against established Arab traders in the East Indies as well as against rival European venturers, the carracks were armed with cannons mounted at first only in the fore- and after-castles, but later, following experiments by the Frenchman Des Charges of Brest in 1501, on the main and lower decks of the hull, pierced to provide gunports.

Mediterranean carrack, c. 1490. Note the two-piece yard-arm. Science Museum, London

Development of the Square Rig

By the early sixteenth century the ocean-going ship had assumed all the main features that were to persist throughout the age of sail, such variations as were adopted during the next four hundred years with regard to hull design and rigging being of the order of improvements rather than basic alterations.

For instance, the large armed carracks, which it became *de rigueur* for every maritime nation to build, usually had a second or 'bonaventure' mizzenmast carrying two lateen sails, while on the other three masts top-gallant sails might be hoisted above the topsails, though these were probably rarely spread and only in the gentlest breezes. Below the bowsprit a square sprit-sail was spread on its own yard.

One of the earliest of these prestige ships was the Scottish *Great Michael*, built in 1511, which was 240 feet in length over all. Three years later, Henry VIII of England built the famous *Henry Grace à Dieu* or, more familiarly, the *Great Harry*, a ship of 1,500 tons which was reputed to carry no fewer than 184 guns. Many of these, however, must have been the little 'serpentines', not much bigger than small arms and firing small shot. There was, indeed, plenty of space in her towering castles for numerous guns. At the same time all this top-hamper must have made her a clumsy craft. More typical of the large armed ship of the period was the Swedish *Elefanten* built for Gustave Vasa in 1532 which was rigged with the orthodox rig of fore- and mainmasts with square courses and topsails and a mizzen with two lateen sails.

During the turbulent centuries up to the end of the Napoleonic wars, it was not unnatural that refinements

Columbus's 'Santa Maria', 1492; a conjectural reconstruction as no accurate plans or pictures of this ship have survived.

Crown Copyright. Science Museum, London

133

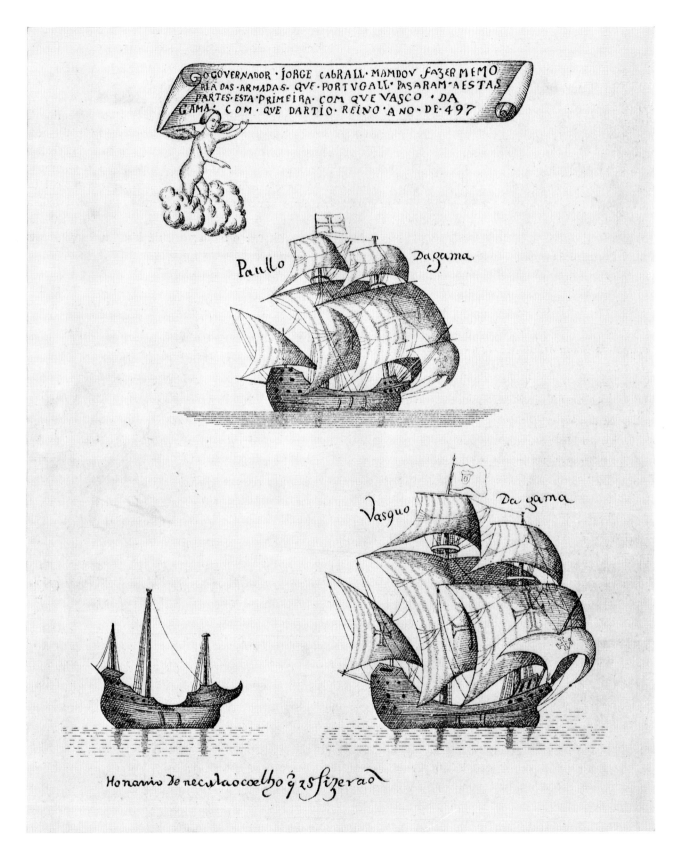

Vasco da Gama's ships, 1497. These are early carracks,
  square-rigged as opposed to the lateen sails of the cara-
  vels which they superseded.

Science Museum, London

Three Dutch ships lying at piles. Note the painting on the stern of the ship at left, a feature of Dutch ships of the sixteenth century. Engraving after Zeeman.

National Maritime Museum, Greenwich

of rig and design were applied to the specialized fighting ships. Merchantmen remained quite small; prime requirements being maximum cargo-carrying capacity and minimum crews, they retained some of the hull characteristics of the 'round' ship, which did not make for speed, and they often carried only the simple rig with six sails, two on foremast and main, a lateen on the mizzen and a sprit-sail.

The first specialized fighting ship developed was the 'galleon', a Spanish word applied originally to oar-propelled galleys. This, however, was a true sailing ship, borrowing only from the galley a slimmer, straighter hull design than that of the carrack and a low beak-head projecting forward of the bow below the bowsprit. At the same time the lofty forecastle was cut down and soon abolished while the after-castle was reduced to three decks. The finer lines and reduction of top-hamper, particularly in the English galleons designed for the Elizabethan Navy by Sir John Hawkins, greatly improved the sailing qualities of these ships. The English took advan-

Galleon of early sixteenth century, by Breughel. Note the lower lines, absence of forecastle, and larger bowsprit, compared with earlier vessels. The sides and stern are pierced for the use of guns.

National Maritime Museum, Greenwich

135

Dutch carracks, by Breughel.
National Maritime Museum, Greenwich

tage of this to engage successfully with their long-range cannon (culverins) the larger, less handy Spanish ships which relied on closing an enemy and boarding with the numerous soldiers they carried for the purpose. It was with these tactics that the Spanish Armada was continuously harried and kept from achieving its object in 1588. The Spaniards then copied the design to produce the class named after the Twelve Apostles which cornered and captured Sir Richard Grenville's galleon *Revenge* in 1591.

So far as the larger ships of war were concerned, English ship-builders retained their pre-eminence into the first quarter of the seventeenth century. The foremost of them was Phineas Pett whose *Prince Royal*, launched in 1610, mounted her fifty-six guns on three decks and provided an early example of the elaborately carved decoration or 'ginger-bread' which was a feature of many ships of that period. Even more revolutionary in design

Galleon, the 'White Bear', flagship of Lord Thomas Howard in the battle of the Armada, 1588. Note the absence of a forecastle.

National Maritime Museum, Greenwich

136

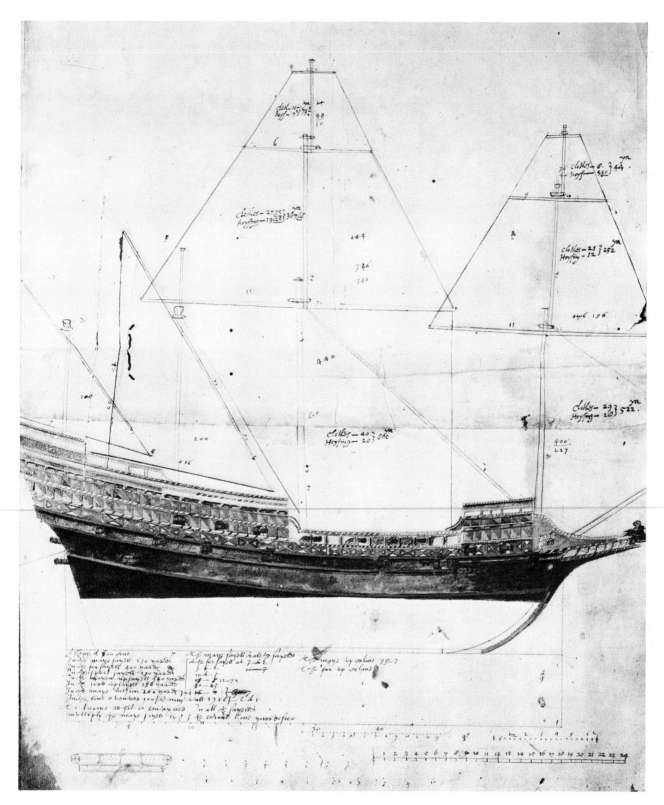

Draught of ship and sail plan, late sixteenth century, from 'Fragments of Ancient English Shipwrightry' in the Pepysian Library. This ship is generally similar to the 'White Bear' on page 136. Science Museum, London

was his *Sovereign of the Seas*, built by Phineas's son Peter in 1637, which mounted 100 guns on three decks. Her sail-plan included top-gallants and royals on the fore- and mainmasts, a square topsail and top-gallant above the lateen mizzen and a square sprit-sail topsail. It was perhaps a sign of the deterioration in English ship-design, which set in at this time and was to persist until the nineteenth century, that Pett's famous masterpiece was to prove so unhandy and top-heavy that she was later cut down to a two-decker and her sail-plan reduced.

Both the French and the Dutch excelled the English at this time, but it is the latter to whom many of the innovations in sailing ships are ascribed. In their merchant ships they developed a distinctive hull which had a narrow, almost pointed stern as compared to the broad, rounded stern of other types, and sides which curved inwards and upwards from the water line to a narrow upper deck. Known as 'fluyt' ships, their design was intended to circumvent the tax system of the Baltic States with whom an essential trade in timber and other maritime stores was carried on.

It was the Dutch who in the middle of the seventeenth century first introduced the stay-sail into the ocean-going square rig, firstly as a storm sail set on the mainstay only when most of the other sails had had to be furled, but later on the other stays also. Not until the eighteenth century, however, did the jib replace the awkward sprit-sail topsail in large ships, and the lateen on the mizzen give way to the gaff-sail 'driver' or 'spanker'.

Another feature which was developed surprisingly late,

Peter Pett's masterpiece, 'Sovereign of the Seas', built 1637 from the proceeds of Charles I's Ship Money taxes at a cost of £65,586 16s. 9½d. Science Museum, London

138

Dutch man o' war, 1665. Note the highly decorated stern, a feature of ships of this period which added greatly to their cost. Science Museum, London

considering the seaman's proverbial handiness with a rope and tackle, was the steering wheel, the basic mechanics of which was simply the transmission of movement of the wheel to the tiller or helm by means of a simple run of pulleys and ropes. The tiller, of course, applied this movement to the rudder. Until the end of the seventeenth century a much less satisfactory steering device known as the 'whipstaff' was in use to enable the ship to be steered from a position a deck or two decks higher than the tiller whence the steersman could hear the orders of the master on the poop or quarter-deck and see the set of the sails.

The whipstaff was a long pole with at one end a ring holding the end of the tiller, the other end passing up through the deck or decks to the steering position, and pivoted in such a way that it could slide up and down as well as rotate on the pivot. The whipstaff could thus, by being tilted to one side or the other, move the tiller through its horizontal arc.

So far as the hull form was concerned, progress was steadily away from the 'high-charged', 'round-ship' concept and towards a more horizontal fore and aft configuration with a single, short poop deck right aft above the quarter-deck.

Varieties of Small Trading Ships

Trade, in the age of sail, was carried on, of course, in multifarious types of small ships differing in one way or the other from the standard ship-rigged merchantman. Their names were bewildering, referring sometimes to their hull design, at others to their rig. Of the former, one of the best-known types was the 'cat-built', or simply 'cat' ships (the name being of Scandinavian origin), which were broad-bellied, almost flat-bottomed and immensely strong craft to be seen in great numbers engaged in the coal trade on the east coast of England. The majority were two-masted brigs, though many had a full three-masted ship rig. Captain James Cook, the great explorer, who started his career in such ships, selected one, renamed *Endeavour*, as the most suitable for his first voyage of discovery, 1768–71; two other Whitby colliers, *Resolution* and *Adventure*, were used on his second and third voyages.

A type known by its rig was the 'hooker', again a word of Scandinavian origin. In the age of steam this became slang for any small tramp steamer; but originally it was a two-masted ship carrying three square sails and a gaff-sail on the tall mainmast, a gaff-sail and square top-sail on the mizzen and, in the absence of a foremast, three large triangular head-sails. Amongst the plethora of types of small sailing ships with their often loosely applied type names, a distinctive variety was the 'snow'. This was a square-rigged, two-masted ship or brig with, in addition, a short, separate mast close abaft the main-mast and fixed under the maintop, on which a gaff-sail was set.

A type of ship developed by the Dutch in the early seventeenth century was the 'yacht'. Introduced for patrolling the waterways of Holland, the yacht was a small, graceful craft drawing little water and fitted with 'leeboards' to act as a keel when beating to windward. It had usually a single mast on which was hoisted a fore-and-aft 'gaff' mainsail and a square topsail, while a triangular stay-sail was spread along the forestay and another, the 'jib', along a stay leading to the end of the bowsprit. The gaff-sail and stay-sail were at this time features of many types of small craft. In these craft a second mast might be stepped forward of the poop, on which was hoisted a gaff mizzen, the rig becoming that of a ketch.

The application of the name 'yacht' to pleasure craft came about as a result of the presentation by the Dutch of one of them, the *Mary*, to King Charles II on his restoration in 1660. He and his brother, James, Duke of York, were so taken with her that they ordered others to be built in English yards, but with deeper hulls and fixed keels, in which yacht racing became a new sport.

A familiar rig in the Mediterranean was that of the 'polacca' or 'poleacre', a small ship with polemasts, usually square-rigged on fore and main and a small mizzenmast with a gaff- and boom-sail or 'driver'. The polemasts allowed the yards and sails to be lowered on deck if required, when shortening sail, instead of furling the sails aloft. Common also in the Mediterranean was the 'xebec', a lateen-sailed two- or three-masted adaptation of the galley developed originally by the Arabs of the Barbary States to be propelled by oar or sail as required and much feared as pirate vessels.

In the Indian Ocean the lateen-sailed Arab 'dhow' was everywhere to be seen as, in smaller numbers and restricted to the western shores of that ocean, it is still to be seen today. Though Arab traders ventured as far as China, where one of the signs left of their impact is the eye in the bow of southern Chinese vessels—the Egyptian Eye of Horus transmitted through them—the Chinese otherwise displayed an independence in naval architecture to develop their 'junks' of many different varieties. Though all had in common the unstayed masts and fore-and-aft lug-sails of matting spread on horizontal bamboo battens, each main sea-trading centre developed its own hull design. The majority were small

Mediterranean craft, sixteenth century. Square-rigged carracks in the foreground, and behind them a lateen-sailed caravel and a galley.

National Maritime Museum, Greenwich

craft of no more than 500 tons; but there were large ocean-going ships of up to 1,000 tons also. The most conspicuous feature of many of them was the brightly painted, intricate decorative work on their sides and on the flat bow. In general they were good sea-boats, as they needed to be in their typhoon- and monsoon-swept seas; but they were slow. Western influence in the mid nineteenth century brought about the development of a hybrid craft of greater speed in the shape of the 'lorcha', which combined the battened sails so efficient when close-hauled, with finer hull lines of Western design. These found favour as pirate ships as well as for dispatch-vessels and police patrols.

In every sea and ocean, of course, swam a myriad of even smaller craft engaged in the coastal trade so vital in an age when alternative local transport depended upon a sparse system of rough, unmetalled highroads, or in the

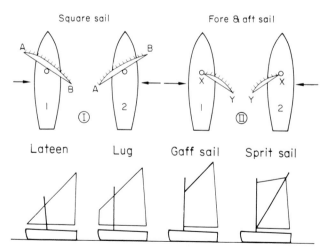

The difference between square sails and fore-and-aft sails; and types of fore-and-aft sails. Based on diagrams in *The Sailing Ship*, by R. and R. C. Anderson, by permission of the publishers, George G. Harrap & Co. Ltd.

141

Two sailing vessels, early sprit-sail craft. Engraving after Zeeman. National Maritime Museum, Greenwich

equally vital fishing industry. Though the square ship-rig was to be seen in quite small craft, the majority, besides the lateen-rigged craft of the Mediterranean and Indian Oceans, were at least partly fore-and-aft rigged.

In northern waters the Dutch played the greatest part in the development of the fore-and-aft rig. Their narrow off-shore channels and the maze of inland waterways constructed during and after the fifteenth century called for such a handy rig. The answer was found initially in the sprit-sail. This must not be confused with the square sail spread below the bowsprit of a seventeenth-century ship. The fore-and-aft sprit-sail, a quadrilateral sail the forward edge of which was laced to the mast, was spread by means of a diagonal spar—the sprit—between its foot and its peak. A rope attached to the peak, called a 'vang', and a sheet, by which the sail was controlled, were both held by the steersman in a small boat, where the sprit-sail might be the solitary sail. For a larger craft, however, not only did it become necessary to balance the sail-plan by a triangular head-sail, but, as the sprit became too long and heavy to control by a simple vang, a tackle from the top of the mast was rigged.

The sprit-sail remained in use until modern times in some craft, notably the Thames barges which used to throng the estuary; but in others it gave way to the gaff-sail which had a spar along its top edge with jaws at one end embracing the mast. To furl the sail, 'brails' to fold it in to the mast were fitted. Such a gaff mainsail enlarged by a 'bonnet' laced to its lower edge was the chief feature of the Dutch 'sloepe'-rig, later anglicized as 'shallop' or 'sloop'.

Another principal fore-and-aft type of vessel developed was the schooner with two masts, the taller of which was aft and carried the largest sails. When these craft added square topsails and top-gallants above the fore-and-aft mainsail, they became 'topsail schooners' or, with such additions to both masts, 'two-topsail schooners'.

The great majority of small merchant ships combined square and fore-and-aft sail in one way or another. And while the various localized types and the names given to them are legion and too many to be included here, the eventual nomenclature generally accepted gives the name 'barque' to a three- (or more) masted vessel in which the mizzen is fore-and-aft rigged, the remainder

The 'Transit' four-masted barquentine. Aquatint after Whitcombe. National Maritime Museum, Greenwich

Collier brig 'Unity', typical of the commercial ships which plied around Britain's shores in the nineteenth century. Science Museum, London

square; 'barquentine' to a three- (or more) masted vessel with only the foremast square-rigged; 'brig' to a two-masted ship, square-rigged on both; 'brigantine' to a two-masted ship square-rigged on the main and fore-and-aft rigged on the mizzen.

East Indiamen and Clippers

When peace between the great maritime powers at last came with the end of the Napoleonic Wars, there arose a great incentive for commercial competition in overseas trade. Prior to this, trade with India and the Orient was a monopoly of the East India Companies, the two most important of which were the English and Dutch, incorporated respectively in 1600 and 1602. They were fierce rivals until the Anglo-Dutch wars came to an end with the Treaty of Breda in 1667, after which Dutch sea-power steadily declined. Thereafter the English and French strove for more than a century for mastery in the Indian Ocean.

East Indiamen, though they sailed in escorted convoys as far as the Azores, were thus expected to, and did,

143

The 'Essex', East Indiaman, at anchor in Bombay harbour.
  Aquatint after Luny.
                National Maritime Museum, Greenwich

East Indiaman 'Warren Hastings'. Aquatint after Huggins.
                National Maritime Museum, Greenwich

defend themselves against attacks even by enemy ships of war, as well as to carry freight and passengers. They therefore carried large crews, bound by a discipline as strict as in the Royal Navy, enforced even by courts-martial, to work the guns of the powerful broadside batteries they mounted. Crews could expect far better pay, prospects and food than in the Royal Navy, however, and being all volunteers, posed less of a disciplinary problem. Their officers enjoyed almost as much prestige as those of the Royal Navy and apprenticeships were eagerly sought.

Cargo space in East Indiamen was sacrificed in favour of the armament. To make them suitable for long voyages away from dockyard support, they were massively built. Thus, although with such large crews they could spread a huge area of canvas, with such romantically named sails as 'sky-sails', 'moonrakers', 'cloudscrapers' and 'star-gazers', as well as royals above the top-gallants, and studding sails hauled out on studding booms beyond the yard-arms, with no competition to face there was little call for speed; they would take in all but 'plain sail' before dark and shorten sail drastically at the first signs of a blow. Oddly enough, the East India Company actually owned few of the ships they operated. Instead they sailed them under charter from the Blackwall firms that built them, the most important of which was Wigram's. At Blackwall, too, they were refitted and laid up between voyages and the forest of tall masts and spars

Many ships ended their days as convict hulks. This is the 'Discovery', built 1789, as a convict ship at Deptford in 1828. Science Museum, London

Chesterfield packet rescuing crew of sinking ship. Note the Red Ensign flown upside-down, to indicate distress.
National Maritime Museum, Greenwich

Mail Packet 'Lady Hobart' threatened by iceberg, 1803.
National Maritime Museum, Greenwich

of the ships tightly berthed in the basins was one of the sights of the Thames waterside.

In the West Indian trade, ships were compelled to travel in escorted convoys. There was thus less need for armament. Nor was speed of prime importance, however, and their design aimed at maximum cargo-carrying capacity and minimum crew. The typical West Indiaman was therefore a broad-beamed ship—rarely more than four times as long as she was broad—and with an un-ambitious sail-plan.

Without the shelter of a monopoly such as that of the East India Company, when peace finally supervened in 1815 there was a real incentive for British ship-builders to improve the design of ships in the transatlantic trade. Complacency bred of long freedom from competition offset this, however, and it was in the United States that new ideas and designs blossomed. The first impact of these was felt during the war of 1812 when American frigates proved themselves greatly superior to their British opponents in a number of single ship actions. In the design of merchant ships, too, the Americans soon

went rapidly ahead. How this led eventually to the production of the first clipper ships will be examined later.

The virtually sovereign status of the Honourable East India Company, as it was officially called, began to be whittled away in 1773 when an Act of Parliament centralized under a governor-general the administration of the various provinces it had acquired and gave the British Government some control over its civil and military affairs. Subsequent reviews of its charter further reduced its privileges, and by 1833 it had ceased to trade and had become merely an administrative agency.

Even earlier than this, however, the East India monopoly had been abolished and 'free-traders' had begun to compete in the commerce with India. Many of them were built and operated by the same firms which had owned the East Indiamen, particularly Green and Wigram (as the original firm of Wigram's had become). They were at first by no means 'flyers', being little ships of less than 700 tons register, sometimes barque-rigged, and of rarely more than four-to-one length to breadth ratio. In 1837, however, the first of a new and improved type of pas-

East Indiaman 'Sir David Scott' at entrance to the straits of Sunda, between Sumatra and Java, 1830. Indonesian craft in foreground. National Maritime Museum, Greenwich

East Indiaman 'Wellington', 1839.
National Maritime Museum, Greenwich

The 'Duff', employed as a missionary ship to Tahiti.
National Maritime Museum, Greenwich

senger ship was built by Green and Wigram. This was the *Seringapatam*, of 818 tons, and she and her successors were admiringly known as the Blackwall Frigates, though similar ships were also built on the Tyne by T. and W. Smith & Co. Record passages to India began to be made, the *Seringapatam*, for instance, reaching Bombay from England in eighty-five days; while the Tyne-built *Minden* in 1848 made Calcutta in ninety days.

To obtain these results the design of the ships had been much improved, largely by increasing the length-breadth ratio. Blackwall Frigates dominated the traffic to and from India until the opening of the Suez Canal in 1869. They continued to run for a time successfully to Australia. But the inspiration needed to bring the sailing ship to its ultimate perfection was lacking in prosperous Victorian England. It was found, instead, in the bustling, progressive shipyards of the United States, where before the end of the eighteenth century fast schooners of a revolutionary hull design were being built, mainly in Virginia and Maryland.

Known as 'Baltimore Clippers', their most distinctive

characteristics were the sharp, raked stem and an inclined, overhanging stern, which reduced the hull area in contact with the water. Rigged with two raking masts, each carrying a gaff mainsail and square topsail and topgallant, with three forestay-sails, they were the fastest and handiest ships in the world, as they often demonstrated during the war of 1812, when, fitted out as privateers, they were able to cut out and destroy a ship from a convoy, contemptuous of the slower British frigates. To make them economic commercial units in time of peace was difficult, however, as cargo space was limited in their graceful hulls. As a result, many were diverted to the slave trade which still persisted, in spite of naval efforts to suppress it, until well into the nineteenth century.

Meanwhile American shipping lines with American-built ships were transforming the old, haphazard trans-atlantic passenger trade with fast packet ships sailing to a regular schedule in defiance of the weather and driven hard by rough, tough officers. One of the first and best known was the Black Ball Line which began to run in 1816. Their first packet ships were no more than 500 tons;

Blackwall frigate 'Malabar', 1860.
Science Museum, London

but their regular sailings from New York to Liverpool on the first of each month brought them popularity and prosperity from the start.

Amongst other American lines were the Dramatic Line which had some forty ships running to Liverpool, London and Le Havre, one of which, the *New World*, was one of the first to be built by Donald Mackay of Boston, of whom more later; the Black Cross Line, one of whose sailing packets, the *Toronto*, gained renown in 1846 by beating both a Cunard steamship and another from London to New York; the Red Star Line; and the Swallow Tail Line.

Fast as these early western packet ships were, they were to be outclassed by the new design of ship that was to come from American yards from about 1845 onwards —the 'clipper'.

As early as 1832, an enlarged Baltimore Clipper, the *Ann McKim*, had been given a ship-rig. But it is the *Rainbow*, built in New York in 1845, which is generally considered to be the first of the 'clipper ships'. Three years later, the incentive to concentrate on speed in

sailing-ship design was given a sharp impetus by the discovery of gold in California, which led to demands for the fastest possible passages from the American east coast to San Francisco. American ship-builders and, in particular, Donald Mackay of Boston, setting out to meet these, were inspired by the Baltimore tradition to produce the clipper ships which were to reign supreme on the trade routes for the next twenty years. They found a fresh field for their products when, in 1849, the British repealed their Navigation Acts which had until then barred foreign ships from taking freight into British ports. American ships could now compete in the highly profitable trade with China. Though they were already taking their share in the latter, their ships going on from San Francisco across the Pacific to bring back cargoes of tea to America, a far bigger market was now opened up for them. The first American clipper to arrive in England with tea was the *Oriental*, of 1,003 tons, in 1850.

Clippers under the Stars and Stripes were thus already famous on the route from New York to San Francisco round the Horn and in the China trade when the dis-

149

covery of gold in Australia in 1850 called for similar ships to make fast passages from England to Melbourne. British ship-builders were at last beginning to shake off their complacency. Alexander Hall and Sons of Aberdeen, already famous for their fast, schooner-rigged

Model of China Clipper, c. 1850.
Crown Copyright. Science Museum, London

packets in the passenger trade between Scotland and England, such as the record-breaking *Scottish Maid* built in 1839, built the first two British clippers, *Stornoway* and *Chrysolite*, in 1850 and 1851 for the China trade, but they were little ships of barely 500 tons.

Thus it was across the Atlantic that aspiring Liverpool ship-owners turned, notably James Baines, founder of the (English) Black Ball Line (quite independent of the American line of the same name, though both used the same house-flag). He turned first to Smith's of St John, New Brunswick, where his first record-breaker the *Marco Polo* was built in 1850. John Pilkington and Henry Wilson, founders of the White Star Line, at the same time ordered several ships from W. & R. Wright, also of St John, N.B. All these ships made famous passages to Australia.

But it was not until Donald Mackay began to build clippers for the Black Ball Line that the Red Ensign was to be seen on the fastest sailing ships in the world. Mackay had set up in partnership with the American ship-owner Enoch Train at Boston in 1844, where in the next six years he built a number of splendid Western

Ocean Packets for Train's White Diamond Line. In 1850 he built the revolutionary *Staghound* for the firm of Sampson and Tappan, his first clipper. On her first trip round the Horn she reached Valparaiso in sixty days, the fastest passage but one up to that time, in spite of losing her main topmast and all three top-gallant masts in a gale when six days out from New York. Even with her jury rig she was able to log 17 knots with a fresh gale on the quarter. The most famous clippers built for American owners were *Flying Fish*, *Flying Cloud* and *Westward Ho*, which made their names on the San Francisco run, and the *Sovereign of the Seas* which ran for the American Swallow Tail Line on the Australian emigrant route. For the English Black Ball Line he built the equally famous *Lightning*, *James Baines*, *Champion of the Seas* and *Donald Mackay*. W. H. Webb of New York was another builder of fine ships for British as well as American lines. Perhaps the most successful, as well as notorious, was the *Challenge*, famous for fast passages to California and notorious for the savage discipline imposed on her crew by her murderous master, Bully Waterman, and her bestial bucko mate, Douglas.

In 1857 the United States suffered a disastrous financial depression followed four years later by the Civil War. Ship-owners were ruined; many American clippers passed into British hands, and the building of them ceased. By that time, however, British shipyards, mostly Scottish, had acquired the art and were building clippers. Though they had the slender, raked bow and overhanging stern of the American clippers, they were smaller ships, rarely more than 800 tons, and their sailing qualities were quite different. It is doubtful if any were ever as fast as the best of the California 'flyers' in a hard gale on the quarter; but they could ghost along in light airs which would hardly give the bigger ships steerage way, an essential quality to get them as quickly as possible through the doldrums along the Equator.

The most successful builder was Robert Steele of Greenock, whose *Falcon*, *Taeping*, *Serica*, *Ariel*, *Sir Lancelot*, *Lahloo* and *Titania* were all famous tea clippers and perhaps the most beautiful ships ever built, though Hall of Aberdeen and Connell of Glasgow also built many fine ships. *Taeping*, *Ariel* and *Serica* took part in the famous tea clipper race of 1866 when all three left Foochow on the same tide on 30th May and docked on the same tide in London on 6th September. Another Aberdeen ship-builder, Walter Hood, built the famous *Thermopylae* in 1868, designed by Bernard Waymouth. The following year the *Cutty Sark*, designed by Hercules Linton, was built at Dumbarton partly by Scott and Linton and completed by Denny Bros. These two ships,

*West India Docks, London, from the south-east, c. 1850.
The forest of masts gives an idea of Britain's importance
as a maritime power at this time.*

Science Museum, London

*The clipper ships 'Taeping' and 'Ariel' racing up the English
Channel at the end of the voyage from Foochow, which
they had left 99 days before. The 'Ariel' won by ten
minutes.* Science Museum, London

throughout a long career, first in the tea trade and later carrying wool from Australia, were fierce rivals from the famous occasion when, in 1872, both left Shanghai on the same day to make a race of it to London. The *Cutty Sark* had established a good lead when, in a severe gale to the south-west of the Cape of Good Hope, she lost her rudder. In spite of six days hove-to while a jury rudder was constructed and shipped, and the need to carry reduced sail for the rest of the voyage, she arrived only six days after *Thermopylae*.

The majority of British tea clippers were composite ships, with hulls of hard wood (as compared to American soft-wood ships) but interior framework and fittings of iron. Of them all, only the *Cutty Sark* still survives, having been saved from the breaker's yard in 1957 and preserved as a museum ship at Greenwich near the National Maritime Museum.

The Last Days of Sail

The advent of the steamship and the opening of the Suez Canal signalled the eventual disappearance of the sailing ship from the oceans. Nevertheless by adapting design in pursuit of larger cargoes, smaller crews and cheaper maintenance, they persisted in ever dwindling numbers until the outbreak of the Second World War. The little tea clippers were uneconomical on all these counts. Larger ships were, therefore, built of iron. Top-gallant as well as topsails were divided into two smaller sails able to be handled by fewer men; refinements such as studding sails were discarded.

The first iron sailing ship had, in fact, been launched in 1838; but such ships were rarities for another twenty years, and it was not until 1860 that iron ships began to replace the wooden clippers on the emigrant run to Australia. The majority there loaded a cargo of wool with which they sailed home, vying one with another for the honour of the fastest passage. Some, however, carried Australian horses (walers) to India and Burma for the Army, and loaded jute at Calcutta or rice at Rangoon before returning home. The average size of these ships was about 1,500 tons.

Though they lacked the yacht-like finish and embellishments of the little tea clippers, they were still beautiful ships; some, indeed, were built in the same yards as the later tea clippers, Robert Steele building the splendid *Hesperus* and *Harbinger* while Hood of Aberdeen launched the *Patriarch*, first of a number for G. Thompson & Co., in the year after he completed the *Thermopylae*. New shipyards came to prominence also mostly on the Clyde, as builders of iron ships: Barclay Curle,

Lowrie, Connell and Thompson, all of Glasgow, built the majority of the numerous 'Loch' class for the General Shipping Co.

During the 1880s all the 'Loch' ships were converted to barques by removal of the yards from their mizzenmasts; performance was little affected and smaller crews could be employed. As ships increased in size to 2,000 tons, the longer hulls provided the space and a balanced sail-plan called for a fourth mast, square-rigged at first, but later fore-and-aft rigged. Amongst the first four-masted barques were Barclay Curle's *Loch Moidart* and *Loch Torridon*, launched in 1881.

An interesting innovation in some of these ships was the perforated sail. The idea was attributed to an Italian shipmaster who believed that in the 'belly' of any sail, particularly when close-hauled, there was a cushion of 'dead wind' which acted as a buffer, preventing the sail from receiving the full strength of the wind. Other advantages of the holes in the sails, which had to be correctly sited to function properly, were that they made them easier to furl by preventing them from ballooning up over the yard and they stopped the maddening flogging of canvas against the mast when becalmed.

Another route on which sailing ships were run economically until about 1880 was that between England and New Zealand. Until 1873 the trade was largely in the hands of two companies, Shaw, Savill & Co., and the Albion Shipping Company owned by Patrick Henderson. Both ran wooden and composite ships and barques as well as iron. In 1873 the New Zealand Shipping Company was formed by a number of New Zealand merchants. Their ambitions to run a crack line were served by the acquisition of a number of fine iron ships, some by purchase from other owners, but the majority were specially built for them by Blumer of Sunderland, Palmers of Newcastle and Stephen of Glasgow.

By the turn of the century most British ship-owners had abandoned sail for steam. The French, Germans and Scandinavians, however, continued to build, or have built for them in British yards, steel sailing ships, often more than 4,000 tons gross registered tonnage and rigged as five-masted barques or barquentines; the Americans specialized in four-, five- and six-masted schooners. Of these, the six-masted *Wyoming*, built in 1910, was the longest (350 feet) wooden sailing ship ever built; while the *Thomas W. Lawson*, built in 1902, had no fewer than seven fore-and-aft-rigged masts.

European owners succeeded in making their big sailing ships paying propositions by confining them to carrying freights not requiring rapid passages on long, direct routes between the ports of origin and destination, by

Model of the clipper ship 'Cutty Sark', 1869.
Crown Copyright. Science Museum, London

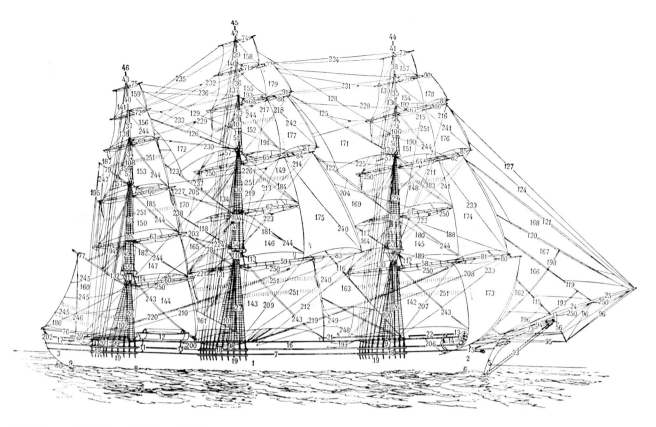

Sail-plan of full-rigged ship, c. 1890.
Science Museum, London

making them highly mechanized, with winches for working the braces and for hoisting the yards, and by dividing all sails into two smaller ones, thus requiring fewer hands. Steel masts and spars and steel-wire rigging cut down maintenance costs. So rigged, they were employed carrying grain or wool from Australia or taking coal to South America and returning with saltpetre or nitrates.

From the last years of the nineteenth century right up to the outbreak of the First World War Ferdinand Laeisz of Hamburg operated his famous ships, the names of which all began with the letter 'P'. One of them, the ship-rigged *Preussen* of 5,081 tons, was probably the largest sailing ship ever built. Although such ships could not sail very close to the wind owing to the limited degree to which there was room for their yards to be braced, they were very fast with a fair wind. The routes they followed were therefore chosen primarily so as to make use of the constant winds such as the Trades. Nevertheless the five-masted barque *Potosi* of 4,026 tons made

eleven consecutive voyages between Hamburg and Peru at an average speed of 11 knots.

The 'P' line began operating again after 1918. The majority were barquentines, fore-and-aft rigged on the four aftermasts and square-rigged only on the foremast. Others, which had square topsails and top-gallants on the first and third masts only, were more properly classed as topsail schooners. The number of ships in service had fallen, however, to just two, the barques *Padua* and *Priwall*, by 1938. Another company that operated large barquentines until the 1920s was Dom Borde Fils of Bordeaux.

The Second World War finally brought the end of the ocean-going sailing ship. In 1939 no fewer than thirteen tall steel barques took part for the last time in the race home with grain from Australia; ten of them belonged to the Norwegian Gustav Erikson of Mariehamn whose four-masted barque *Moshulu*, built by William Hamilton of Glasgow in 1904, was the winner.

154

Model of four-masted barque 'California', 1890.
Science Museum, London

*Model of seven-masted schooner 'Thomas W. Lawson',
1902.* Crown Copyright. Science Museum, London

3
Steamships

Model of Jouffroy's steamboat, 1784.
Science Museum, London

Early Experiments

There is evidence that propulsion of boats by means of
paddle-wheels was employed, or at least attempted, as
long ago as the classical age. Experiments with man-
driven paddle-wheels both in Europe and in China have
been recorded. The Jesuit Fathers in Peking mentioned
such a craft in their *Mémoires*, published in Paris in 1782.
As with all the other developments of the Industrial
Revolution, however, it was the invention of the steam
engine that was at last to free sailors from the thraldom
of the wayward winds or the labour at the rower's bench.

Steam as a source of power was vaguely perceived as
early as 130 B.C. when Hero of Alexandria constructed his
'aeolipile', a mechanical toy in which a hollow pivoted
ball was made to revolve by the action of steam escaping
from it through angled exhaust nozzles. Not for another
1,820 years was the power of steam first harnessed to a
practical purpose by the Huguenot Dr Denis Papin, who
settled in London in 1675 and was elected a Fellow of the
Royal Society of which he was curator from 1684 to 1688.
He was then appointed professor of mathematics at
Marburg University, and in 1690 he published a description of a cylinder in which a piston was first forced

John Fitch's paddleboat, on the Delaware River, opposite Philadelphia, 1786. Science Museum, London

upwards by steam generated under it and then descended again when the steam was allowed to condense.

He had, in fact, described the principle of the atmospheric engine more generally associated with the name of Thomas Newcomen, who took out his first patent in 1705. Both men originally visualized their engines as pumps, for which Newcomen's was eventually set up. Papin, however, also sought to harness this new source of power to drive the rotatory paddles he had seen in use in a boat belonging to the Prince of Hesse-Cassel. In 1707 he did so with such success in a boat on the River Fulda in Hanover that he set off in her down-river with the intention of navigating across the sea to London. Not for the last time in the history of steam power, its success excited envious opposition. The watermen of Münden attacked this first steamboat in history, smashing it to pieces. Papin's experiment was not repeated. Newcomen's and Papin's engines had a basic weakness as power units for ships (or locomotives) in that after each upwards stroke there was a pause while the steam under the piston was condensed. It was not until 1769 that James Watt's engine, embodying a separate condenser, a 'sun and planet' system of cog wheels to convert the up-and-down

movement of the pivoted beam into a rotary movement, and a flywheel to maintain a smooth motion over the whole piston stroke, made further progress towards a steamship possible.

The first to make use of such an engine to drive a steamboat was a Frenchman, Claude François, Marquis de Jouffroy d'Abbans, who first installed a single-acting Watt engine in a 42-foot boat in 1776 and then, in 1783, an improved, 2-cylinder engine driving a pair of paddle-wheels in a 150-foot boat at Lyons. In this craft he navigated the Saône for some sixteen months, though he did not put it to any practical use and, meeting with discouragement from the French Academy of Sciences, he abandoned his experiments.

At about the same time experiments were being made in America by James Rumsey which culminated in 1787 in a model steamboat which made successful trials on the Potomac, achieving a speed of 4 knots, and by John Fitch in whose boats a double-acting steam engine drove banks of paddles in a motion similar to that of a canoeist. The latter steamed the 20 miles from Philadelphia to Burlington in a 60-foot boat in 1788, and in the following year constructed a larger vessel which achieved 8 knots

157

William Symington's double-hulled steamboat, built for Patrick Miller, 1788. Science Museum, London

and ran regularly on the Delaware for some years. In 1796 the same remarkable man fitted a boat with an engine driving a screw. None of these inventions inspired faith in his financial backers, however, and when the last of them abandoned him he committed suicide in 1798.

Meanwhile a Scottish engineer, William Symington, was following a career equally productive in the development of the marine steam engine and, alas, equally unrewarding financially. He had taken out a patent for such an engine in 1786, but it was not until 1788 that the opportunity came to fit one in a small double-hulled 25-foot boat built for an Edinburgh banker, Patrick Miller, who had been experimenting with man-powered paddle-boats.

On one hull Symington placed his boiler; on the other a 2-cylinder atmospheric engine using the separate condenser as patented by Watt and driving two paddle-wheels, placed in the space between the two hulls, by means of chains which rotated drums with a pawl-and-ratchet gear to allow rotation in one direction only. When

this little craft successfully made up to seven knots on Dalswinton Loch, Dumfries-shire, Miller commissioned the Carron Iron Works to construct similar machinery to be installed in a 60-foot boat on the Forth and Clyde Canal, which in December 1789 towed a heavy load at 7 knots.

For some reason the association between the two men ceased soon after this. Miller's boat was dismantled and a project for a third lapsed. Symington, however, persisted and indeed was working on a simple conception of universal application today, but of which no one had previously thought—the conversion of the reciprocating motion of the piston rod to a rotary one by means of a crank and connecting rod. He secured the support of Lord Dundas, who had an interest in the Forth and Clyde Canal, and in 1801 a 56-foot vessel, the *Charlotte Dundas*, was launched on the canal as a steam tug, fitted with a stern paddle-wheel driven by an engine of this type, the first direct-acting steam engine ever constructed.

Success was immediate; in 1802 the *Charlotte Dundas*

towed two 70-ton loaded barges nearly 20 miles in 6 hours against a stiff wind. But the opposition so often suffered by innovators came from the canal owners, who complained of the damage to the banks likely to occur from the resultant wash. The vessel was withdrawn and left to rot. Symington was to die in poverty.

The seed had been planted nevertheless. It was to

Model of the 'Charlotte Dundas', showing engine.
Crown Copyright. Science Museum, London

germinate first and most successfully under the hands of the American inventor, Robert Fulton. A man with an immensely varied turn of inventive talent, he had earlier offered and demonstrated in Britain and France a practical, man-powered submersible, the *Nautilus*, as well as ingenious methods of attacking ships with towed explosives.

The Steamboat in America

Fulton now received the patronage and became the partner of Mr Chancellor R. Livingston, the United States Minister to France. Having visited Symington and made a trip in the *Charlotte Dundas*, he borrowed a Watt engine from a M. Périer, who had unsuccessfully experimented with a steamboat earlier, and built a paddle-boat on the Seine in which it was installed. The machinery proved too heavy for it and it broke in two and sank in a gale. Undaunted, he salved the engine and built another boat which in August 1803 achieved a speed of 4½ knots.

Fulton was now fired with the ambition to repeat his success on the Hudson River. In the autumn of 1806 he reached New York and at once set about building a ship to be called the *Clermont* after the country house of his partner, Livingston, powered by a single-cylinder, Boulton & Watt beam engine.

Fulton had, in fact, been forestalled by John Stevens (Livingston's brother-in-law and early partner) and Robert Livingston Stevens. Both had developed during 1804 original concepts of John Fitch, the former with a stern-wheel paddle-steamer in which he had crossed the Hudson River, the latter with a steamer in which the first tubular boilers ever to be built provided the power to drive a screw very similar to the four-threaded helix that was to be generally adopted decades later. Such a concept was far in advance of its time, however, and the paddle-wheel was to hold the attention exclusively for another thirty years.

During the winter of 1806-7, while the ship-builder Brownne of New York worked to construct the *Clermont* to Fulton's plans for a hull 150 feet long with a beam of 13 feet, the Stevenses, having refused to join Fulton in partnership, were engaged on another paddle-steamer, the *Phoenix*. The *Clermont* was the first to be completed and on 17th August 1807 she set out on her maiden voyage from New York to Livingston's country estate, 110 miles up the Hudson River. As she thrashed her way up-stream under a cloud of black smoke which, mingled with showers of sparks from the pine-wood fuel, billowed from her funnel, her unboxed side paddle-wheels splashing manfully round and a cloud of steam shrouding the mid-ship section where the boiler and engine were situated, she excited incredulity from a large proportion of the crowds that watched her, none of whom imagined that 'Fulton's Folly' would reach her distant destination and many of whom were certain she would blow up. Amongst others, more simple-minded, she spread terror; crews of ships she passed were seen to flee ashore or to fall prayerfully on their knees asking for protection from so fearful a monster.

The *Clermont* was rigged with a spanker on her mainmast and a yard and square sail on her foremast; but with a contrary wind she made no use of these during her first voyage which took her to Clermont in just twenty-four hours and on to Albany, a further 40 miles, in eight hours —a speed of 4·6 knots which qualified Fulton and Livingston for the monopoly of steamboat operation on the Hudson.

At her original dimensions the *Clermont* was somewhat unstable; and during the winter of 1807-8 she was given a greater beam—16 feet at the water line, 18 feet at deck

159

Robert Fulton's paddle-steamer 'Clermont', 1807.
Science Museum, London

Machinery of the 'Clermont'. Science Museum, London

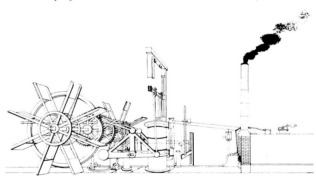

level. In 1809 she was rebuilt and renamed *North River* and her ultimate fate is not known. In the next six years before his death in 1815 Fulton designed and had built seventeen craft of various kinds, the immediate successor to the *Clermont* being the *Car of Neptune*. Few exceeded a speed of 7 knots, but the whole enterprise was a financial success, aided, of course, by the monopoly it enjoyed. When a would-be rival, Captain Bunker, introduced two steamers, the *Hope* and *Perseverance*, to the Hudson River, the law was invoked and the vessels confiscated.

Undaunted and evidently bearing no ill-will, Bunker transferred his activities to start the Long Island Sound Line with a steamer designed by and named after Fulton in 1813. The *Fulton* was the first American steamer to break away from the wall-sided, flat-bottomed design in favour of a rounded bottom as in sailing ships. The two Stevenses, meanwhile, also forbidden to operate the *Phoenix* on the Hudson, steamed her in 1809 to the Delaware, giving her an honoured place in history as the first steamship to navigate the open sea, and with her inaugurated the successful Philadelphia Line.

Fulton's activities extended to the Mississippi in 1811 when he pioneered the steamship service on that river with the *New Orleans*, which made the voyage down the Ohio and Mississippi from Pittsburg to New Orleans in fourteen days. Another 'first' scored by Fulton was when his steamer the *Firefly* made the open sea voyage from New York to Newport, Rhode Island, in 1817 after his death. At that time, too, there was building on the Hudson for Fulton and Livingston the *Chancellor Livingston*, designed by Henry Eckford, a leading naval architect, the finest boat the partners ever owned and, at 500 tons, the largest steamboat in the world, but which Fulton was not to live to see completed. Comfort for the passengers was by this time catered for, and in the *Chancellor Livingston* a two-storied deck-house covered her square stern, its roof being extended forward under awnings as far forward as the paddle-boxes to form a promenade deck. She had three masts which carried a fore-and-aft rig of sails as well as a square sail on the foremast. Her engines, which were of the 'steeple' type, gave her a speed of a little over 7 knots.

By this time steamboats had become a familiar sight on the Hudson, between New York and Albany, where ten were in operation, on the Delaware between Trenton, Philadelphia, Newcastle and Wilmington, as well as numerous steamers on the Mississippi where such ships as the *Etna* and *Vesuvius* of 450 tons were plying, able to carry 280 tons of merchandise, 700 bales of cotton and 100 passengers. The development of American river steamers is dealt more fully elsewhere in this volume. Here we are more concerned with sea-going craft. Of these, there were a number running between New York and the ports of Connecticut and New Jersey and between Baltimore and Norfolk, Virginia. All these were of wooden construction and driven by side-wheel paddles.

It was natural that the steamboat should soon also be seen on the lakes of North America, which offered easy communications through the still wild forest lands of the interior. Lake Champlain, the natural extension of the Hudson River route to Canada from New York, had its first steamer, the *Vermont*, in 1808 and, for the next sixty-seven years, until the completion of the New York and Canada Railroad in 1875, steamers of the Champlain Transportation Company were an important link in the

Model of the paddle-steamer 'Savannah', 1818.
Crown Copyright. Science Museum, London

161

route. Thereafter they continued to run for the summer tourist trade.

The Great Lakes saw their first steamer in 1818, when the 338-ton *Walk in the Water*, appropriately named after a famous Wyandotte Indian Chief, was launched on the waters of Lake Erie where Buffalo soon grew to be the starting-point of a regular passenger service.

Development of Ocean-going Steamers

Of a wider significance for the future than the river-boats was the *Savannah*, built at New York in 1818 as a full-rigged ship of 350 tons, but while on the stocks fitted with a steam engine and detachable paddles. Although this engine was only an auxiliary means of propulsion, the *Savannah* undoubtedly made history when she crossed the Atlantic between 24th May and 17th June 1819, arriving at Liverpool having used her engine for eighty hours of the passage, which used up all her fuel. The time was not ripe, however, for the ocean-going steamship. Nor was the American genius directed towards such a development, being preoccupied rather with the navigation of the broad inland waterways of the country. On her return, the *Savannah*'s engine was removed and she spent the rest of her days under sail only.

Meanwhile in Europe, or, more specifically at this epoch, in Great Britain, progress had been slower, chiefly no doubt owing to the absence of large, navigable waterways such as the Hudson and the Delaware in which development could naturally take place. Following the withdrawal of the *Charlotte Dundas* no steamboats were built until 1811. Then it was Henry Bell, an hotel pro-

Paddle-steamer 'Comet'; the 150th anniversary replica, built in 1962. Science Museum, London

prietor of Helensburgh, who had accompanied Fulton on his visit to Symington and seen the trial trip of his steamboat, who now had the idea of running a steamboat service between Helensburgh and Glasgow. He commissioned John Wood & Co. of Glasgow to build a 42-foot boat which he named the *Comet*, for which John Robertson constructed a 4-hp engine, the single piston of which drove a pair of side levers which turned the crankshaft by means of a connecting rod. The boiler, set on one side of the engine, was constructed by David Napier. Originally provided with two paddle-wheels on each side, driven through spur gearing, but later reduced for simplicity to a single pair, the *Comet* had a speed of about 6 knots.

Though she was a commercial failure, the *Comet* was the inspiration for a stream of subsequent ventures on the River Clyde. Between 1813 and 1814 the steamboats *Clyde*, built by John Wood & Co., *Tay*, *Caledonia* and *Humber*, built at Dundee, were all engined by John Robertson. In 1813 another little steamboat, the *Elizabeth*, powered by an 8-hp engine, became the first British steamer to make a sea voyage, surviving a violent gale on the way, when she was sent from the Clyde to Liverpool for service on the Mersey. Two years later the *Marjory* and the *Argyle*, small, wooden paddle-steamers of about 70 tons, both steamed from the Clyde to the Thames where the former began a daily service between Wapping Stairs and Gravesend. The latter, renamed *Thames*, inaugurated the service of pleasure steamers between London and Margate which was to become a well-known and popular feature of London life. Her average speed was 10 mph. In 1816 the English Channel was first crossed by a steamboat, the *Majestic*, which steamed from Brighton to Le Havre. In the same year James Watt, Junior, bought the *Caledonia* mentioned above; and, having fitted her with new engines, steamed her from the Thames to Rotterdam and thence up the Rhine to Coblenz.

By this time steamboats on the Thames had become a not uncommon sight, driven mostly by Boulton & Watt engines of some 20 hp. More significant of the future was the inauguration of a regular steam packet service between Greenock and Belfast in 1818 by David Napier, who revolutionized ship design by introducing the sharp stem in place of the customary bluff bow in the little 90-ton *Rob Roy*, which he had built by William Denny, driven by a 30-hp engine. In the same year he had the 156-ton *Talbot* built to inaugurate a steam packet service between Holyhead and Dublin. It was the *Rob Roy* too which in 1819 opened the Dover to Calais packet route.

Except perhaps for the *Talbot*, all these were indeed

only steamboats, as opposed to steamships; this may be why to the English-speaking people the passenger ship has, popularly, always been a 'boat'; to the French, too, it is a *paquebot*. In the third decade of the nineteenth century, however, bigger steamers took the water. From the firm of Wigram & Green, famous for their crack Blackwall Frigates, came the *City of Edinburgh* in 1821 for the London to Edinburgh passenger trade, and the *James Watt*, a 420-ton ship built by Wood & Co. of Glasgow, each driven by a 100-hp Boulton & Watt engine. The *Lightning*, a 200-ton, 80-hp steamer, was the first to carry mails.

Marine steam engines at this time were almost always of the 'side-lever' type. The original engine was the 'beam' engine in which the piston rod acted directly on one end of a pivoted beam above, the up-and-down

Side-lever engine from the P.S. 'Leven', 1823.
Crown Copyright. Science Museum, London

motion of the other end of the beam transmitting a rotary motion by means either of Watt's 'sun and planet' arrangement or by means of a crankshaft. Such an engine, with the massive beam projecting high above the hull, remained adequate for steamers in sheltered, inland waters and, indeed, was to be seen until well into the twentieth century in American river steamers.

For an ocean-going steamer, however, it was necessary to get the machinery more compact and lower in the hull.

163

*Paddle-steamer 'Sirius', the first vessel to steam the whole
way across the Atlantic, 1838.*
Science Museum, London

Model of the 'Great Western', 1837.
Crown Copyright. Science Museum, London

The paddle-steamer 'President', 2,360 tons, 1839.
Science Museum, London

The beam was therefore transferred to the bottom and to the side of the engine mounting. One end of this 'side-lever' (or pair of side-levers) was driven by the piston rod through a cross-head and connecting rod, the power being delivered to the crankshaft through a connecting rod at the other end of the side-lever.

•Such was the type of engine with which, during the 1820s, the *Falcon* of 176 tons and the *Enterprise* of 470 tons successfully made the long haul round the Cape of Good Hope and across the Indian Ocean to Calcutta. Then in 1833 the *Royal William*, of some 600 tons and equipped with a Boulton & Watt engine, made the passage from Picton, Nova Scotia, to Cowes in seventeen days. All of these were primarily sailing ships; their engines were auxiliary.

It was finally the Queen Steam Navigation Co. that achieved the first Atlantic crossing with a ship that steamed the whole way in 1838. This was the *Sirius*, a 703-ton brigantine, 178 feet long and powered by a 320-hp engine, which had been built for the London to Cork run. The company's own first large steamer was still being built and it was perhaps in order to forestall a rival firm that they chartered the *Sirius* and sent her forth from London with ninety passengers and, after coaling at Queenstown, across the ocean to New York. Her captain had to deal with a near mutiny by his fearful crew when a westerly gale was met. Fuel ran low and had to be augmented with the ship's spars; but she arrived at New York on 22nd April, seventeen days out.

The next day she was joined by her rival, a more famous ship, Brunel's *Great Western*, almost double her size at 1,321 tons and 236 feet in length, which had made the trip in 15 days at an average speed of 8 knots. Her 2-cylinder, side-lever engine, the product of the firm of Joseph Maudslay, was supplied with steam from four boilers. One quarter of her coal supply still remained when she arrived. This was one dividend that accrued from building so large a ship. The other was that unlike the *Sirius* and another steamer, a second *Royal William* which the City of Dublin Steam Packet Co. also tried on the Atlantic route, of much the same size as the *Sirius*, the bigger ship could beat the Atlantic rollers. The *Royal*

Model of the paddle-steamer 'Britannia', 1840.
    Science Museum, London, courtesy of Cunard Steam-ship Company

Charles Dickens's cabin aboard the 'Britannia'.
    Science Museum, London, courtesy Cunard Steamship Company

William and *Sirius* were soon withdrawn. The *Great Western* ran regularly and was a financial success, carrying some 150 passengers to and fro across the ocean at a fare of 35 guineas each, enabling her directors to declare a 9 per cent dividend after the first year's operating. The Queen Steam Navigation Co.'s own ship, *British Queen*, which was completed in 1839 at a cost of £60,000, was even bigger than the *Great Western* and averaged more than 10 knots on her first trip in April of that year, reaching New York in fourteen days. She too proved a success.

The Paddle-wheel Passenger Liner

The success of the *Great Western* and the *British Queen* made it clear to the discerning eye that the time had come for the supersession of the Western Ocean Sailing Packets by the steamship. First to react to the implications was the Board of Admiralty, so often held up to ridicule for

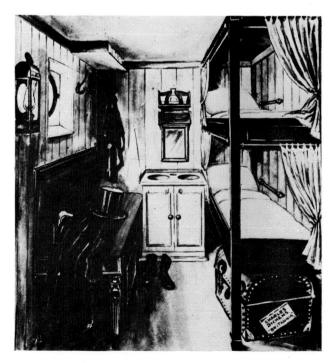

excessive conservatism. In 1838 they still held responsibility for negotiating overseas mail contracts; they now decided that steamships should replace the Falmouth Packets in carrying mail to America, and invited tenders.

News of this reaching Samuel Cunard, a Halifax, N.S., merchant and ship-owner, he crossed at once to Britain to raise the necessary capital. There he obtained the support of the Clyde ship-builder and engineer Robert Napier who introduced him to George Burns and David MacIver. The new company, the British and North American Royal Mail Steam Packet Company, was to build four ships to carry on a service with fixed, fortnightly dates of sailing.

Such was the origin of what was soon known as the Cunard Company. During 1840 their first four wooden

Navigation Company, famous as the P & O and still the best-known passenger line from Europe to the Orient and Australia.

The former named all their ships after rivers, and it was with the *Thames* that they inaugurated their service, at first from Falmouth like their sailing predecessors, and later from Southampton. They soon extended their service to South America; firstly to Panama where their cargoes were transported across the isthmus and re-embarked for onward passage along the Pacific coast by ships of the associated Pacific Steam Navigation Company, whose steamers *Chile* and *Peru* had been the first such ships to navigate the Magellan Strait.

The latter, as the Peninsular Company, had been running small paddle-steamers to Lisbon and Gibraltar

Models showing comparative sizes of the 'Britannia' (1840) and 'Queen Mary' (1934).
Science Museum, London, courtesy Cunard White Star Ltd

paddle-steamers, *Britannia*, *Acadia*, *Caledonia* and *Columbia*, which, by contract, had to be adaptable for use as troop transports in war, were built on the Clyde at various shipyards and on 4th July of that year the 1,154-ton *Britannia* sailed for Boston, arriving on the 18th, having touched at Halifax *en route*. Her 740-hp side-lever 2-cylinder engines were built, as were those of all four, by Robert Napier's Glasgow firm, and supplied with steam from four boilers. Her average speed was $8\frac{1}{2}$ knots and she could accommodate 115 cabin passengers and 225 tons of cargo. As with all steamers for many years to come, these were all rigged for sail; but by this time it was the sails which had become the auxiliary, the paddle-wheels the main propulsion.

Closely following the Cunard Company in the date of their incorporation came the Royal Mail Steam Packet Company which in 1840 contracted to take over the mail service to the West Indies in place of the Admiralty's gun-brigs, and the Peninsular and Oriental Steam

since the 1830s. In 1840, as the P & O, it extended its service through the Mediterranean to Alexandria; two years later its first steamer made the voyage to India via the Cape of Good Hope, the 1,800-ton, 500-hp *Hindostan*. In 1844 the P & O initiated a mail service to India and China which transported passengers, cargo and mail from Alexandria to Suez by boats on the Mahmoudieh Canal to the Nile, by steamers up the river to Cairo and thence across the desert on the backs of camels, often as many as three thousand of them, to Suez. This laborious route was maintained until the opening of the Suez Canal in 1869.

As noted earlier, American ship-builders at that time were absorbed with development of river and lake steamers rather than ocean liners. On the Great Lakes by 1849 there were registered twenty-nine side-wheel steamers of up to 1,500 tons displacement. Thirteen years later the number had grown to 147 paddle and 203 screw steamers.

Meanwhile on the great rivers and on Long Island Sound which, so far as steamship types are concerned, can be considered with the more strictly defined inland waterways, the operation of passenger steamships had expanded even faster. By 1835 the side-wheel paddle-steamers *Lexington* and *John W. Richmond* were rivalling each other to make the fastest passage between New York and Providence. As was to be the case for another fifty years, these shallow-draught ships were of wooden construction and all had a longitudinal weakness, a tendency to 'hog' or 'sag'. To obviate this a system devised by the Stevenses, making use of stump masts, struts or 'hog-frames' and iron ties to stiffen them, was to be seen on a great many American river steamers.

The other feature common to all the passenger boats on the American north-eastern inland waters was the wide overhang of the main deck, covering the paddle-boxes and tapering towards bow and stern. Rising from this broad, oval platform were the double, triple or quadruple tiers of enclosed passenger accommodation, two-berth state-rooms for perhaps 120 with another 600 in open berthing areas, besides a saloon and promenade area.

The decade 1840–50, before competition from railroads began to eat into their trade, was the golden age for the Hudson River steamboat companies. Twenty steamers famous for their speed and elegance plied between New York and Albany, carrying passengers at some 20 mph in all the comfort of an American hotel for as little as 12½ cents. Crack boats occasionally staged races such as that in 1847 between the *Oregon* and the *C. Vanderbilt* for $1,000, which the former won by 400 yards after having had to burn much of her furniture when fuel ran low.

On the Mississippi, and its tributaries too, large, shallow-draught steamers with immense side or stern paddle-wheels, high superstructures and tall funnels were being built. Their operations were not without dangers and disasters. In 1838 the *Moselle*'s boilers blew up and more than 150 passengers perished. A similar catastrophe overtook the *Oroonoko*. Rival steamers would race, beam to beam, down the narrow channels, and their captains were not above ramming their opponents to gain an advantage. A famous race in 1855 was that between the *Eclipse* and the *Natchez*, pictures of which show the two steamers rushing through the night, their towering funnels red-hot. Another, later, *Natchez*, sixth of her name, ran a famous race in 1870 with the *Robert E. Lee* (immortalized in song) from New Orleans to St Louis.

The machinery of most of these steamers for many years to come was the old-fashioned vertical beam or 'steeple' engine, slow-running, but driving paddle-wheels as much as 40 feet in diameter, very reliable and almost impossible to wear out. They were very suitable for river steamers, unlike the sea-going ships being developed mainly across the Atlantic; and this fact accounts, to a large extent, for American backwardness in marine engineering during the nineteenth century.

Another fast-growing transport industry in America during that epoch was the carriage of freight through the Great Lakes. The completion of the Welland Canal between Lakes Ontario and Erie and the Sault Ste Marie Canal between Lakes Superior and Huron connected up 30 per cent of the world's navigable fresh water. This was a great stimulus to construction of freight-carrying steamers designed specially for the Lakes and for easy passage through the canal locks. The principal freight traffic was the carriage of iron ore from the upper end of Lake Erie and Hudson and returning with coal. At the end of the summer, too, there was a heavy traffic in grain.

Thus it was the bulk carrier which dominated the scene on the Lakes. One type originating there, the 'whaleback', invented by Alexander McDougall, is described later. The typical Great Lakes bulk cargo ship has been variously described as a huge self-propelled barge or an immense box-girder on account of its long, obstruction-free, vertical sides and stem with even the anchors stowed away internally. Like canal barges everywhere they are unusually long for their beam. The largest of them in 1910, the *William M. Mills*, was also typical for that period: 607 feet in length, with a beam of 60 feet, her boiler room and her triple expansion steam reciprocating engines were situated right aft, while her crew accommodation and bridge were on the forecastle. Between these two stretched 447 feet of cargo-hold obstructed only by three screen bulkheads for grain, of which she could carry 514,500 bushels. Alternatively she could load 12,380 tons of ore. As these cargoes were loaded through spouts, a large number of small hatches was provided so that a score or more of these spouts could be delivering simultaneously.

We have gone somewhat ahead of our story; but it was necessary to show why American ship-builders and engineers, fully occupied with the busy, expanding shipping industry of their inland waters, played a comparatively minor part in developing that on the oceans at that time. One American line did emerge during the 1840s, however, to offer serious competition to the Cunard for a while; this was the Collins Line which during 1848 and 1849 built four of the finest steam ships afloat at that time, the *Arctic, Atlantic, Baltic* and *Pacific*. At an average speed of 13 knots the *Baltic* and

River paddle-steamer 'New World', 1849.
Science Museum, London

*The celebrated race between the Mississippi paddle-
steamers 'Natchez' and 'Eclipse' in 1855.*
Science Museum, London

Beam engine used in American river steamer, 1884.
Crown Copyright. Science Museum, London

Pacific won the west-bound and east-bound Blue Ribbon for Atlantic crossings in 1851. With side-lever engines driving paddle-wheels, this was a great strain on their wooden hulls, however, and they suffered numerous defects; after the *Arctic* was lost in collision in 1854 the line declined and ceased to run in 1864.

Screw Propulsion

While these several companies had been forming, a number of innovations of dominating influence on the development of the steamship had been offered but not at once accepted. That with the longest history was the screw propeller. Although Archimedes of Syracuse had demonstrated it centuries earlier, Joseph Bramah had patented the idea in 1785 and John Stevens had actually

made use of it in 1804 to drive his boat on the Hudson, it was not until 1836 that two engineers patented different types of screw which caught the interest of backers to give them practical application.

John Ericsson, a Swedish engineer working in England, devised a system with seven helical blades on the outside of a wheel and three more blades inside it, forming its radii. Two of these wheels contra-rotated on the same shaft. Ericsson successfully demonstrated this propeller, fitted in a 45-foot boat named *Francis B. Ogden* after his patron the American consul in Liverpool, by towing a barge carrying Admiralty officials down the Thames at 10 knots. This invention was turned down, however, on the grounds that the steering of his craft was unreliable, perhaps because his propeller was mounted behind the rudder. Ericsson persisted, however, again proving the

170

Beam engine and paddle, American river steamer, 1884.
Crown Copyright. Science Museum, London

worth of his invention when used to drive a larger vessel, the *Robert F. Stockton*, the name of his other American patron, who persuaded him to take himself and the vessel to the United States. There he was to gain fame as the inventor of the gun turret and designer of the U.S.S. *Monitor* during the Civil War.

Better success attended the efforts of Francis Pettit Smith with a two-bladed propeller which he demonstrated firstly in a 6-ton steamboat which he navigated successfully from Blackwall to Folkestone. A syndicate was then formed which built the 240-ton *Archimedes* on the Thames and sent it on a successful tour round Great Britain and then from Plymouth to Oporto, when she set up a record for the passage by steam. In 1839, Winshurst, the builder of the *Archimedes*, launched the first screw-driven cargo steamer, the *Novelty*.

The screw continued to have many opponents, nevertheless, and it was not until a convincing demonstration staged by the Admiralty in 1845 in the form of a tug-of-war between a paddle-sloop and the Navy's first screw-propelled sloop, the *Rattler*, which the latter convincingly won, that its superiority was conceded. The forward-reaching mind of Brunel, who had seen the *Archimedes*, had been at once convinced, however, and he was now to use the screw propeller in his latest great design. This was the *Great Britain* which he had designed as a paddle-steamer for the Great Western Company and whose design he now altered to screw drive.

This huge ship (for its day) of 3,618 tons was also to be revolutionary in that she was to be constructed of iron. So huge in comparison with any other ship afloat was the *Great Britain* that no shipyard would undertake to build

Collins Line paddle-steamer 'Atlantic', 1849.
Science Museum, London

Model of the stern paddle-steamer 'Inez Clarke', built in London in 1879 for mail service on the Magdalena River, Columbia.
Crown Copyright. Science Museum, London

her. The Great Western Company therefore laid down plant at Bristol and proceeded to build her themselves. In July 1845, after proving trips to London and Liverpool, she sailed for New York. Her 1,000-hp engine with four direct-acting cylinders driving a large drum which, in turn, by means of four chains drove the propeller shaft, thus producing the effect of gearing, gave her a maximum speed of 12 knots, but on her maiden voyage she averaged 9½ knots, making New York in fifteen days.

Apart from her status as the first iron ocean-going ship, the biggest screw-ship until Brunel's *Great Eastern* took the water fifteen years after her, and the first to cross the Atlantic, the *Great Britain* also enjoyed such innovations as water-tight compartments and bilge keels, later to become universal.

This second masterpiece by Brunel was originally to have been called the *Mammoth*. Some contemporary writers accounted her a resounding failure and suggested that she might have been better called the *White Elephant*. The fact is that, like the *Great Eastern*, she was ahead of her time.

In September 1846 she ran aground on rocks in Dundrum Bay, Ireland. It was seven months before Brunel was able to salvage her. But the amazingly small amount of damage she had suffered during that time was a great advertisement for iron construction and for Brunel's design. When she had been repaired, however, her owners sold her for the paltry sum of £100,000; she was then used on the Australian run for a time and finally, with her engines removed, as a sailing ship before being laid up as a coal hulk at Port Stanley in the Falkland Isles.

There she lay until a body of ship-lovers, interested in having her brought back to England as a memorial to Brunel's genius and British marine engineering of that epoch, approached the wealthy Englishman, Mr Jack Hayward, for assistance. He contributed £150,000 for the *Great Britain* to be reconditioned, hoisted on to a raft and towed back to Bristol. This remarkable feat was completed on 5th July 1970; fifteen days later the ship was berthed in the dry-dock where she was built. Her final berth is yet to be decided at the time of writing.

There were still practical objections to screw propulsion in ocean-going ships when the *Great Britain* was

Paddle-steamer 'Wilhelm Tell', one of five used on Lake Lucerne, Switzerland. Built in 1908, she was still in service in the summer of 1970. G. N. Georgano

The screw-steamer 'Archimedes' on a voyage from Gravesend to Portsmouth in the spring of 1839.
Science Museum, London

Match between the sloops 'Rattler' (screw) and 'Alecto' (paddle), 1845. The 'Rattler' succeeded in towing the 'Alecto' stern foremost at a speed of nearly three miles per hour. Science Museum, London

launched. In head seas which caused pitching, the screw raced as it lifted clear of the water. As passengers, by immemorial custom, still had their accommodation in the stern they complained bitterly of the resultant vibration. This 'racing' also put a heavy strain on the gearing which was necessary to produce an adequate propeller speed at a time when engines could not be run very fast. The Cunard Company did not adopt either iron construction or screw propulsion until 1852, when they built four ships for the emigrant trade. They were not popular, however, and after six more had been built for the Mediterranean trade, they reverted in 1856 to the paddle-wheel for a time.

Other developments at this time were an improvement in the hull design of ships as a result of the theories and experiments of John Scott Russell with regard to what was later to be called 'streamlining', and the introduction of the oscillating engine which was to become almost universally fitted in paddle-steamers.

This had been patented as long ago as 1827 by Joseph Maudslay, but was not appreciated until it was re-introduced and perfected in 1838 by John Penn. In this engine the cylinders were mounted on trunnions which permitted them to oscillate so that the piston rod could drive the crankshaft without the medium of a connecting rod. Steam entered the cylinders through the outer trunnions and escaped to the condenser (situated between the two cylinders) after it had done its work, through the inner trunnions.

Though this type of engine saved considerable weight and space, it was more particularly adapted to driving paddle-wheels. At about this time, therefore, there was invented by the same John Penn the trunk engine for screw-steamers. In this the reverse process to that of the oscillating engine took place. The cylinders remained stationary; the piston rod was discarded and the connecting rod, able to oscillate within a trunk which passed through a steam-tight gland in the cylinder cover, drove the crankshaft. This type of engine was to be satisfactory

Model of the 'Great Britain', 1843.
Crown Copyright. Science Museum, London

The 'Great Britain' in heavy seas.
Science Museum, London

so long as steam pressure remained low, but thereafter the piston rod and connecting rod conjunction had to be re-introduced.

In the field of boilers, too, there had been a great advance at this time. The earliest boiler had been simply a water tank set in brickwork with a furnace beneath it. It produced steam at no more than atmospheric pressure —15 lb. per square inch. The next development was to situate the furnace inside the tank, the gases passing through flat-sided flues, thus increasing the area being heated. This type was the 'box' boiler, in which steam up to 33 lb. per square inch could be generated. About 1850, however, boilers were built round a number of tubes through which the hot gases from the furnace passed to heat the water surrounding the tubes. In these tubular boilers, higher pressures were possible. Slowly and with some trepidation these were introduced in steamships, bringing simultaneously advantages and complications.

The time was now ripe for a big advance in the design and performance of steamships. As before, it was to be Brunel who blazed the trail. As before, his concept was to

Sectioned model of early tubular boiler, 1844.
Crown Copyright. Science Museum, London

Maudslay's oscillating engine, 1827.
Crown Copyright. Science Museum, London

be in advance of the times and receive less than its due credit.

His idea was for a ship of such a size that she could carry a large number of passengers as well as a great quantity of cargo to Australia at 15 knots without having to coal during the voyage. She was to be driven by paddles as well as a screw, and to have six masts square-rigged on the second and third, fore-and-aft rigged on the remainder. The Eastern Navigation Company was persuaded and Scott Russell's firm at Millwall received the contract to build the 680-foot ship and the oscillating engines for the paddle-wheels, while James Watt & Co. were to provide the 4-cylinder horizontal direct-acting engine to drive the screw. Laid down in May 1854, she was finally launched on 31st January 1858 after a three-month delay following an initial failure to leave the slipway, a delay which ruined her builders.

The *Great Eastern*, as she was named, seemed to contemporary critics a monstrosity. Nevertheless she fulfilled much that Brunel had prophesied for her. Under paddles and screw power she made her 15 knots; she was immensely strong and her great length proved a great advantage in the Atlantic rollers; her novel system of double-bottom compartments demonstrated its value when she struck a rock, tearing open her bottom for more than a hundred feet, but was able to complete her voyage with the integrity of her inner hull unaffected.

She was, however, a financial failure, largely because the company which bought her after the failure of the Eastern Navigation Company before she was completed put her to compete on the short transatlantic run for

176

The 'Great Eastern', 18,914 tons; 1858.
Science Museum, London

Oscillating engines of the 'Great Eastern'.
Crown Copyright. Science Museum, London

which she was unsuitable. After being used to lay the Atlantic cable, and many others, she was finally broken up in 1888.

The Ocean Greyhounds

The prestige as well as profit of the transatlantic passenger trade led to the foundation of several competing lines during the 1850s and '60s. The North German Lloyd started an Atlantic service in 1858, though it was not to become a serious competitor for another thirty years. The French Line, or more properly the Compagnie Générale Transatlantique, was inaugurated in 1864 with British-built paddle-steamers. The following year, however, the *Pereire*, on the stocks at the yard of Robert Napier & Sons on the Clyde, was converted to screw propulsion, as were her successors the *Ville de Paris* and *Saint Laurent*. Cunard's chief competitor at that time, however, was the Inman Line founded in 1850, whose screw-driven *City of Paris* took the west-bound Blue Ribbon in 1867 with a speed of 13·77 knots.

How far American design and construction of ocean-going steamers was lagging behind the British at this epoch is to be seen from the ships with which the Pacific

Mail S.S. Company fulfilled their contracts for the mail service with China. These, the *America*, *China*, *Great Republic* and *Japan*, built in 1866 and 1867, were of wooden construction—the largest wooden commercial steamers ever built—and their paddle-wheels were driven by vertical beam engines.

This is a further indication of the influence on Ameri-

S.S. 'City of Richmond', 1873. Science Museum, London

The first turbine-driven ship, the yacht 'Turbinia', 1894.
Science Museum, London

can ship-building practice of the decades of concentration on lake and river steamers. Although iron had begun to replace wooden construction in these by 1883, when the Fall River Line put the double-hulled *Pilgrim* on the Long Island Sound route from New York to Boston via Newport and Fall River, she was still propelled by paddles. So too was the Line's famous *Commonwealth*, built of steel in 1907 and powered by double inclined compound engines which gave her a speed of 22 knots. In the wide, four-tiered superstructure there was sleeping accommodation for two thousand passengers. This splendid ship was in operation until 1937. Another well-known flyer of this type was the *City of Cleveland* which, with others of her sort, spectacularly plied the Great Lakes.

Except for the Pacific Mail ships mentioned above, screw propulsion had superseded the paddle-wheel everywhere on the ocean routes by 1870.

In 1873 the Stars and Stripes returned to the Atlantic passenger trade with the *Pennsylvania* of the American Steamship Company, and four other ships followed her. Another American line was the Guion whose *Arizona* not only held the Blue Ribbon in 1879, but by surviving a head-on collision with an iceberg led to the more general adoption of water-tight bulkheads and compartments.

The White Star Line had been founded in 1871 to take over the Australia passenger service from the sailing clippers as well as to compete on the Atlantic Line. Their first liner, the *Oceanic*, built, as were her sisters *Atlantic*, *Baltic* and *Republic*, by Harland and Wolff of Belfast, made the successful innovation of accommodating their first-class passengers amidships. In 1890 the Canadian Pacific Railway secured the British mail contract across the Pacific and inaugurated the service with the first of their famous Empress ships, the *Empress of India*.

By this time steel construction, twin-screw propulsion by fast-running triple-expansion engines of horse-power as great as 30,000, with steam pressures of 150 lb., were

Original turbine of the 'Turbinia', 1894.
Crown Copyright. Science Museum, London

S.S. 'Mauretania', 1906.
   Science Museum, London, courtesy Cunard White Star Ltd

Stern of 'Mauretania'.
   Science Museum, London, courtesy Cunard Steamship Company Ltd

combining to produce 20-knot liners such as the Inman Line's *City of Paris* and *City of New York*, the White Star's *Majestic* and *Teutonic*, and the 13,000-ton *Lucania* and *Campania* of the Cunard Line, the last of which, built by Fairfield's of Glasgow, beat all records with a speed of 22 knots. In 1897 the North German Lloyd captured the Blue Ribbon with the *Kaiser Wilhelm der Grosse*, built by the Vulcan Company of Stettin, which made the crossing at 22·35 knots.

The marine steam turbine, invented by Sir Charles Parsons in 1894, was installed in a small merchant ship, the *King Edward*, built by Denny Brothers of Dumbarton in 1901, which achieved a speed of 20·48 knots, running with notable success between the Clyde and Campbeltown. In the same year the Allan Line, running passenger ships between Liverpool and Canada, had Parsons turbines and triple screws installed in their new liners, *Victorian* and *Virginian*. It was not until 1904 that the Cunard Line followed suit with the *Carmania*; but from this time onwards the superiority of the turbine for fast steamers was established, and the Cunard's next two ships, *Lusitania* and *Mauretania*, which made 27 knots on trials, held the Atlantic speed record between them from 1907 to 1929.

The fast Atlantic liner has been steam-turbine driven ever since. The record for the fastest crossing passed to the North German Lloyd *Bremen* in 1929, to the Cunard White Star *Queen Mary* in 1936 and again in 1938 after she lost it temporarily to the French Line *Normandie*, and finally in 1952 to the state-owned *United States* which averaged speeds of 35·59 knots east-bound and 34·51 knots west-bound. For sheer size the *Normandie*, with a displacement of 83,243 tons, holds the record; but the two Cunard ships *Queen Mary* and *Queen Elizabeth* of nearly the same size will probably always be remembered as the finest all-round examples of the giant liner. Today the advent of air travel has so reduced the volume of passenger traffic by sea that the most modern Atlantic liner, the Cunard *Queen Elizabeth II*, displaces only 65,863 tons and is content with a speed of 28·5 knots.

We have concentrated, perhaps inevitably, on the more spectacular and newsworthy transatlantic liners to the detriment of the very many other types of ships, from the smaller passenger liner on the longer routes down to the humble tramp and coaster.

T.S. '*Titanic*', *setting out on her maiden, and fatal, voyage, 1912.*
Science Museum, London, by courtesy of the National Maritime Museum, Greenwich

T.S. '*Empress of Britain*', *1930.*
Science Museum, London, courtesy Canadian Pacific S.S. Company

T.S. 'Queen Elizabeth', 1938.
Science Museum, London, courtesy Cunard White
Star Ltd

So far as the smaller passenger ships are concerned, with the space available to us it is perhaps sufficient to say that they followed the same trends as their bigger sisters in general except that on the long routes the very high speeds were barred by the high fuel consumption rate they entailed. The short-run packets, such as those between England and the Continent or between England and Ireland, were designed for as much speed as the machinery space available would allow after accommodation of a large number of passengers had been provided for. This today is in the region of 25 knots.

An unusual propulsion system with which small, shallow-draught steamers on the Rhine are equipped must be mentioned here. This is the vertical-axis Voith-Schneider propeller, which can provide thrust in any desired direction. When it is placed aft like a normal screw, as in the *Köln*, a ship 224 feet in length which draws less than 3 feet, no rudder is required. A later development of the system is to be seen in the diesel-driven Rhine steamer *Berlin*, which runs between Köln and Mainz making no fewer than forty landings on

passage. The *Berlin* is propelled by Voith-Schneider propellers situated one on each beam which can be made to transmit a sideways motion, so making the manœuvre of going alongside a jetty in the fast-flowing current a comparatively simple matter. Triple rudders are fitted, however, in the normal way, to steer her.

Two types of craft invented in recent years are often predicted by enthusiastic advocates as supplanters of these conventional packet-boat ferries. These are the hovercraft or, as they are known in America, ground-effect machines (GEM) and the hydrofoils. The former makes use of a powerful horizontal fan to build up sufficient air pressure inside a surrounding skirt to lift the hull a short distance off the water (or ground). The whole is then supported on a frictionless cushion of air, taking it clear of wave-tops or ground irregularities of moderate height over which it can be moved at high speeds by an air propeller.

The hydrofoil has a boat hull from beneath which on vertical columns is projected a horizontal plane designed in the same way as the plane of an aircraft to give lift

T.S. 'United States', 1951.
Science Museum, London, courtesy United States
Lines Company

when propelled through the water. As such a craft, driven either by a water-jet inducted through the vertical column and ejected astern or by a water propeller on a downward-inclined shaft, picks up speed, it is lifted by this hydrofoil clear of the water and of wave tops of a certain height. It can thus proceed at high speed in rough waters which would force a normal craft to a crawl.

Both these craft are well suited for ferry work across short sea passages and, within certain limiting weather conditions, can be greatly superior to the conventional ship. The hovercraft has the advantage that it can travel over land as well as water and at the ferry terminus can run straight up on to the beach. It cannot operate in such rough water as a water-jet propelled hydrofoil of similar size; but the hydrofoil needs a sheltered jetty with a fair depth of water alongside it from which to operate.

During the second half of the nineteenth century, while the 'ocean greyhounds' caught the eye, there were many scores of small iron single-screw steamers of some 2,500 tons carrying immigrants and cargo. Of the specialized cargo steamers the majority, by the turn of the

century, were of the 'three-island' type, with a raised poop, forecastle and midships bridge superstructure with the machinery amidships. These were by that time invariably powered by triple expansion engines and could make 10 knots in calm weather.

The three-island type of cargo steamer which, of course, varied greatly in size, was suitable for carriage of mixed cargoes as opposed to homogeneous bulk cargo such as grain, mineral ores, coal or oil. For these, specialized ships were constructed.

A type employed in the carriage of coal, ore and timber was the 'turret' ship, a development from the 'whale-back' type invented in America. In the latter the ship's side merged with the deck in a continuous curve from water-line to water-line, leaving virtually no flat deck, a design which enabled the largest amount of cargo to be carried for a particular registered tonnage. It had the disadvantage of making movement about the deck hazardous in bad weather except by means of the narrow gangway which ran fore and aft from the bridge superstructure right aft, while its spoon-shaped bow caused pounding in

183

R.M.S. 'Windsor Castle', 1959, one of the Union Castle company's liners used on the regular run from South-ampton to Cape Town.

Union Castle Mail Steamship Co. Ltd

First-class dining saloon on the 'Windsor Castle'.
Union Castle Mail Steamship Co. Ltd

a seaway. It was usually to be found on the Great Lakes or along the Pacific coast.

In the turret ship, the flat sides curved inwards at the top for about one-third of the beam to form a main or 'harbour' deck which curved upwards again to form a flat-topped turret running the whole length of the ship between the bridge superstructure aft to the poop. Apart from advantages of this design for stowage of bulk cargo—coal, ore, etc.—it attracted lower port dues which were often based on deck area in which the turret was not included, an advantage also enjoyed in the calculations under the Suez Canal measurement rules. When used to carry timber, this could be stowed on the harbour deck.

The 'trunk' ship was another type which enjoyed some of the advantages of the 'turret' ship. This has a continuous trunk of rectangular section about half as wide as the beam of the ship, rising from the main deck and

Model of Voith-Schneider vertical axis propeller.
Crown Copyright. Science Museum, London

185

Hovermarine Transport Ltd hovercraft HM-2.

Beken & Son

SRN-4 hovercraft operated by British Rail Hovercraft on their 'Seaspeed' service between Dover and Boulogne. The SRN-4, which went into service during 1968, can carry 250 passengers and thirty cars.

British Hovercraft Corporation Ltd

Hydrofoil Supramar PT-150.

Hovering Craft & Hydrofoil

extending from the poop to the bridge superstructure amidships and from the superstructure forward to the forecastle.

Other commodities besides the bulk cargoes for which these ships were most adapted, and which required specialized vessels, were fruit, dairy produce and meat. All these are now transported in ships with insulated holds and refrigerating machinery. The carriage of bananas from the West Indies to Europe and the U.S.A. began with fast brigs and schooners at a time when these could still outpace the early steamers. The American United Fruit Company grew out of the enterprise of Captain Lorenzo D. Baker, who started with one schooner in 1870. The risk of spoilt cargoes soon led to auxiliary steam machinery and then to specially designed steamers with refrigerated holds. Other well-known banana-carrying companies are Elders and Fyffes and Elder Dempster. Their ships are fairly fast and often have accommodation for a small number of passengers. A famous shipping company which also operates refrigerated fruit ships was one of the last to own and operate sailing ships, the Laeisz Company of Hamburg whose four- and five-masted sailing ships and barques only ceased to run in 1939.

A very large trade in refrigerated cargoes is carried on by the New Zealand Shipping Company. Typical of their ships built between the two world wars was the *Otaio*, a twin-screw motor ship of 10,048 tons, driven by two diesel engines developing a combined bhp of 9,450 at a speed of $15\frac{3}{4}$ knots.

The diesel engine which, since the end of the First World War, has been replacing the steam reciprocating engine in the majority of cargo liners, was the invention of Dr Rudolf Diesel. An internal combustion engine, it does not, as does the petrol engine, explode a mixture of fuel and air by means of a sparking plug, but makes use of the heat generated by the compression of air by the piston in the cylinder to ignite injected oil fuel. Besides saving the large amount of space required for boilers in a steamship, the diesel is comparatively very economical in fuel. Many different varieties have been developed which may utilize a 2-stroke or 4-stroke cycle and be single- or double-acting. Improved flexibility in manœuvring, especially in the early days of diesel machinery, was sometimes achieved by diesel-electric drive, the diesel engines driving electric generators from which current was taken to direct-drive electric motors. The first ocean-going merchant ship to be equipped with diesel engines was the

187

Midship section of turret-deck steamer, 1895.
Crown Copyright. Science Museum, London

small Dutch tanker *Vulcanus*, built in 1910. By 1939, 25 per cent of the world's merchant shipping was being propelled by diesel engines, 14 per cent by turbines and 61 per cent by reciprocating steam engines. By 1967 diesels had captured 59 per cent with 30 per cent turbine-driven and only 11 per cent still using the steam reciprocating engine.

Diesels, indeed, are being more and more favoured as the machinery for all ships other than the very high-speed types. Little coasters as well as the huge super-tankers being built today are almost exclusively diesel-driven. The former are no longer the rust-streaked, coal-dust-covered steamers which thronged the coastwise routes,

trailing a plume of thick black smoke in the years following the First World War. The diesel engine has abolished the dirt and grime and with its instant readiness for service at all times has greatly improved the efficiency and regularity of coastal passages. Coasters, in the development of which in European waters the Dutch have led during the last fifty years, vary between that typical little Dutch craft the *schuyt* of light draught and some 200 tons displacement which can reach the wharves of towns up the smallest rivers, to the 700- to 1,000-ton cargo carriers which connect the bigger ports. All have their diesel machinery, bridge structure and crew accommodation right aft. Bulk carriers are usually of the trunk ship design; dry cargo carriers have a single mast amidships with associated derricks plumbing the two long hatches of their holds.

The placing of the machinery right aft, which began with tankers, has spread to all types of ships, passenger liners as well as cargo ships. For a long time the obvious advantage of a short propeller shaft was offset by problems of trim; but the latter have now been largely resolved and the silhouette of a general cargo ship may be distinguishable from that of a bulk cargo carrier only by the numerous derricks and king-posts of the former.

Before we pass on from discussion of general cargo carriers mention must be made of the latest trend which is producing a revolution in the large commercial ports—the container ship. One kind of these received its inspiration from the landing ships of the Second World War in which vehicles and supplies were put ashore or embarked over ramps. This is the Roll-on, Roll-off (RO-RO) type in which cargoes in special containers are passed over

Russia and the transport of it by canal and river from Baku to St Petersburg, ordered a fleet of 1,500-ton-capacity tankers from British and Swedish shipyards for their Black Sea Steam Navigation Company to carry oil to Europe. In the same year the Swedish Lindholmen Yard and the Newcastle yard of Sir W. G. Armstrong, Mitchell & Co. built tankers with the same general features as those of modern types—the machinery aft, coffer dams separating the tanks from other spaces to obviate leakage from one to the other, and a separate pump room situated right forward. The Swedish-built ship was the *Sviet*, of 1,827 tons, for the Russian Steam Navigation Company of Odessa. The Armstrong ship was the 2,307-ton *Glückauf* for the German-American Petroleum Company.

In the United States the first tanker for Standard Oil was built in 1886. Within five years there were between eighty and ninety operating across the Atlantic. An early development was that of tankers towing huge barges, a

Sectioned model of an early oil tanker, c. 1895.
Crown Copyright. Science Museum, London

ramps through doors. In another type standard containers are hoisted on board by special loading systems and stacked in cellular holds and on deck. This system is likely to make existing cranes and dock layouts obsolete.

We have left to the last the consideration of the most numerous of all the types of cargo carriers, the tanker, which today, in its various forms, represents more than half the world's total tonnage. The first tankers to carry crude oil in bulk appeared at about the same period both in European waters to transport it from the Black Sea oilfields of Baku, and in America to carry it across the Atlantic. In 1885 the Swedish firm of Nobel Brothers, which controlled most of the petroleum production in

system primarily for use along the seaboards, but which was also used for transport of oil round the Horn to Japan and across the Atlantic. A famous pair built in 1907–8 at Belfast for the Anglo-American Oil Company were the *Iroquois* (tanker steamer) and *Navahoe*. The latter, which carried 9,250 tons of oil, had no propulsion machinery but was rigged as a six-masted schooner. This pair made no fewer than 148 Atlantic crossings.

Tankers naturally had design problems different from those of dry-cargo carriers. Besides the coffer dams mentioned earlier, there was need for expansion trunks, mechanical venting, steam heating to reduce viscosity in cold weather and for segregation of 'clean' and 'dirty'

cargo. The transverse frames which provide much of the strength of other types of ship were a nuisance in bulk carriers. This led to the invention of a system of longitudinal framing by Sir Joseph Isherwood in 1908 which revolutionized tanker construction. In 1925, also, there came the Isherwood Bracketless System.

During the Second World War the tankers built to replace the tremendous losses from enemy action tended to belong to a few standard types. From British yards emerged the 'Ocean' or 'Three Twelves' type, 12,000 tons deadweight, consuming 12 tons of oil a day at a speed of 12 knots; or the Standard Fast Tanker developed from the Norwegian type, 11,900 tons deadweight, turbine-driven with steam from water-tube boilers at 15 knots, all of which were eventually bought by the Admiralty and given 'Wave' names.

The Americans built some 525 of the 'T2' type besides many smaller. The majority had a speed of $14\frac{1}{2}$ to 15

Examples of today's super tankers, both built at Yokohama by Ishikawajima-Harima Heavy Industries. 'King Alexander the Great', about 227,000 long tons deadweight. 'Universe Ireland', about 326,000 long tons deadweight. The 'Universe Ireland' and her six sister ships were the largest tankers in service in the summer of 1970.
Ishikawajima-Harima Heavy Industries Ltd

Nuclear ship 'Savannah', 1959. Science Museum, London

knots, but some were more powerfully engined to make 16 knots. All, however, were 16,800 tons deadweight and had a standard hull 523 feet long, 68 feet beam.

The post-war period saw the rise of huge tanker-operating companies such as those of Onassis and Niarchos, making use of 'flags of convenience', registering their ships in Panama, Liberia, Costa Rica and Honduras to reduce cost of operation. Construction by welding in place of riveting has become universal. And, finally, the closure of the Suez Canal has high-lighted the economies to be achieved by operation of enormous super-tankers to transport crude oil to the refineries being set up near the main areas of consumption. When ships such as the Norwegian *C. J. Hambro* of 24,900 tons deadweight began to be built about 1949 they created a sensation and were called super-tankers. Soon, however, Japanese yards had been redesigned to build ships of 100,000 tons; today tankers of more than twice that size are going to sea and research is in hand by British ship-builders on designing tankers of between 400,000 and a million tons.

Furthermore, special types of tankers are in operation to carry such bulk cargoes as asphalt and bitumen, molasses, wine, alcohol, chemicals and liquefied petroleum gas. The last of these, in particular, has proved very successful, and construction costs have been greatly reduced by liquefying natural gas by refrigeration and so carrying it at atmospheric pressure.

Finally, before we close this account of the development of sea-going merchant-ships over the ages, mention must be made of the most recent type of power unit adapted to their propulsion—the nuclear reactor, providing heat to steam boilers to serve turbines. Developed first and most effectively for propulsion of submarines, in which it offers such enormous advantages that its high cost is acceptable, it has so far been installed in only one merchant ship, the American *Savannah*. This ship of about 14,000 tons was built in 1959 on a primarily experimental basis. She was not expected to be commercially competitive. On the other hand she was no doubt intended to be the forerunner, if possible, of other ships which could be economically built and operated. That no other such ships have yet been laid down, and that research in other countries into the possibility has so far led to nothing, perhaps indicates that the use of nuclear power for merchant ships is not, for the present, a viable concept; *Savannah* has meanwhile been laid up.

Enough has been said in this inevitably brief survey of sea-going merchant ships of the mechanical age to show how immensely varied are the types which have been developed in the 160 years since the early experiments of Papin and Jouffroy d'Abbans, of Miller and Symington, Fitch, Rumsey and Fulton: so wide a variety that only a small proportion can receive mention in the limited space available in this volume. Ships remain today and must surely continue into the foreseeable future by far the most important means of transport of the world's trade, even though they may have been superseded to some extent by aircraft for that of passengers.

VII. *1968 Cadillac* coupé de ville. General Motors Corporation

VIII. *1915 Harley-Davidson motorcycle.* National Motor Museum at Beaulieu

MODEL-K. PRICE. $2,500 COMPLETE

Stoddard=Dayton

THE DAYTON MOTOR CAR CO., DAYTON, OHIO

V. 1907 Stoddard-Dayton Model K roadster. G. Marshall
Naul Collection   *VI. 1919 Australian Six tourer.* Gilltrap's Auto Museum

III. Burrell Showman's Traction Engine, built in 1922.
National Motor Museum at Beaulieu

IV. 1903 Panhard-Levassor 7-hp rear entrance tonneau.
Veteran Car Club of Great Britain

I. Pedlar and pack pony. J. Parker, c. 1830   *II. Gloucestershire ox wagon, 1813. Drawing by R. Hills*

IX. Liverpool and Manchester Railway 0-4-2 Lion, *built in 1838, now restored to working order and the property of the Liverpool Engineering Society.* K. Cooper

X. The Great Western Railway's 4-cylinder 'Castle' class 4-6-0s were built from 1923 to 1950, but this design dates back to 1907. No. 4079 Pendennis Castle *is one of several that have been preserved.* K. Cooper

XI. *Before the days of bulldozers, earthmoving jobs of all kinds needed fleets of small two-foot gauge locomotives to haul trainloads of soil.* Britomart, *dating from the 1890s, spent its working life in a North Wales slate quarry.* K. Cooper

XII. *Rarest now of the descendants of the Semmering contestants is the Fairlie locomotive; the last two working anywhere are on the 2-foot gauge Festiniog Railway.* Earl of Merioneth, *built in 1885, shunting at Portmadoc Harbour.* J. B. Snell

XIII. One of the oddities of the American railway scene nowadays is the Chicago & North Western's commuter service, whose trains are colourful, clean and profitable. Several other companies also use similar double-decked coaches. J. B. Snell

XIV. The train at Knott's Berry Farm, a popular attraction in Los Angeles, is a genuine relic of the 1880s, even if the paint job is twentieth-century. J. B. Snell

XV. One of the last large-scale users of main-line steam power are the South African Railways. A 25NC-class 4-8-4, polished and decorated, on a Johannesburg to Cape Town run near Modder River. J. B. Snell

XVI. The last main-line steam locomotives to be built in Europe, which had only a ten-year lifespan, were these 2-8-2+2-8-2 Garratts built for the Spanish National Railways in 1960: one of them climbing near Valencia with a freight for Madrid. J. B. Snell

XVII. One of the most spectacular main lines of Europe, electrically-worked since it opened in 1908, is that of the Berne-Lötschberg-Simplon company. A train descending into the Rhone valley near Brigue, crossing the valley at Hohtenn. J. B. Snell

XVIII. Though dwindling fast now, Yugoslavia still has a considerable length of 2 ft. 6 in. track largely worked by steam power. On the Lasva-Jajce line, two 97-class 0-6-0 rack and adhesion engines meet at Turbe. J. B. Snell

XIX. China Clipper Sir Lancelot, *of 1865. Colour lithograph by T. G. Dutton.* National Maritime Museum

XX. Queen Elizabeth 2 *at anchor in the West Indies.*   *XXI. Container ship* Atlantic Causeway, *14,946 tons.*
Cunard Lines Ltd   Atlantic Container Line

XXII. *Russian-built hydrofoil on the Danube, 1969.*
Charles Hadfield

XXIII. *SRN-1 hovercraft on test near Beaulieu river.*
National Motor Museum at Beaulieu

XXIV. Scene on the canalized Moselle, 1968. Charles
Hadfield

XXV. The Ford Tri-motor transport monoplane. First built in 1926, it still serves with at least one airline. John W. R. Taylor Collection

XXVI. A Boeing 707 jet-engined transport aircraft of B.O.A.C. B.O.A.C.

up in medieval times by the Dutch, Germans and Italians. The Dutch were concerned with water control, and built river extensions, many of which also had a drainage purpose. In Germany the Stecknitz Canal was finished in 1398, the first in Europe to be built up and over a summit level. In Italy a number of canals were cut in the fifteenth century in the area of Milan, Parma and the River Po.

From the beginning, river and canal engineers had been faced with the problem of changing water levels. If the current of a river is to be slowed down, and its navigable depth increased, then steps must be inserted in it, up and down, on which boats can be lifted. Most canals too, and all those over a watershed, have to change level.

A weir across the waterway, with a staunch or flash-lock inserted in it to allow craft to pass, was the earliest solution. A vertically rising gate within a frame built over the weir opening was the commonest form of staunch—there were others. When a boat wanted to pass, the staunch was partially opened to allow water to run under the gate, and maybe sluices as well. This raised the level of the river section below the staunch down to the next weir, and lowered that above, until the two nearly equalized. Then the staunch was fully raised, and the boat either shot through the opening on the current, or was winched up against it. The staunch gate was then shut, and the river levels restored themselves. Such staunches were used in China at least in the first century B.C., the Romans were familiar with them, and they were common in Europe by the late thirteenth century.

Working staunches was a slow business, depending upon the distance apart of the weirs. The Chinese sometimes used slipways, paved ramps up which barges were hauled by rope and capstan. It was a canal engineer, Chhaio Wei-Yo, who found the best answer in the pound-lock, still fundamental to waterway engineering. Instead of a single gate inserted in the weir, he built a chamber big enough to take craft using the canal, with gates at each end. By opening the gate at one end to allow a boat to enter the chamber, and then filling or emptying it before opening the other, a barge could be raised or lowered without disturbing the main water levels above or below the weir and chamber. Chhaio Wei-Yo's lock was built in 983, and thereafter in China further pound-locks began partially to replace the awkward slipways. The Romans do not seem to have known the invention, which appears again in 1373 at Vreeswijk in the Netherlands where a canal from Utrecht enters the River Lek (one of the Rhine channels), at Damme near Bruges in 1396, and on the Stecknitz Canal about the same time.

Vertically rising gates have advantages on river navigations liable to flooding and variations in water level, but

Briare Canal; seven locks at Rogny (Yonne), built in 1605.
Service Central des Ports Maritimes et des Voies Navigables

Canal du Midi; tunnel at Malpas.
Service Central des Ports Maritimes et des Voies Navigables

198

1
Canals

The use of natural rivers for carrying goods and people is older than history, the building of artificial waterways nearly as old.

Men early turned their engineering arts towards making rivers easier to navigate, by digging short canals to cut off bends, by-pass dangerous stretches or extend the navigation above its natural limits. It was then not a great step further to join two rivers together by a cut over the intervening watershed. Such canals were river-based; but there was another kind, that built to connect two seas, or to extend the sea inland.

Canals of both kinds in developed form were built in

classical times: the pharaoh Necho built a canal from the Nile to the Red Sea by way of the Bitter Lakes in the seventh century B.C., which was later adapted in turn by the Ptolemies, the emperor Trajan, and seventh-century Arabs; the 'Magic' Canal of China was built in 219 B.C. over the watershed between two rivers in Kwangsi, and was followed by others before the first lengths of the Grand Canal were opened in A.D. 610; the Romans built canals linking the Meuse to the Rhine and the Rhine to the Zuyder Zee, and in Britain the Caerdyke and the still navigable Fossdyke from Lincoln to the Trent.

In Europe the work the Romans laid down was taken

Model of a lock on the Stecknitz Canal, in use from 1398 to 1896. Deutsches Museum, Munich

*XXVIII. Astronaut Alan Bean assembling the Bendix
Apollo 12 lunar surface experimental package on the
Moon.* NASA

*XXVII. A Sikorsky S-64 Skycrane loading timber in the
Bavarian Alps.* John W. R. Taylor Collection

Canal and locks of the mid eighteenth century.

Deutsches Museum, Munich

they are less suitable for canals and the lower gates of river locks. Mitre-gates, each of which lies flat against the lock wall, and opens out when required to meet at a point facing uphill, were invented by Leonardo da Vinci in about 1495, when he was building a canal for the Duke of Milan.

Now that lock construction had been made easy, river navigations were improved and canals built. The slipway method of transferring craft from one level to another was not, however, lost. Used in classical times to enable boats to cross the isthmus of Corinth, it is also found in the Netherlands from the twelfth century, and later in Italy. It was to develop into the modern inclined plane, whereby boats are carried in wheeled tanks along railways laid down a slope connecting two water levels.

The sixteenth and seventeenth centuries saw rivers improved, and small canals built, in many European countries, including the Netherlands, Germany, Italy and Sweden. The most important work, however, was done in France, first on the Briare Canal between the Loire and the Loing, with its thirty-five locks, opened in 1642, and then by the astonishing Languedoc or Midi Canal between the River Garonne at Toulouse and the Mediterranean.

Financed by the French Government, built by Pierre-Paul Riquet, opened in 1681, this canal, 150 miles long, with its locks, great aqueducts, tunnel at Malpas, probably the first on any canal, and elaborate system of intakes and feeder-channels to supply the summit level with water, was the finest piece of waterway engineering Europe had produced, and evidence of what could be done by state money and indigenous engineering skill to develop national economies. Today many of Riquet's structures still remain to delight the eye of the visitor who cruises the Canal du Midi.

From the beginning of the eighteenth century waterway construction spread more and more widely. Rivers were improved, to make it easier to sail craft when this was possible, and towpaths built so that they could be hauled from the banks by groups of men or horses when it was not. On the River Inn, for instance, a towpath was built to its junction with the Danube at Passau, whence the

Locks on the Ludwigs Canal, near Forchheim, 1845.
Deutsches Museum, Munich

Ludwigs Canal; harbour at Nuremberg, looking westward, 1845. Deutsches Museum, Munich

Ludwigs Canal; bridge over the River Pegnitz, near Doos, 1845. Note the railway train on a separate bridge in the background. Deutsches Museum, Munich

salt convoys could be partly towed, partly sailed down into Austria and beyond.

Canals were cut, as branches from rivers or to connect them, from Russia to the Atlantic. In Russia the Neva and the Volga were joined to give a through route from the Baltic to the Caspian; in Sweden the Göta Canal, with Thomas Telford as consulting engineer, was completed in 1832 between the Baltic and Gothenburg on the Kattegat, and enabled craft to by-pass the Danish-controlled Sound; in Germany the 112-miles-long Ludwigs Canal from the River Main, itself a branch of the Rhine, to a tributary of the Danube, opened in 1845. The Dutch in 1825 by-passed the Zuyder Zee by the Great North Holland Ship Canal, 50½ miles long from Amsterdam to the North Sea at what is now Den Helder. The Belgians built a network of canals connecting the coalfields round Charleroi to Brussels and to France, and linking Brussels to Ghent, Bruges and the sea at Ostend, that culminated in the ship canal from Ghent to the sea at Terneuzen, opened in 1827. The French constructed a system that gave access to Paris from the Channel and the Scheldt, and notably the Canal du Centre from the Loire to the Saône that in 1793 provided a through waterway from the Channel to the Mediterranean, and the Rhine–Rhône Canal in 1834.

Many thousands of miles of canal had been built, and rivers improved, throughout Europe by the mid nineteenth century, notably by governments, municipalities or other public bodies, the motive being economic development. As the continent moved into the nineteenth century, and the impetus of the Industrial Revolution spread from Britain, so did the scale of work, and the size of craft, grow. This tendency increased when, during the first third of the century, steam-towing began on such rivers as the Danube, the Rhine and the Seine, and experiments were first made with the system later to be widely used on rivers and occasionally on canals, chain-towing, when a steam tug hauled itself and the barges it was pulling along a chain laid on the river bed.

This period also saw passenger services being worked on many European waterways, notably in Belgium and Holland. Accounts of journeys in *trekschuits* (literally: towboats) often occur in contemporary British travel books.

Because the Industrial Revolution began in Britain, development there was different. Canals did not precede or even accompany industrial development, as they so often had on the Continent; they followed it. Pressure to build came from industrialists, mine owners, merchants anxious for better transport and wider markets for products already available. Therefore money could be

Old Runcorn locks that led from the Bridgewater Canal to the Mersey (and later to the Manchester Ship Canal) in 1962, not long before they were filled in.

Hugh McKnight Photography

201

Marple aqueduct, built by Benjamin Outram just before 1800, carries the Peak Forest Canal over the River Goyt not far from Stockport, Cheshire.

Hugh McKnight Photography

found from those who stood to gain by improved means of carriage, and there was no need for the government to step in, except to build such canals as the Caledonian and Royal Military, which had a primarily defence purpose.

When the main impact of the Industrial Revolution began in about 1760 Britain had some 1,400 miles of navigable waterways, mainly rivers, though with a very few canals like the Exeter, originally built in Elizabeth I's reign, and later enlarged. When the canal age ended and railways were supreme, say in 1850, she had some 4,025 miles. The difference, of 2,625 miles, had been built in ninety years, a more intensive and faster growth than in any other European country at that time.

The growth began round Manchester. The first of the Industrial Revolution canals was the Sankey Brook, authorized by an Act of 1755 from St Helens, mainly to carry coal to the Mersey and then up the already navi-gable River Weaver to be used in the making of salt, or else to Liverpool. By 1762, when it was completed, the first part of the better-known Bridgewater Canal had been built from the Worsley collieries to the outskirts of Manchester, and an Act had just been passed to allow its extension to the Mersey estuary at Runcorn.

This in turn was joined at Preston Brook by the Trent & Mersey Canal to near Nottingham on the Trent, completed in 1777 and nearly a hundred miles long, the impetus to build which had mainly come from Josiah Wedgwood and his fellow manufacturers of the Potteries. From it in turn the Staffordshire & Worcestershire Canal, opened in 1772, ran to the Severn with a side-link to Birmingham, and another had by 1790 been opened to London. To the south, canals, notably the Kennet & Avon, linked Thames to Severn; in the north three straddled the Pennines from Liverpool and Manchester,

A horse-drawn passenger boat on the Welsh Canal beside the Dee near Llangollen early in the present century.
British Railways Board, Western Region

all joining the Aire & Calder river system of Yorkshire, dating from 1699, which led on to Hull. In Scotland the Forth & Clyde Canal, opened in 1790, ran across her industrial waist from sea to sea, and farther north the much bigger Caledonian; in south Wales waterways down the valleys carried coal and iron to Swansea, Neath, Cardiff and Newport.

British canals were on the whole built small, to take either narrow boats carrying some 25 tons, or barges of perhaps 60 tons capacity. This was partly to save cost, partly to save water that was also urgently wanted to provide factory power, partly because actual present needs were more urgent than hypothetical future increases in traffic. Their varying sizes, and a capacity that had been outgrown by the time steam railways had become practicable, were later to prove a handicap.

The men who built them had problems to solve that

had not been found so constantly anywhere else except in France, notably those of keeping as level a line as possible by passing through hills and over valleys, and of rapid changes of level. Britain probably had a greater mileage of canal tunnel—some 42 miles—than the rest of the world put together; her largest, Standedge through the Pennines on the Huddersfield Canal, being over 3 miles long. She also built the world's highest canal aqueduct, Pontcysyllte near Llangollen, opened in 1805 and still serving those who take a pleasure cruiser on the Welsh Canal.

Great flights of locks were built to overcome changes of level: thirty at Tardebigge near Birmingham, twenty-nine at Devizes on the Kennet & Avon, twenty-one at Wigan and at Wolverhampton, among others. Inclined planes also were built to carry small boats quickly from one level to another in hilly country such as Shropshire,

203

Part of the flight of thirty locks at Devizes on the Kennet & Avon Canal, in the early 1900s. These locks were opened in 1810.

British Railways Board, Western Region

Trench inclined plane on the old Shrewsbury Canal in 1921. This plane raised small boats 75 ft from one level of canal to another.

Waterways Museum, Stoke Bruerne

Somerset, Devon, Cornwall and south Wales, the biggest, on the Bude Canal in Cornwall, having a vertical rise of 225 ft. And lifts, which enabled similar boats to be lifted vertically from one level to another, were successfully used in Somerset, and experimented with elsewhere.

The engineers who built Britain's canal system were a small group of highly paid, incredibly hard-working, very skilled men, the older generation, men like James Brindley and John Smeaton self-taught, their successors, notably William Jessop, Robert Whitworth, Thomas Telford and John Rennie, able to profit by the experience of their predecessors.

The engineers planned and directed: the work was done by many hundreds of subordinate engineers, contractors and foremen, and many thousands of navvies (the word derives from 'navigator', a man who builds navigations). These last were at first locally recruited to do one job only, but were transformed into a body of itinerant professionals who later formed the nucleus of the much bigger army who built the railways. Behind these again

stood the canal officials, lock-keepers, toll-takers, boat-builders, accountants, clerks and the rest, and the men who manned the boats that moved ceaselessly about Britain's network of waterways.

The canal business has always been—and still is—one which breeds and demands independent men, and sometimes women, sons often succeeding fathers for many generations. In this period, before the days of the telephone or the penny post, lock-keepers, maintenance men, toll-clerks, wharfingers, were very much on their own. A lock-keeper worked all the hours the canal was open; if he wanted time off, his wife or son took over, and if two boatmen quarrelled for precedence at the lock, he had to stop the fight and settle the argument. If the bank threatened to burst, out came the maintenance men, at night, in rain or snow or hail, and got to work, while a boy flew for the engineer. And when he arrived on horseback, he would expect repairs to have been started and the canal to be on the way to re-opening.

Such men were well paid by contemporary standards.

Boatwomen on a narrow boat owned by Fellows, Morton & Clayton about 1909. A group of boats are held up due to repairs to a lock near Stoke Bruerne on the old Grand Junction Canal.

Waterways Museum, Stoke Bruerne

*A steam grab dredger and hopper boat, working on the old
Grand Junction Canal in 1898.*

Waterways Museum, Stoke Bruerne

A lock-keeper, for instance, also had his house and garden, and probably a coal allowance—a useful insurance against the temptation to take it off passing boats. When he was old, he could look forward to a company pension, often with part-time employment also, like Thomas Lancaster of the Aire & Calder, who after his retirement was employed as a carpenter and when he was too old for that, was in 1790 given an annual pension of £10 ($40) and was also to be 'paid a reasonable Allowance for such Work . . . as he shall be capable of doing'.

Before railway competition boatmen also were prosperous. Canal boats then carried all-men crews varying from one or two and a boy on a narrow boat up to five or more on a big sailing barge. Men were accustomed to sleep on board or in regularly used canal-side lodgings, but they also had their homes beside the water, where wives and children would watch the canal for father's boat to appear. Sometimes a man would own one or several boats and employ his own crews; often, too, fleets would be run by trading companies, such as the

Grocers' Company of Manchester which ran its boats to and from Liverpool on the Bridgewater Canal; or by colliery or iron companies; or by the canal company itself. Paid usually by the voyage, boat captains, or steerers as they were often called, were something of an élite, as engine-drivers were later to be.

The canal age in Britain was shorter than it had been on the Continent; in North America it was shorter still, hardly starting before 1800. We may date it from the Louisiana Purchase of 1803 and the end of the war of 1812. The Louisiana Purchase made the Mississippi American. Traffic along it, and along its great tributary the Ohio, increased rapidly as settlement increased, and steamboats began to be used.

The end of the 1812 war made Canada and the United States nervous of developing the St Lawrence route to Lake Ontario, on which some small boat locks had already been built. It was too near their common frontier. The Canadians developed a military and trading water route to the lake by way of the Ottawa River (three falls in which were by-passed by short canals

206

completed in 1834) and the Rideau Canal, opened in 1832, from Ottawa itself for 124 miles to Kingston. Farther inland, private companies built the Welland Canal, finished in 1829, to link Lakes Ontario and Erie, which was later bought by the Upper Canada Government, and that at Sault Ste Marie between Lakes Huron and Superior, opened in 1855. To the south, the Americans developed their own route from the Hudson River at Albany, whence there was access to New York, to Buffalo on Lake Erie, with a branch to Oswego on Lake Ontario. This was the famous Erie Canal, 363 miles long with a 38-mile branch, built by New York State and opened in 1825.

The needs now were for direct lines between the eastern seaboard and the Ohio River, and between the river and Lake Erie. Three of the former were begun, but only one succeeded in surmounting the Allegheny mountain barrier, the Pennsylvania Canal & Railroad, from Philadelphia to Pittsburgh. This extraordinary route, opened in 1834, began as a railway from Philadelphia to Columbia. A 170-mile canal stretch followed, then a railway to take passengers and freight up five inclined planes to the mountain summit level at 2,334 ft, then down another five to Johnstown, whence a second canal, 105 miles long, carried them to Pittsburgh. The other two canal routes

Two typical American passenger-carrying packet boats meet at a bridge.
Pennsylvania Historical & Museum Commission, Harrisburg, Penn., U.S.A.

had only reached, and not surmounted, the mountains when they were overtaken by the rapidly developing railways.

To link the Ohio river with Lake Erie, and so to the Erie Canal and the Welland and St Lawrence route, a number of canals were opened during the twenty years from 1833 from near Pittsburgh to Erie, from Portsmouth to Cleveland, from Cincinnati to Toledo, and, longest canal ever built, the Wabash & Erie, over 450 miles long from Evansville to Toledo.

Water transport in North America had only a brief predominance: but without the barges, scows, flatboats, steamboats and passenger-carrying craft of the lakes, rivers and canals of the time, development would have been slower and the great expansion to the West would have had less force.

As we move from the mid nineteenth century to modern times we meet a new kind of waterway, product of steam and expanding ocean trade, the ship canal. The oldest, at Suez, developed from the idealism of Ferdinand de Lesseps, the Frenchman who promoted and built it, and Anglo-French rivalry for Middle Eastern influence and the route to India. Opened in 1869, its success encouraged de Lesseps to cut a similar sea-level canal at Panama. But there he failed, defeated alike by the geology

of the central mountain spine through which he had to cut, and the malaria that carried off his workmen. In 1889, broken by the task, the French company gave up, and in 1914 the Americans, who had taken over the enterprise and defeated the mosquito, completed their lock canal.

The world's most spectacular isthmuses had been conquered, as had two others—that at Corinth in 1893 by a canal hewn deeply through the rock, and that from the North Sea to the Baltic at Kiel in 1895. Other ship canals have followed, among them the North Sea Canal from Ijmuiden to Amsterdam completed in 1865, in 1894 a 30-mile cut from the Mersey above Liverpool to Manchester, and others in the United States.

From 1850 onwards railways greatly affected waterway trade and prospects, as later did the motor lorry and the pipeline. The First World War broke up many established transport patterns, as wars do, and after it the canals found themselves with less traffic and higher costs. By the

The last stroke of the pick-axe (by His Excellency Ali Pasha) joins the two ends of the Suez Canal, 1869.
Deutsches Museum, Munich

Steamer in lock on the Trollhätte Canal. Charles Hadfield

inter-war period horse-drawn barges had become fewer; many had been replaced by steam-driven craft, which in turn had begun to give place to diesels. On the narrow canals the pair, a motor boat towing an engineless butty, was replacing the single horse-boat. The pair could be worked by a boat family, whose predecessors had been forced to live on the water by the cut in incomes brought about by railway competition. Before that, men had been able to maintain homes ashore. On the broad canals of the north, however, many boats continued to be crewed by men only, as they are today. There too, and on the larger navigations elsewhere such as the Severn, the big self-propelled craft, often an oil tanker, now appears.

The Second World War once more dislocated familiar patterns. Then in 1948 most, though not all, canals were nationalized, first as part of the British Transport Commission, but from 1962 onwards under the separate British Waterways Board.

Early in the post-war period it was becoming clear that there was no transport future for Britain's smaller canals: they were too small, too slow and often in the wrong places. Instead they offered over 2,000 miles of varied waterways for pleasure cruising. The prescient began to buy boats and put them on the canals; the solitary pre-war firm hiring cruisers was joined by many more; boatyards began to open, canalside pubs to be refurnished, and local authorities to be interested in canalside amenities. The Board's plans for a network of cruiseways was supported by public opinion, influenced by the Inland Waterways Association and the enthusiast bodies, and accepted by the Government.

Bigger waterways have been modernized, and some, notably the Aire & Calder and the Gloucester & Sharpness Canal, are now taking larger craft than ever before. On the former, too, big 180-ton coal carrying compartment boats have been introduced, these also being tipped in the biggest apparatus of its kind in the world. But their future is uncertain, for, unlike railways or roads, Britain has not yet developed a waterways transport policy.

The last hundred years in North America have seen the decay of one navigation system and the growth of another. Almost all the old canals have gone: the Rideau, the Erie, the Pennsylvania and its companions and those from the Ohio to Lake Erie. Only one major line remains, the New York State Barge Canal, replacing the old Erie, opened in 1918 and taking 2,500-ton barges.

Instead the Mississippi from Minneapolis downwards sees a heavy traffic pass its great locks, mostly push-tows made up of barges lashed together and pushed by a powerful diesel-tug, the whole making one rigid body. Its tributaries, such as the Ohio, the Missouri and the

*The building of the 30-mile-long Manchester Ship Canal
between 1887 and 1893.*
Manchester Ship Canal Company

A steam-driven barge or flat near Vale Royal on the River Weaver in Cheshire early in the present century.

Hugh McKnight Photography

An early use of containers: boxes of coal are transferred from horse tramroad to boat at Little Eaton on the Derby Canal.

Waterways Museum, Stoke Bruerne

A train of nineteen compartment boats carrying some 700 tons of coal, behind a tug on the Aire & Calder Navigation. Note the false bow on the leading boat. At Goole each boat is lifted by a hoist and its contents tipped into a sea-going ship. British Waterways Board

Arkansas, have been dredged to a uniform 9-ft depth, and in turn give access to other lines. Below New Orleans the Mississippi waterway joins the Gulf Intracoastal, a sheltered part-canal, part-lagoon, part-sea route that runs from Brownsville, Texas, to Florida, whence the 107-mile-long cross-Florida canal is now being cut to link it to the Atlantic Intracoastal, another protected waterway along the eastern seaboard to Norfolk, Virginia. A separate 500-mile waterway system running inland from the Pacific to Newiston, Idaho, is also now being built.

In Canada the Rideau and the later Trent Canal from Lake Ontario to Georgian Bay, Lake Huron, are now major pleasure cruising routes. But along the line of the St Lawrence the huge seaway, built by Canada and the United States in partnership, was opened in 1959 to replace the older late nineteenth-century waterway, and today the Welland, already twice rebuilt, is again being enlarged to take the ocean-going vessels and Lake freighters that work through to Detroit, Chicago and Duluth.

On the Oxford Canal, between Upper and Lower Heyford.
British Waterways Board

On the continent of Europe waterways developed quite otherwise than in Britain. Because nearly all had been built with public money, the state encouraged their modernization for bulk goods carrying, so that railways, often state owned also, would supplement and not supplant them. The result was a more balanced growth of the means of transport, and a less intensive railway network.

In France, where there were some 7,500 miles of canals and navigable rivers, the late nineteenth century saw a great drive to standardize the dimensions of most older waterways, and also to build new ones such as the canal from the Marne to the Rhine, to take 270–300-ton family barges (*péniches*), a drive associated with the name of Charles de Freycinet, Minister of Public Works from

1877. Bigger waterways took the 600-ton *chaland*. France, unlike other continental countries, introduced a system of electric towpath haulage, using locomotives or tractors, that lasted to 1969. Cable towing was used also on rivers like the Seine, Saône and Rhône, and through long tunnels such as that at Riqueval, $4\frac{1}{2}$ miles long, on the St Quentin Canal over the watershed of the Scheldt and the Oise.

In Belgium canal links with France were developed, as were the ship canals from the Dutch coast at Terneuzen to Ghent, and from Ostend to Bruges. On the Antwerp–Brussels waterway, made up of the River Rupel to Willebroek and a large canal thence to the capital, chain-towing was used on the canal section, one tug being able to haul up to thirty barges. In the Netherlands the exist-

212

The Ronquières inclined plane on the Brussels–Charleroi
Canal in Belgium, opened in 1968, lifts 1,350-ton barges
220 ft in 20 minutes. J. H. Boyes.

*Anderton lift, which can raise two narrow boats at once,
50 ft from the River Weaver in Cheshire to the Trent &
Mersey Canal. Opened in 1875, its present mode of
operation dates from 1908. L. A. Edwards*

ing network of canals was enlarged and extended, and in
Germany after the foundation of the empire in 1871, a
programme was undertaken that over the next forty
years produced some 400 miles of new navigable rivers
and, among others, the 167-mile-long Dortmund–Ems
Canal.

By the end of the nineteenth century chain-towing was
giving way to self-propelled steam craft or trains of
barges behind a tug. The tendency was still to increase
waterway dimensions, improve inland harbours and
enable craft to travel faster. By about 1930 the tonnage
carried on French canals reached its peak, and then began
slowly to decline as the Freycinet dimensions proved
relatively uneconomic. Elsewhere, as in Holland, traffic
on the smaller waterways started to fall off, while that on
the larger ones continued to increase. Our own century,
therefore, has seen continuous enlargements and much
new construction.

In Western Europe today the future seems to lie with
barges of 1,000 tons and upwards. Most new waterways

are indeed being built to the 1,350-ton barge standard. These are usually self-propelled diesel craft, but one now often sees them travelling in pairs, one pushing the other. Tugs hauling barge-trains become less common: the move is to self-propelled craft on the one hand, and push-towing on the other where waterway dimensions allow it. These big barges tend to be run by barge lines owned by carrying or product firms, the latter especially in the oil business. But smaller and older barges, many owner-run, still work beside their bigger and more modern brethren, their numbers slowly decreasing.

Operation becomes increasingly sophisticated. Economy requires barges to keep moving day and night: so we get locks arranged in pairs or triplicate, and engineered for quick operation; tracks illuminated for night running, and many craft fitted with radar, sonic equipment and short-wave radio. As they move, water-boats and oil-tankers come alongside to fill tanks without the need to stop, and floating shops enable the barge-housewife to replenish her larder. In port, equipment is being steadily improved to give better turnround times.

Waterway engineering, too, has greatly changed. Locks, thanks to steel and concrete, can now be built with rises once thought impossible. In Britain we have no canal lock with a rise even of 20 ft, but that on the Rhône at Donzère-Mondragon, for instance, can lift craft 79 ft, and greater rises still are found in the United States. These are supplemented, when necessary, by inclined planes and vertical lifts. Canal planes seemed to have died out, until the Belgians in 1968 opened their giant mile-long structure at Ronquières, each tank of which can raise or lower a 1,350-ton barge 220 ft in 20 minutes, to be followed in 1969 by the French, with their 350-ton plane at Arzviller-Saint Louis on the Marne–Rhine Canal; each replaced a flight of locks. Modern vertical lifts stem from the British example at Anderton on the Weaver, opened in 1875. Larger structures of similar design were then built in France and Belgium. Today Germany is the only European country building new lifts. Before the war she had three, the Henrichenburg lift at Dortmund, that at Rothensee near Magdeburg on the Mittelland Canal and a third at Niederfinow on its extension to the Oder. Since the war a new Henrichenburg lift was opened in 1962 to take 1,350-ton barges, and another at Lüneburg is being built for the new North–South Canal from Hamburg to the Mittelland Canal.

The picture today in continental Europe is one of waterway development. The navigation of the Rhine between Strasbourg and Basel is being improved by building eight pairs of locks, seven of which are now in use. Farther south, that difficult river the Rhône is being tamed by other locks, six of which are open and a seventh under construction, and the French plan a 1,350-ton link between the two rivers that will give a large barge route from the Mediterranean.

From the lower Rhine the Moselle, with thirteen locks to take 1,500-ton barges, was opened in 1964, the result of joint enterprise by Germany, France and Luxembourg. Higher up at Mainz, the navigable River Main runs to Bamberg. Here the first section of the new Rhine–Danube Canal, taking 1,350-ton barges and replacing the old and disused Ludwigs Canal, was opened in 1972 to Nuremberg on its way to the Danube above Regensburg.

In north Germany the most interesting new work is the North–South Canal, begun in 1968, to run upwards from Hamburg beside the Elbe and provide a connection with the Mittelland Canal, and so with the rest of the west European waterway system, that does not pass through East Germany, as does the navigable Elbe itself. In Belgium Ghent saw the opening of the Circular Canal in 1969, which enables traffic between the Ghent–Terneuzen ship canal and the Scheldt to by-pass the city's waterways, an interesting example of modern waterway development. Not far away, the Belgians and Dutch are collaborating in a new waterway being built between Antwerp and the Rhine.

The French commercial system has now shrunk to about 4,500 miles. But much effort and money is being put into modernizing certain of the Freycinet-standard canals, and notably that from the Marne to the Rhine, which has seen the opening in 1969 of the Arzviller–Saint Louis inclined plane to by-pass seventeen locks, and the new Réchicourt deep lock, with a fall of $52\frac{1}{2}$ ft, far the biggest on the Freycinet network, which avoids six old locks. France too, like Holland, is seeing the growth of pleasure cruising on its canals.

From a deck-chair on one of the comfortable Rhine passenger steamers that run between Rotterdam and Basel, watch the traffic. Tugs with strings of barges, self-propelled craft flying their line-flags, push-tugs behind their tows, tankers, fuelling craft, floating shops, police launches, passenger boats, never less than a couple of dozen in sight at any time, all show the part played by inland waterways in continental transport. Or, in the United States, do the same from another chair, on a Mississippi steamer. In Britain the picture is more likely to be one of pleasure craft: consider, for instance, Hurleston locks near Nantwich, at the entrance to the Llangollen Canal, on a summer week-end.

Canals and navigable rivers are very old as a means of transport for men and goods—older indeed than history. Yet they flourish today, meeting modern needs.

PART SIX
Aviation
by David Mondey

Except where otherwise stated, pictures are from the John W. R. Taylor Collection.

1

From Prophecy to Practicality

The time will come, when thou shalt lift thine eyes
To watch a long-drawn battle in the skies,
While aged peasants, too amazed for words,
Stare at the flying fleets of wond'rous birds.

Thomas Gray. *Luna Habitabilis*. 1737

Thomas Gray, like many before him, spilt ink to record the vision of man in flight that must, one day, become reality.

For centuries man had dreamed of flight. Perhaps 'centuries' is an inadequate word to express how long the dream had been maturing. It may well be that in prehistoric times our first ancestors had looked to the sky as they—to corrupt Gray's words a little—'had homeward plodded their weary way'. Envious of the birds that moved so effortlessly above their heads, they must have thought how quickly they could regain the safety of their caves if they too could fly. So began what must have seemed an endless period of frustration for man who, with his superior strength, could crush the frail structure of a bird within the palm of his hand: who, by the cunning of his brain, could capture the will-o'-the-wisp bird to fill his cooking pot. But he could not wrest from them the secret of flight.

Inevitably, he tried to copy them: and failed. During the fifteenth century Leonardo da Vinci made the first serious studies of bird flight. He concluded, wrongly, that man's muscular power, so much superior to that of a bird, should be adequate to enable him to fly. Two centuries later Borelli, another great figure in the early studies of bird flight and related aeronautical problems, came to an opposing and more accurate conclusion; so much so that it virtually ended all heavier-than-air experiments until the nineteenth century. 'It is impossible,' he wrote, 'that men should be able to fly craftily by their own strength.' Experimentation did not end because of this basic statement alone; it was his

The opening gambit. A model of the hot-air balloon built by the Montgolfier brothers. The original was 74 ft high and 48 ft in diameter. Qantas Empire Airways

detailed analysis of bird flight that convinced the hopefuls that they must now class themselves the hopeless.

By this time, of course, man had already flown—in a way. True, it was in a precarious manner, but the Chinese had been sending kites into the air since goodness knows when. It has been suggested that four centuries B.C. was a starting point, but man-lifting kites undoubtedly came very much later. Nevertheless, Marco Polo (1254–1324), the Venetian traveller, has described the use of such kites to forecast the success or failure of a sea voyage. Apparently some poor unfortunate was sent aloft on a kite: if he landed in one piece all would be well, if not, no voyage.

Then, at last, on 15th October 1783, Jean-François Pilâtre de Rozier remained airborne in a captive Montgolfier hot-air balloon for 4 minutes 24 seconds. It was

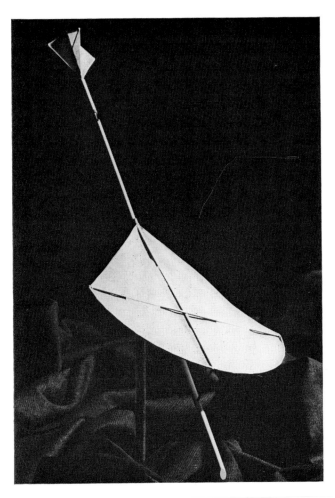

Sir George Cayley's first successful glider utilized a 'kite' wing, as shown by this model from the Qantas collection.
Qantas Empire Airways

the beginning of lighter-than-air flight. Less than two months later, on 1st December 1783, Professor J. A. C. Charles, in company with Marie-Noel Robert—one of the two Robert brothers who had assisted him in the design and construction of his hydrogen balloon—made a successful two-hour flight. This was a remarkable craft, and one which in its essential details differs little from a sporting ballon that might be flown today. Unfortunately, the balloon has a will of its own, progressing in the direction of its own inclination, or that of the breeze. Nearly seventy years were to pass before it became elongated and almost controllable when, in 1852, Henri Giffard flew a steam-powered airship from Paris to Trappes at the immense speed of 6 mph. But the balloon had stimulated man's determination to fly, far and near, high and low, in the direction that he wished to travel.

Most important of the early experimenters was Sir George Cayley who, at the end of the eighteenth century, designed an aircraft that got away from flapping wings. He had already made a serious study of the kite—the 'wing' that had been in existence for centuries. He mounted such a kite at the end of a 5-ft-long pole, with its forward edge set up a few degrees. At the opposite end of the pole was a cruciform tail, attached by a swivelling joint that allowed him to move it up or down and from side to side, to pre-set the direction of flight. When launched from a hill top it flew, surely and steadily, like any well-proportioned glider.

From this humble beginning he went on to produce a full-size glider, capable of carrying a small boy for a few yards of never-to-be-forgotten flight. The culmination of his work came in 1853, when he built the world's first man-carrying glider. Its reluctant passenger, his name unrecorded in history, was Cayley's coachman. Breathless and astonished to find himself still alive after traversing a small valley, he found he had just sufficient breath remaining to resign on the spot. Thus ended the first recorded man-carrying aeroplane flight. Cayley—long regarded as the 'Father of British aeronautics'—was sufficiently astute to realize that this was as far as he, or anyone else, could progress until the development of a compact, lightweight power plant.

Inspired by the theories so clearly expounded by Cayley, William Samuel Henson believed that he would succeed, utilizing a compact and cleverly designed steam engine constructed by John Stringfellow. In 1843 Henson had produced the design of an aircraft that was fifty years ahead of its time, introducing a wing remarkably similar in construction to that of a modern aeroplane. Together with Stringfellow, Henson built a 20-ft span model of this aircraft—known as the Aerial Steam Carriage. When launched from an inclined ramp, in 1847, it managed only a brief hop. Unfortunately the power plant was not powerful enough. It was not the failure of this model which destroyed Henson. His enthusiasm for the potential of this aircraft was much greater than his common sense. When he had tried to float a company to operate passenger services with Aerial Steam Carriages, press, public and even Parliament subjected him to such ridicule that he gave up and emigrated to America.

You may, if you wish, see his model. It is on permanent exhibition in Britain's National Aeronautical Collection at the Science Museum in London. Look at its workmanlike lines and see if you too have the impression that given a suitable power plant it might well have been the world's first successful heavier-than-air craft. But Henson has his place in history, far-sighted enough to be thinking seriously about the transportation of passengers by air more than 120 years ago.

W. S. Henson's Aerial Steam Carriage 'in flight'. It was publicity of this nature that made Henson a subject of ridicule. Science Museum, London

Henson was followed by a number of 'hoppers'—men who added, little by little, to the steady advance of aeronautical technology. All were defeated for lack of a suitable power plant. Félix du Temple, a French naval officer, patented the design of a steam-powered monoplane in 1847. Seventeen years later a full-size version of this machine, then powered by a hot-air engine, made a short hop through the air after being launched down an inclined slope. This is regarded as the first man-carrying powered aircraft to leave the ground.

Ten years later came the turn of a Russian inventor, Alexander Mozhaisky, whose large steam-powered monoplane could only manage a short hop following a ramp launch.

More convincing were the results achieved by Clement Ader in France, with his two bat-wing aeroplanes. These looked so odd that it seems unreasonable that anyone could have expected them to fly: but the first one, the

Eole, nearly did, in 1890. Powered by a 20-hp steam engine, it managed a short hop from level ground without any assistance from a ramp, thus becoming the first man-carrying powered aircraft to lift itself from the ground.

But all this spade-work of the hoppers was not confined to the land masses that stretched out from the shores of France. On the other side of the Channel at Bexley, in Kent, Hiram Maxim was busy building an immense aircraft with wings which spanned 104 ft, and which was powered by two very lightweight 180-hp steam engines. A length of steel track was provided to launch this machine, with guard rails to prevent its lifting for more than a few inches. When, one day in 1894, the engines were opened up to full power, the aircraft developed so much lift that it broke away from one of the guard rails and almost flew, before crashing to the ground.

By this time the more serious pioneers realized it was useless to continue with experiments of this nature until

Félix du Temple's monoplane in model form. It looks as if it could fly and was, in fact, the first powered aeroplane to leave the ground. Qantas Empire Airways

A wealth of artistic licence shows Alexander Mozhaisky's monoplane in flight: it is unlikely, however, that it made more than a brief 'hop'.

the power plant materialized. Their ingenuity could be employed more usefully in developing the efficiency of the airframe itself. Thus it was that Otto Lilienthal, in Germany, began to refine the design of the glider. Over a period of six years he made thousands of flights in his graceful aircraft, gradually improving performance and carefully recording progress and results. During a flight made on 9th August 1896 he lost control and crashed, dying from his injuries on the following day. Percy Pilcher of Britain met a similar fate in his *Hawk* glider. Impressed by reports of the German's achievements, Pilcher had crossed the Channel to meet and learn all he could from Lilienthal at first hand. When he returned to England he built gliders similar to those that he had seen flying so easily, but added wheels so that they could be towed into the air. Pilcher might well have been the first man to achieve true powered flight, for he built a remarkable little oil engine which he intended to fit to one of his

gliders. This fame was not to be his, for he died following a crash in the *Hawk* on 30th September 1899, and the experiment never took place.

But by this time the essential power plant was almost within reach, for in 1876 the German Nicholas Augustus

Hiram Maxim's enormous biplane photographed on its launch and restraint rails at Bexley, Kent.

This model, from the Qantas collection, shows well the graceful and practical construction of Otto Lilienthal's gliders. Qantas Empire Airways

Otto had built a successful 4-stroke internal combustion engine, which used coal gas as fuel. The four strokes—induction, compression, power and exhaust—soon became known universally as the Otto cycle. Otto had been assisted in his work by a fellow countryman, Gottlieb Daimler, and in 1885 this latter engineer constructed the world's first single-cylinder internal combustion engine utilizing the Otto cycle, and burning petroleum fuel. One year later he adapted it to drive a motor car. Clearly it was but a matter of time before this type of engine would be developed to the point of having an adequate power/weight ratio for utilization as an aircraft power plant.

The men who were to be the first to achieve success with such an engine, Orville and Wilbur Wright, had learned of Lilienthal's experiments through a fellow American named Octave Chanute. Chanute had been inspired by Lilienthal's work and endeavoured to make even greater progress. He built well-constructed gliders with a rigid wing structure and utilized cambered surfaces of the kind suggested by Cayley. But since, like Lilienthal and Pilcher, he relied upon body movements for control and stability, he was still a long way from achieving controlled flight. However, he produced a book in which he enumerated the important advances in aeronautical design. It was this book that encouraged the Wrights to ask Chanute for more detailed information.

From this evolved the decision to build a powered aeroplane, but the Wright brothers sensibly chose to work slowly and patiently to overcome the failings that had doomed all earlier attempts. They began by building a biplane kite and introduced the technique of wing warping (or twisting) to control its direction of flight. When the kite was airborne, control wires enabled them to warp the wingtips. The idea worked so well that next they built a full-size glider embodying the wing-warping technique. This too was successful, and in the two years that followed they built improved versions of this. Their No. 3 glider had a front elevator control surface as well as a rudder, and with this craft they made hundreds of successful piloted glider flights. It was an efficient machine, and the Wrights decided they had now learnt enough to add a petrol engine.

It should not be thought that this success had come easily. The results had been achieved by painstaking care. They had even tested innumerable wing sections in a home-made wind tunnel in their attempts to arrive at the most efficient lifting surface. And this same care went into the construction of their 12-hp 4-cylinder engine, and the two propellers that were to push their frail craft through the air. The moment was fast approaching when

nearly four and a half years of hard work would be put to the test.

But they had an American rival who nearly snatched triumph from their hands. This was Dr S. P. Langley, who had built an enormous machine which he called an *Aerodrome*, powered by a remarkable 5-cylinder radial petrol engine designed by Charles Manly, who was to pilot this aircraft. When it was launched from a catapult mounted on a house-boat in the Potomac River, the *Aerodrome* hit part of the launching gear and crashed into the river. Taken from the water and hurriedly repaired, the *Aerodrome* made a second attempt on 8th December 1903. The accident of the first launch was repeated, and Langley had lost his chance.

Nine days later, on 17th December 1903, the Wright *Flyer*, piloted by Orville, completed a switchback-like flight of 120 feet to earn its niche in the halls of fame as the first aircraft to complete a powered, sustained and almost-controlled flight. On the same day Wilbur achieved a flight of 59 seconds—which was more nearly controlled—during which the *Flyer* covered a distance of 852 feet. At last man had broken free from the chains which had bound him to the earth for so long.

In America, Octave Chanute developed a more refined structure for his gliders. He is shown at the World's Fair at St Louis in 1903.

*Dr S. P. Langley's hopes of achieving powered flight are
dashed for a second time as his 'Aerodrome' plunges into
the Potomac River on 8th December 1903.*
Smithsonian Institution, Washington, D.C.

In Britain, at the turn of the century, ballooning had become the sporting event of an elegant age.

2

Ugly Duckling

The Wright brothers had flown. Heavier-than-air flight was an accomplished fact. Yet this world-shattering event aroused just about as much excitement as news of a pin being lost in a haystack. And the persons responsible for

this amazing situation were the Wright brothers themselves. When, in 1904, they carried out a demonstration for the local pressmen of their No. 2 *Flyer*, it could not be coaxed into the air: the sceptical men of the newspaper world doubted that it had ever flown. And then, almost eighteen months later, when *Flyer* No. 3 had just notched up a 24-mile non-stop flight, they simply packed away their aeroplanes and gave up flying for nearly three years. As the year 1906 neared its end, Wilbur wrote to a friend, saying: 'We do not believe there is one chance in a hundred that anyone will have a machine of the least practical usefulness within five years.' This was their most serious error.

At about the same time, in France, a flamboyant little gentleman named Alberto Santos Dumont succeeded in

Not the original 'Flyer', but a delightful picture of an early Wright biplane piloted by Wilbur. In the foreground is the gantry of their falling-weight launch catapult.

getting his strange-looking 14-*bis* biplane into the air to cover a distance of 200 feet. His was the name that attained the headlines and made the world in general aware of the fact that real powered flight, authenticated by eye-witnesses and photographs, had at last been accomplished.

It was France that continued to lead the way, soon becoming the centre of world aviation. And it was a Frenchman, Louis Blériot, who became first to demonstrate that international travel by air was no longer a figment of the imagination. On 25th July 1909, in a monoplane of his own design, he successfully crossed the English Channel from a point near Calais, landing thirty-seven minutes later almost in the shadow of Dover Castle. This single event brought immediate awareness of

the fact that natural boundaries would soon have no real meaning—that island insularity was no longer an adequate means of defence. And just as quickly came the realization, summed up by one Sydney Walker in an early aviation book, that '. . . it is supposed also that aeroplanes will be able to drop bombs over fortifications, towns, and on the decks of men-of-war'.

There are few of us who are now unaware that his suppositions were correct, but it was a very long time before the upper echelons of the military services were to hold a similar view. They could see the aeroplane only as an extension of field glasses: ideal for reconnaissance if it happened to be a fine day, and the wind wasn't blowing too strongly, or in the wrong direction. Cruel comment, but fairly accurate.

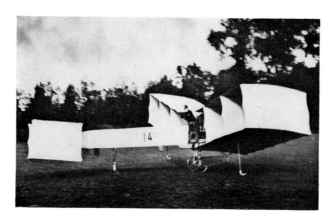

Alberto Santos Dumont, almost dwarfed by his strange-looking tail-first 14-bis biplane.

Louis Blériot flying his No. 11 monoplane, in which he made the first historic crossing of the English Channel on 25th July 1909.

The early years of flight were dominated by the vagaries of the weather and all too often the slightest zephyr was sufficient to prohibit flying for the day. Thus it was that so many of the pioneers were compelled to fly at dawn or dusk, when the air was often in its most gentle mood. This explains why Britain's first pioneer, a young man named Alliott Verdon Roe, was almost hauled up in court for disturbing the sleep of tramps who frequented the Lea Marshes, east of London. After seven years of struggle, concerned principally with lack of finance and the indifference of authority in general, he had succeeded at first light on 13th July 1909 in flying his diminutive triplane, powered by a 9-hp J.A.P. engine, for a distance of 100 feet. This duly became recorded as the first flight in an all-British aeroplane by a British pilot. Fortunately for Roe, Blériot's successful cross-Channel flight caused such glowing accounts of aviation's future to appear in the press that it would hardly have been fair to laud Blériot and punish Roe. But due to the fact that military interest in aviation was only slowly awakening prior to the beginning of the First World War, the public regarded the aeroplane principally as a sporting vehicle—an airborne version of the racing car—a rich man's toy. This was true of Britain and France at any rate. Germany held quite different views.

In 1909, when the British War Office was expressing its alarm at the vast sum of £2,500 ($12,500) that had been thrown away on experiments with aircraft, German spending on military aviation had already risen to the startling sum of £400,000 ($2m.) per year. And the Germans had also been more far-sighted in respect of the peaceful applications of air transportation, albeit lighter-than-air. On 16th November 1909 the Deutsche Luft-schiffahrts A.G. Direktion (German Air Transport Company) was founded at Frankfurt-am-Main. During the years 1910–14 this company, known universally as Delag, began the operation of regular but unscheduled passenger services from its base at Friedrichshafen. A fleet of four airships were employed, the *Hansa*, *Sachsen*, *Schwaben* and *Viktoria Luise*, each equipped to carry about twenty passengers in Pullman-like comfort. Even buffet meals were served to the some 34,000 passengers who travelled by Delag services, and when the First World War brought an end to operations a total of more than 170,000 miles had been flown without a serious mishap.

However comfortable, reliable or exciting travel by airship had been, these huge craft had no long-term future despite development, between the two world wars, of craft like the R.100 and R.101 in Britain, and the *Graf Zeppelin* and *Hindenburg* in Germany. It should not be forgotten, however, that in the early thirties the German airships pioneered transatlantic passenger services, at a time when no commercial aircraft were capable of the task. But the burnt and tangled wreckage of the R.101 at Beauvais, France, and that of the *Hindenburg* at Lakehurst, New Jersey, ended the hopes of the lighter-than-air advocates.

But in 1909, Germany apart, the aeroplane was largely unwanted by the military, as yet unsuitable for the carriage of passengers or cargo—in a commercial sense—and, in fact, almost an ugly duckling.

However, Igor Sikorsky in Russia could foresee the advantage of an aircraft able to take off and land vertically and, as early as 1909, he began to build rudimentary helicopters. After comparatively little work he

A. V. Roe flying his frail triplane with which, on 13th July 1909, he entered British aviation history: first Briton to fly a British-built aeroplane.

was sufficiently astute to realize that success in this field needed a strong and lightweight structure allied with a power plant offering much better power/weight characteristics than anything then available. Sensibly, he pigeonholed his ideas until a more suitable moment of time and produced, instead, the world's first four-engined aeroplane, *Le Grand*, with the then enormous wing span of 92 feet. From it he developed the improved *Ilia Mourometz*, heavier and larger, which was powered by four engines, two of 140 hp and two of 125 hp, and this introduced a cabin in which meals could be served, a toilet and even a promenade deck. Admittedly this latter feature was suitable only for a brave minority, for it was an external deck atop the fuselage!

It is safe to say that in the early 1900s the technique of building aircraft structures, that is the airframe, had far outpaced the development of power plants. By and large, the aircraft engine of that day was even more unreliable than the British weather: to such an extent that forced landings were accepted as a normal accompaniment to any flight. Fortunately landing speeds were such that it was possible to drop a biplane down safely into practically any field worthy of the name, provided it had a reasonable surface, but a cross-country journey demanded that the pilot should keep his weather eye open constantly for a suitable field within gliding range.

Then, overnight, Laurent Seguin of France changed all this, with the construction of a rotary engine which he

Igor Sikorsky's 'Ilia Mourometz' in flight, complete with passengers enjoying the 'promenade deck'.

227

Handley Page V. 1500 'Atlantic', after erection at Harbour Grace, Newfoundland, preparatory to an attempted transatlantic crossing.

called the Gnome. This should not be confused with a radial engine, which has stationary cylinders and crankcase within which the crankshaft rotates. The propeller is driven by the crankshaft, usually through a train of reduction gearing. The rotary engine, on the other hand, had a fixed crankshaft, and the crankcase and cylinders rotated around this. Why such a revolutionary design, one regarded initially as a freak and given the barest attention when the engine was first exhibited publicly? Seguin was aware that overheating was the prime cause of engine failure. The radial engine was cooled by the air flowing past its cylinders: but since low-powered engines meant also low forward speeds, there was a vicious circle of inefficiency. Seguin realized that if the cylinders rotated, cooling would be more efficient and, furthermore, that the flywheel action of the rotating engine mass would make for a smoothly running engine. Even more important, his engine had a compact, strong, steel crankcase and short crankshaft, resulting in low weight per horsepower of output. In fact the average engine of the day produced about 30 hp and weighed around 180 lb: 6 lb/hp. The 7-cylinder Gnome of 1909 weighed 172 lb. and developed 50 hp: 3.4 lb/hp. Thus, Seguin had produced a power plant that almost doubled the power/weight ratio

of aircraft engines, and one that provided what was undoubtedly the biggest single advance in the history of powered flight to that date. Little wonder, then, that immediately the aviation fraternity realized that this odd-looking piece of machinery was really *the* engine they had all been seeking, they adopted it rapidly and almost universally, and it completely dominated the aero-engine scene for a number of years.

And so we have arrived at the aeroplane available to the belligerent nations at the beginning of the First World War: still very much stick-and-string, but capable of a fair degree of reliability over short ranges.

What did four years of war contribute to the development of the aeroplane? It has often been suggested that but for the First World War many more years would have passed before it would have become a viable commercial transport vehicle. This is not strictly true, for airframe design and construction had developed little beyond becoming bigger and heavier because power plants were able to drag or propel a far greater weight through the air.

The aero-engine, on the other hand, had developed almost beyond recognition, with greatly increased power output and reliability, offering the potential of flight over ranges very different from those accepted as normal at the war's beginning. The rather daring Channel crossing, for example, had become routine. The lightweight structures imposed by low-powered engines had given place to aircraft like the Handley Page V/1500. This, the largest British bomber of the First World War, was designed to bring the German capital of Berlin within range of R.A.F. bases in England, and was the first practical British bomber designed to hit strategic targets from home bases. It was powered by four 375-hp Rolls-Royce Eagle VIII engines, had a wing span of 126 ft, and when fully loaded with some $3\frac{1}{4}$ tons of bombs had an all-up weight of nearly $13\frac{1}{2}$ tons.

Times had changed indeed. Perhaps the only good thing to come out of the war was the emancipation of the aeroplane. The scene was set for a new dimension in transport, to be available to men and women in civilian clothes.

A charming picture of the early days: British pioneer Claude Grahame-White about to carry a daring young lady in his flying machine.

3

The Swan Emerges

To the average man and woman of 1919 the Atlantic Ocean was a mighty, stormy barrier separating the Old World from the new, insurmountable except by sea. Nobody was surprised when one of Britain's famous pilots, Harry Hawker, in attempting to fly non-stop across the Atlantic, simply finished up in the sea, somewhere in the middle. When Alcock and Brown were successful in a similar attempt four weeks later, it was regarded as such an extraordinary feat that both men received knighthoods in addition to a £10,000 prize.

And although the First World War had generated tremendous progress in aircraft design and manufacture, it had tended to strengthen the popular view that flying was only for supermen. The fact that tens of thousands of people had travelled safely by air services in Germany before the war was little known. In any case, the Zeppelin airships which had provided the service were now, apparently, outmoded by the faster but smaller and less comfortable aeroplane. True, there had been a pioneer aeroplane passenger service in the United States in 1914; but the little Benoist flying-boats which made the 22-mile overwater hop between St Petersburg and Tampa, Florida, twice a day, carried only one passenger at a time and the service was closed after a few months. So there was little evidence to suggest that air transport would prove either popular or profitable in the early post-war period.

Such doubts did not deter the men who began planning international passenger services even before the fighting had ended. There was no shortage of aeroplanes; the Royal Air Force alone had 22,647 aeroplanes and seaplanes, and the government was prepared to sell thousands of these for whatever price anyone cared to offer. Most of them were unsuited for passenger carrying, but it was possible to convert the ex-bombers into makeshift airliners, until something better became available. The aircraft industry was eager to start building civilian aircraft, as all military orders had been cancelled overnight when the war ended; but the airlines of 1919 could not afford to buy new machines and the industry soon found

itself so short of work that it was grateful for contracts to manufacture motor cycles, milk churns, saucepans or anything else that kept its factories in business.

Strangely enough, it was the newly defeated Germany that opened the first regular airline services after the war. The German Air Ministry authorized the resumption of civil flying on 8th January 1919 and less than one month later, on 5th February, Deutsche Luft Reederei opened a service between Berlin and Weimar, using five-seat A.E.G. biplanes and two-seat D.F.W.s. These converted bombers took 2 hours 18 minutes to complete the 120-mile flight, even when everything went according to plan, and passengers had to pay for their 52-mph trip at the rate of about 4s. ($1) a mile; but it was a start.

Britain was less enterprising and refused to allow flying over the United Kingdom until April 1919. This did not please the French, who reckoned that they had more experience of over-water international flying than anyone else, having started with Blériot's cross-Channel hop in 1909. So, on 8th February, the Farman brothers, who had become leading manufacturers of large aircraft, arranged for eleven passengers to be carried from Toussus-le-Noble aerodrome, near Paris, to Kenley, on the outskirts of London, in one of their Goliath twin-engined bombers, hurriedly adapted for the purpose. They evaded the British ban by offering seats only to military passengers, who were regaled with a champagne lunch over the Channel. Unfortunately it was not always like that. When George Stevenson-Reece took off from Hounslow aerodrome at ten past nine on the morning of 25th August 1919, as the first passenger on the first-ever daily international air service, operated by Air Transport & Travel Ltd, he flew in the back of a D.H.4A that had been built as a small single-engined two-seat day-bomber. Where the gunner had once stood, two seats were crammed face-to-face in the narrow fuselage under a lid containing celluloid windows. As Stevenson-Reece was the only passenger on that historic occasion, he shared the cabin with an assortment of freight, including newspapers, some leather, grouse and a quantity of Devonshire cream. For the privilege of doing so he paid a single fare of £21 ($105). Bearing in mind the drop in value of the pound sterling in fifty years, this was probably equivalent to the cost of a transatlantic flight today.

It was, however, an inexpensive way of becoming a hero. Anyone who could claim to have flown between London and Paris in 1919 acquired a not-undeserved respect from his earth-bound fellows. Some could tell tales afterwards that the pampered passengers of today would hardly believe. There was, for example, the

Alcock and Brown in the Vickers Vimy climb away from St Johns, Newfoundland, at the beginning of their historic first non-stop Atlantic crossing.

Farman Goliaths at Le Bourget. An aircraft of this type was used by the Farman brothers to carry eleven passengers across the English Channel on 8th February 1919.

A de Havilland D.H.34, one of the first specially built airliners with cabin comfort for its passengers. The pilot was still able to 'enjoy' the slipstream.

leather coats, helmets, goggles and gloves, plus a life-jacket in case the aircraft was forced down at sea, and even a hot-water bottle on particularly cold days.

Things improved rapidly in the 1920s. Specially built airliners, like the British D.H.36s and Dutch Fokkers, had neatly furnished cabins by 1922, with tables, curtains at the windows, reading lamps and other homely touches. The Daimler Airway introduced stewards to serve refreshments on flights from London to Amsterdam and Cologne, while the Dutch Company, KLM, invented a unique 'met.' service. If there was rain or strong wind over the Channel, it used a system of blackboards on the ground at points between Amsterdam and the coast to pass a message to its pilots to turn back. There was, of course, no law against low flying in those days and aircraft seldom flew higher than one thousand feet. This made the journeys much more interesting and exciting, but it was frustrating for the pilot when passengers complained about being overtaken by a railway train when the aircraft was battling against a strong headwind. Today KLM, which began operations in 1920 with aircraft hired from A.T. & T., is one of the world's great airlines. It has seen air travel grow, and played its part in making it grow, from the kind of haphazard flying described so far into the highly technical, efficient, worldwide mass transport system of today.

From the very start operators had two primary aims—to make air travel more reliable and to make it profitable for both the customers and themselves. It was clear after a few years that, in general, the small companies started by men with more enthusiasm than capital would have to be replaced by organizations able to afford expensive new aeroplanes, with more than one engine, and with radio to enable their crews to keep in constant touch with airfield staff during flight.

By 1924 the pioneer companies in Britain had just about come to the end of their money and their enthusiasm. There were too many international airlines chasing too few passengers, and commercial aviation might have ended in the U.K. if the government had not come to its aid. This was done not by the drastic step of forming a state-run airline but simply by combining the four surviving companies into Imperial Airways, which was then promised government aid in buying up-to-date aircraft and equipment. In due course, much the same thing happened elsewhere, and the great national carriers like Air France, Deutsche Lufthansa in Germany and Sabena in Belgium began to emerge.

One of the first important policy decisions taken by Imperial Airways was that it would buy no more single-engined aeroplanes. In 1926 it began to open up what

famous occasion when one of A.T. & T.'s 'airliners' made twenty-two forced landings between London and Paris—none of them, fortunately, in the Channel. The real heroes were the pilots, who sat in a tiny open cockpit immediately behind a pounding 350-hp Rolls-Royce Eagle engine, and tried to find their way with a minimum of instruments in the days when meteorological services and radio were non-existent so far as the airlines were concerned. Some people claimed that pilots would always have to sit in the open, exposed to the icy slipstream, so that it would keep them awake and alert during long, slow flights. A better reason was that most pilots found their way by following familiar railway lines and main roads a few hundred feet below, as these were more reliable than their compass. This led to an unfortunate incident one day when a Paris-bound aircraft from London met a London-bound aircraft from Paris, following the same road at the same height. Both pilots had their heads over the side, looking at the road, and the aircraft collided head-on.

In general, however, flying was uncomfortable rather than unsafe. With thousands of ex-military pilots eager to stay in the air, the operators could be choosy when picking their staff and the standards were high. In their primitive way, too, the airlines tried to make their passengers as comfortable as possible. When not even the modest luxury of a cabin hood was available, and the passengers had to sit in open cockpits, they were lent

*Typical of early monoplane airliners is this Fokker F.VII,
once operated by the Dutch airline KLM.*

developed eventually into its great network of Empire
Air Routes from Britain to every corner of the Empire.
The first stage was, surprisingly, in the Middle East, over
the desert between Cairo and Baghdad. The reason is that
the R.A.F. had been operating an air mail service over
this route for several years, for the benefit of British
servicemen in Iraq, and Imperial merely took over the
task when it had aircraft good enough to do so. It then
extended the route at both ends, until it could offer
services all the way from England to India and Australia
in one direction and South Africa in the other. All kinds
of difficulties had to be overcome, both technical and
political. Italy refused permission for British airliners to
fly over its territory; so passengers had to fly from
London to Basle, via Paris, and there catch a train to
Genoa, where a flying-boat was waiting to take them on
across the Mediterranean to Alexandria. Later sectors
were even more exciting, one of the most popular night
stops being a Foreign Legion-type fort in the desert,
where both aeroplane and passengers were given armed
protection through the hours of darkness. It is almost
difficult to believe now that a forced landing in 1929
might have resulted in everyone being held for ransom by
tribesmen, but as recently as a decade ago it was not
unusual for light airliners to be used for target practice
by trigger-happy inhabitants of some of the more remote
areas of the Arabian coast.

In view of the cost, difficulties and unreliability of air
travel in the first post-war decade, it is easy to appreciate
why the carriage of air mail played such an important
part in the growth of commercial aviation. The airlines
realized quite early that sacks of mail had many attractions by comparison with human passengers. They could
be packed one on top of another to fill completely any
available space inside an aeroplane. They were waiting to
be carried in large quantities all the year round. And they
never complained of draughts, noise, bumps, delays,
diversions, poor service and similar inconveniences. This
helps to explain why, when the three-engined D.H.
Hercules airliner entered service in 1926, it carried only
seven passengers but had 465 cubic feet of mail space in
its main cabin. In the U.S.A., the preference for mail was
even more marked; in fact there were virtually no
scheduled passenger services until 1927, although by that
time the U.S. Air Mail Service, using old D.H.4 biplanes,
had flown a total of more than ten million miles, delivering 67,875,000 letters in the peak year of 1923. The Air
Mail Service did far more than simply make America air-
minded. It created a pool of tough, experienced pilots—
men like Charles Lindbergh who won world fame with
his solo transatlantic flight from New York to Paris in
1927—and it was responsible for getting strings of
beacon lights set up along most of the main air routes
across America, so that it could fly by night and day. This

Charles Lindbergh thrilled the world by his solo Atlantic flight in 1927. He is seen here landing at Croydon— escorted by a de Havilland Moth—following a tumultuous reception in Paris.

lighting system, and the network of landing fields used by the mail pilots, were to prove of immense value to the airlines when they did get started.

All over the world aerodromes improved in pace with the development of more efficient airliners—none more so than London's Croydon Airport which became, perhaps, the best-known of all. In the early 1920s Croydon consisted of a rather bumpy meadow with a few wooden sheds in one corner, where passengers could wait if it was raining or if the aircraft's engine refused to start. The airfield was approached along a narrow winding track called Plough Lane, which created something of a problem as the aircraft hangars were on one side of the lane and the landing field on the other. Consequently, passengers who arrived when an airliner was crossing the lane were stopped by the only aircraft level-crossing gates in the world. Safety equipment at the airport was limited to a windsock to indicate the direction of the wind. When an airliner was seen approaching, a look-out on the wooden tower did his best to identify it through a pair of binoculars and announced its imminent arrival. He then signalled for a klaxon hooter to be sounded, to alert H.M. Customs and the ground staff. Passengers' baggage was handled by anyone from the manager of the airline downwards, and valuables were often kept under his bed for safety at night. Aircraft were refuelled manually from two-gallon cans (fortunately they needed only some 65 to 105 gallons of fuel, compared to more than 20,000 gallons carried by modern transatlantic jets). Ground equipment began as no more than a pair of household steps to provide access to the cabin, followed closely by flat wooden baggage trolleys when the aircraft began to carry a greater number of passengers.

After a time, the wooden look-out platform at Croydon was superseded by the square stone control tower, sur-

The sublime memory-picture of many early travellers: Handley Page H.P.42 'Horatius' in front of the control tower at Croydon Airport. The Marconi Company Ltd

Women enter a man's world. On 15th May 1930 Boeing Air Transport employed the first airline stewardesses on its San Francisco–Chicago route.

rounded by a balcony and topped by a wireless aerial, which became the world-famous 'trademark' of London's air terminal. No photograph ever taken creates more nostalgia among pre-war flying enthusiasts than a view of one of the eight big Handley Page H.P.42 biplanes of Imperial Airways parked in front of the old tower. With their girder-braced biplane wings, four engines and massive fixed undercarriage, the H.P.42s had a majesty that no airliner has since recaptured. Anthony Fokker, the famous Dutch manufacturer, described them as 'having built-in headwinds'. It is true that they cruised at under 100 mph, but they offered a standard of comfort and safety that no other transport of their day could match. Because of their huge wings, the 42s had no difficulty in taking off from Croydon's short and hilly grass runways. Their stately pace allowed time for full-course hot meals to be served in flight between London and Paris. For these and other reasons they carried more passengers between London and the Continent in the

Important aircraft on European routes in the 1930s was the Junkers Ju 52/3M: the one shown landing belonged to Deutsche Luft Hansa.

1930s than did all other airliners combined. Together, in fact, they flew about ten million miles, without ever hurting a passenger until the last of them disappeared during a wartime flight in 1940.

The H.P.42s represented a beginning and an end. They introduced enclosed cockpits for the flight crew, who promptly exchanged their old leather flying suits and goggles for smart blue serge uniforms, gold braid and peaked caps. Pilots assumed a new status, rather like the captain of a ship, and an even more startling innovation was tried out by Boeing Air Transport in the U.S.A. On 15th May 1930 they hired eight young nurses to serve passengers on board their aircraft on the San Francisco–Chicago route, and the airline stewardess was born.

So the airliner of the early thirties was big, safe and capable of offering passengers a comfortable journey if the weather was not too rough. But machines like the H.P.42, and the Boeing B.80s in which the stewardesses worked, were anachronisms, leftovers from the Wright brothers' era of biplane design.

The early needs of civil aviation had demanded the retention of aircraft of this type, but there were designers like Fokker in Holland, Junkers in Germany and Ford in America who had been producing big twin-engined and three-engined metal monoplanes, with clean streamlined airframes that eliminated most of what Fokker had called 'the built-in headwinds'. They were not much faster than the biplanes, but they were more economical to operate and the Fords, in particular, were so sturdy and efficient that some remain in airline service today, thirty years after they were built.

But the biplane had not been eliminated from the aviation scene. In 1925 de Havilland in the U.K. had produced a two-seater known as the Moth. One of the most important light planes ever built, it was responsible for the birth of the flying club movement throughout the world. It was an outstanding aeroplane, so reliable that a courageous young woman named Amy Johnson flew one solo half way round the world from England to Australia. A no less courageous man, named Francis Chichester, also used a Moth to brave the extremely hazardous crossing of the Tasman Sea, from Australia to New Zealand, performing one of the most outstanding feats of transoceanic navigation ever recorded.

Nor was flight limited only to aeroplanes of biplane and monoplane configuration. The rotating wing aircraft began to emerge at about this same period when the Spaniard, Juan de la Cierva, invented the 'flapping hinge' rotor which he fitted to an aircraft fuselage in place of conventional wings. The rotor of la Cierva's Autogiro was not power driven: his aircraft had a conventional propeller for traction and the rotor auto-rotated in flight to provide lift. This meant, of course, that the Autogiro could not take off vertically, but it was a first practical step in this direction.

Nevertheless, it was design of monoplane aircraft that led to one of the most significant transport aeroplanes ever built—the Boeing 247. Although less well known than some of the types which followed, the 247 was the first truly modern airliner, from which all the others were evolved. First flown in 1933, it was a highly streamlined low-wing monoplane, with two 550-hp Pratt & Whitney engines, variable-pitch propellers, a retractable undercarriage, control surface trim-tabs, an automatic pilot and de-icing equipment, and was the first twin-engined monoplane airliner able to climb on one engine with a full load.

With the 247, cruising at 160 mph under the automatic control of 'George', the autopilot, commercial flying entered a completely new era. The thousands of people

Interior shot of the Boeing 247-D, which carried a crew of three and provided completely new standards of comfort for its ten passengers.

who watched and cheered as Cunard's great new ocean liner, the *Queen Mary*, slid down the slipway into the water for the first time in 1934 could not know that by the time this fine ship went into retirement she would have conceded pride of place in transatlantic travel to 150-seat, 600-mph descendants of the upstart Boeing 247.

4

Wings Over the Oceans

The Boeing 247 flew for the first time on 8th February 1933: by the end of the following month it had entered service with United Air Lines (UAL) in America. Introduction of this aircraft into commercial airline service sparked off a revolution in travel in the United States. The improved 247B, for example, was able to carry ten passengers at a speed of 160 mph, and for the first time the U.S. coast-to-coast schedule fell below 20 hours. UAL's chief rival was Transcontinental and Western Air (TWA), which had introduced Ford Tri-Motors at the end of 1932 to establish a coast-to-coast schedule of $26\frac{3}{4}$ hours; quite something at the time. Now TWA found they were losing their passengers to UAL and were, perhaps, the first airline to discover that the travelling public will almost invariably elect to fly with the airline able to offer the fastest journey time between any two points. The situation was not one they could accept complacently and little time was lost in approaching the Boeing Company to supply them, also, with the revolutionary 247s. Boeing, however, was closely related to UAL, and so there was no sale; which meant that TWA had to find an alternative, quickly.

Specifications of an aircraft that would be superior to the 247 were drawn up and the Douglas Aircraft Company was approached to build what could prove to be an important aircraft both for constructor and operator. This, indeed, proved to be the case, for the aircraft which resulted finally was one of the most famous in the entire history of commercial aviation. The prototype of this, designated DC-1, was built and flown during the first six months of 1933. When the production version—the DC-2—entered service on TWA's Columbus–New York route, it was found to be more comfortable, faster and able to carry four more passengers; and it introduced trailing-edge flaps which considerably improved take-off and landing performance.

One of many DC-2 customers was American Airlines, and early in 1935 they discussed with Douglas the development of a sleeper version, able to carry the same number of passengers as the standard DC-2. The resulting aircraft had a wider fuselage and was known as the Douglas Sleeper Transport (DST), while the day version had the same wider fuselage, enabling it to accommodate another row of passengers fore and aft, to make it a twenty-one-seater. This was the DC-3, the aircraft that completely revolutionized air travel in the United States. Consider these facts alone: when America entered the Second World War in December 1941 no less than 80 per cent of all scheduled airliners in the U.S. were DC-3s: during a twelve-month period of 1939–40 the airlines of America recorded a 100 per cent safety record. So outstanding was this aircraft that over 10,000 were built during the Second World War: so reliable, so airworthy, so enduring that they are still in service in many countries as these words are being written.

While America was gaining an immense lead in civil aviation—and one that it has retained—what were the European nations doing to stretch their wings? The British, Dutch, French and Italians all had colonial possessions, so their main concern was to extend air services eastwards. Great Britain, in the shape of Imperial Airways, had slowly but surely reached out towards Australia and New Zealand, its most distant relatives in the Commonwealth. When the link had reached Singapore, Imperial Airways and the Australian Queensland and Northern Territory Air Services (QANTAS) formed Qantas Empire Airways to forge the last link of the chain, from Singapore to the Australian mainland across the awe-inspiring Timor Sea. Over this 12,722-mile route the Christmas mail was flown out for the first time in 1934, taking almost two weeks.

The glow of satisfaction which should have accompanied this achievement was completely spoiled by the Dutch. In the early months of 1933 Sir Macpherson Robertson, an Australian patriot, offered prize money to the value of £15,000 ($67,500) for an air race from England to Australia, to help mark the centenary of the state of Victoria and, more far-sightedly, to encourage the development of more rapid communications with the mother country. The result was that on 20th October 1934 a motley collection of aircraft began to take off from Mildenhall, Suffolk, to take part in a race that had, initially, aroused little interest. Gradually, however, aircraft manufacturers had begun to appreciate that the prestige that would attach to the winning machine would be worth far more than the cost that might be involved in its design and construction. So it was that the de Havilland company built a twin-engined aircraft especially for this race, and gave it the name of Comet. Three models were built and one of these was flown by C. W. A. Scott and T. Campbell Black, who won the speed section of the

Ubiquitous, safe and enduring, still in airline service: the Douglas DC-3 Dakota.

C. W. A. Scott and T. Campbell Black arrive at Melbourne in their de Havilland Comet Racer to win the Macpherson Robertson England–Australia Air Race.

race, completing the course in 71 hours 18 seconds. Thus for the first time England became linked with Australia in less than three days. To the astonishment of everyone, and the consternation of Imperial Airways, the second aircraft home was a DC-2 of the Dutch national airline, KLM, flown by K. D. Parmentier and J. J. Moll. It carried three passengers, 421 lb. of air mail, and had completed the journey in 3 days, 18 hours, 17 minutes. It was, at that time, an amazing performance, and demonstrated conclusively the qualities of the aircraft that was beginning to equip the American airlines.

No sooner had the results been announced than KLM ordered 14 DC-2s from the Douglas Company, and this marked the entrance of American civil aircraft into the European scene, a market which the civil products of the American aviation industry have dominated ever since. While KLM was awaiting its DC-2s, the British Government announced, on 20th December 1934, introduction of the Empire Air Mail Scheme, which meant that all

mail to or from Commonwealth countries that were served by Imperial Airways would henceforth be carried by air. To enable the fulfilment of such a programme, Imperial ordered a fleet of four-engined flying-boats, and the first of these Short S.23s, the *Canopus*, made its first service flight on 30th October 1936.

By 26th June 1938 it was possible to fly from Southampton, England, to Sydney, Australia, without a change of aircraft, and the S.23 'Empire Boats'—faster than the DC-3's which by then equipped KLM— acquired a reputation for reliability, comfort, standard of passenger service and amenities which are the subject of nostalgic memory to this day. Incidentally, it was *Canopus* that was the first aircraft to provide a through service from Southampton to Durban, South Africa, in June 1937.

The demand for long-range aircraft had created worldwide interest in flying-boats, for the majority of long-distance routes were above oceans and, in any event, no less than seven-tenths of the earth's surface is covered

'*Canopus*', *first of the original* '*C*' *Class Empire flying-boats, which between them flew more than twenty million miles on regular passenger service.* B.O.A.C.

Pan American's 'Sikorsky S-42 Clipper' II at Auckland,
New Zealand, after completing the first U.S.–New
Zealand survey flight. Pan American Airways

with water. It seemed quite reasonable to assume that a flying-boat, rather than a landplane, stood a better chance of survival if forced down during a long ocean crossing. Furthermore, increasingly heavy aircraft with increasingly heavy loads needed immense airfields from which to operate and these did not exist. On the other hand, vast stretches of water were to be found everywhere and these offered almost unlimited take-off and landing areas. As we have seen already, Britain relied upon the Short 'Empire Boats' to provide their long-range transport. In America, Pan American Airways steadied their commercial gaze across the vast expanses of the Pacific Ocean and ordered two different types of flying-boats simultaneously: the Martin M.130 and the Sikorsky S.42, and it was one of the former aircraft, named *China Clipper*, which made the inaugural mail flight across the central Pacific. Leaving San Francisco on 22nd November

1935 the *China Clipper* arrived at Manila, Philippines—via Honolulu, Midway, Wake and Guam—six days later, but almost another year elapsed before, on 21st October 1936, passengers were carried over this route for the first time.

The most important of the long ocean crossings was the last to be conquered commercially: the Atlantic Ocean, which provided a barrier to trade between the great centres of industrial population in America and Europe. Geographically, it seemed less demanding than the Pacific, but the North Atlantic not only suffered worse weather, it was plagued also by adverse winds and posed severe navigational problems. This explains why France, Germany and Italy considered conquest of the South Atlantic a far easier proposition, and a target more within their reach at the beginning of the thirties. The route of 1,890 miles from Dakar, Senegal, to Natal, Brazil, on the whole enjoyed very good weather and navigation, even at

Martin Model 130 'China Clipper' which made the inaugural mail flight across the central Pacific.

night, posed no great problem. France chose, initially, to use a flying-boat for the service, and on 11th May 1930 the almost legendary Jean Mermoz, a pilot of *Aéropostale*, flew a Latécoère 28 seaplane from Dakar to Natal in 19 hours 35 minutes. Nearly three years later he bettered this time, flying a landplane, but in August of that year—1933—*Aéropostale* became merged into Air France, and it was this latter company that provided a regular and almost routine flight from Toulouse to Santiago in 1936. Germany chose a quite different solution, Deutsche Luft Hansa (DLH) carrying mail from Stuttgart to Las Palmas by air, from where a ship continued to Fernando de Noronha. Finally, an air link completed the journey to Rio de Janeiro. Total time saved over a wholly surface route was ten days.

But so far as Germany was concerned it was the rigid airship *Graf Zeppelin* that provided the first true air services across the South Atlantic, from Seville to Recife, in 1931. In the following year these flights were extended from Friedrichshafen to Recife, and finally to Rio de Janeiro, continuing until 1937 when disaster came to the *Hindenburg*. This was not the limit of German ingenuity on this route, however, for experiments were made with a depot ship equipped to pick up seaplanes from the sea and re-launch them by catapult.

The North Atlantic remained a most formidable barrier, despite advances in aeronautical technology, but the demands of commerce acted as a spur to hasten a solution to the problem. This meant that because the aeroplane of the period had inadequate range with an economic payload, many ingenious ideas were proposed to bring success.

It should be remembered that of the five European nations with a major stake in aviation, it was Germany alone—with no colonial possessions to link by air with the homeland—that was both anxious and able to concentrate its attention upon the development of routes that could offer prestige as well as profitable operations. Their first attempt to resolve the problem lay in the construction of a special flying-boat for the task, the Dornier Do X, launched early in 1929. Then the biggest aeroplane ever built, it weighed 52 tons, spanned 157 feet, was powered by twelve 500-hp Siemens Jupiter radial engines and could seat 100 passengers with little difficulty. Unfortunately, it was gravely underpowered. The twelve Jupiter engines were mounted in tandem on pylons above the wing, each pair being housed in a common nacelle, the forward engines with tractor, the aft engines with pusher propellers. All the rear engines overheated badly, even if left uncowled, and in an attempt to provide more power all twelve were removed late in 1930 and

The German 'Graf Zeppelin' which, in 1929, accomplished the first round-the-world flight by an airship.

replaced by 600-hp Curtiss Conquerors. Even this extra 1,200 hp was quite inadequate and after an Atlantic crossing which began in November 1930 and ended in New York Harbour on 27th August 1931, it was clear that the Do X could hardly be counted a success.

Germany's next serious attempt came when she initiated a slight variation of the technique that had first been used with success much farther south. Her new transatlantic liner *Bremen* was equipped with a catapult to permit the launch of a Heinkel seaplane some 300 miles short of the liner's destination. Proved successful, the idea was extended to her second big transatlantic liner, the *Europa*, and in 1934 the journey time for sea/air mail between any place in Germany and New York was quoted as $4\frac{1}{2}$ days. By then, however, DLH had ample evidence that the depot ship technique, in use on the South Atlantic route, was completely successful and decided to give this a trial on the far more difficult North Atlantic crossing. Accordingly, the depot ship *Schwabenland* was stationed mid-way between the Azores and New York and on 10th September 1936 two Dornier Do 18 seaplanes successfully completed Berlin–New York crossings, via Lisbon, the Azores and the *Schwabenland*.

It was not necessary, then, to continue experimentation, for the *Graf Zeppelin* and *Hindenburg* began scheduled North Atlantic flights in the summer of 1936. When destruction of the *Hindenburg* in May 1937 terminated this service, these two lighter-than-air craft between them had carried rather more than 16,000

Dornier Wal seaplane of the type used by Germany for
early South Atlantic air-mail services.

But for the Second World War the Dornier Do 26 flying-
boat would have been introduced on the South Atlantic
air-mail service.

*The British airship R.100, which crossed the Atlantic to
Canada and back in 1934. She was designed by Barnes
Wallis, better remembered for geodetic-Wellingtons,
bouncing-bombs and swing-wings.*

National Aviation Museum, Ottawa, Canada

passengers safely and comfortably across North and
South Atlantic—no mean achievement for those days.
DLH then came back into the picture, making no fewer
than fourteen crossings with a Blohm & Voss Ha 139
flying-boat, combined with the depot ship technique. But
the moment of success for a landplane was near. On 10th
August 1938 a four-engined Focke-Wulf Condor made a
Berlin–New York crossing in just under twenty-five
hours: three days later the return flight was accomplished
in about five hours less, and experimental flights with the
Condors continued until the approach of war brought to
an end DLH's hopes of a scheduled passenger service.

Although Britain had been concerned principally with
air routes eastward, it should not be thought that she
lacked interest in the North Atlantic route. Nevertheless,
Imperial Airways were aware that however keen they
might be to establish a scheduled transatlantic service,
there would be little long-term satisfaction in attempting
to create a route based on aircraft of marginal range.

The Americans, in their turn, were looking eastward
across the tumbled waters of the Atlantic, equally
anxious to establish an air route to their English-speaking
cousins but they, too, had no aircraft offering adequate
range. So, in 1935, America, Britain, Canada, the Irish
Free State and Newfoundland got together to discuss the
possibility of creating an air bridge over the Atlantic, and
it was agreed that Foynes, on the River Shannon, and
Botwood, in Newfoundland, would be the eastern and
western terminals respectively. America's Pan American
Airways, it will be remembered, had ordered Sikorsky
S.42 flying-boats for their Pacific services: similarly,
Imperial Airways were awaiting delivery of their Short
S.23s, intended for their Commonwealth routes. When
both of these types had entered service, it was decided to
initiate simultaneous survey flights from each side of the
Atlantic, an early example of Anglo-American goodwill
and co-operation in aviation matters. Accordingly, on
5th July 1937, Pan American's *Clipper III* took off from
Botwood, while Imperial Airways' *Caledonia* flying-boat
climbed away from the Shannon at Foynes. Both made
safe and quite uneventful crossings, followed by return
flights to their respective countries. Before the summer of

245

A flying 'boat' indeed: the giant twelve-engined Dornier
Do X, built for the North Atlantic route.

One of the Lufthansa's Heinkel seaplanes mounted on the
catapult of the transatlantic liner 'Europa'.

1937 had ended, *Caledonia* and her sister 'boat *Cambria*
had, between them, completed four more round trips,
while the American flying-boats had made two more,
one of which was over the more southerly route taken
by DLH.

In the following year Britain concentrated her efforts
on an entirely different solution to the problem of providing an aircraft with adequate range, albeit for the
carriage of mail only. It had long been appreciated that
an aircraft could fly quite safely at a weight considerably
in excess of that at which it took off. If some means could
be found to assist an aircraft into the air it would be able
to carry an increased payload; if the extra payload was in
the form of fuel then its range would be extended. A
British consulting engineer called Robert Mayo proposed
and designed a 'pick-a-back' concept, in which the lower
component was a Short S.23, named *Maia*, the upper a
specially designed seaplane called *Mercury*. The two aircraft took off as a single unit, *Mercury* being separated
when both were at a safe height. Following such a take-
off on 20th July 1938 *Mercury*, piloted by Capt D. C. T.
Bennett and carrying 1,000 lb. of air mail, completed
successfully a non-stop flight from Foynes to Montreal in
a record time of 20 hours 20 minutes. The return flight
had to be made without *Maia*'s help, and so followed the

A Blohm & Voss Ha 139 seaplane of Lufthansa being hoisted aboard a depot ship.

Back in her natural element: the Blohm & Voss Ha 139 immediately after catapult launch.

*Focke-Wulf Fw 200 'Condor' with which Lufthansa made
the first landplane transatlantic air-mail flight on 10th
August 1938.*

*Aerial divorce: the moment of separation when seaplane
'Mercury' lifts away from the Short S.23 'Maia'.*

The flight-refuelling technique: a Harrow tanker feeds a
flying-boat as it begins its transatlantic crossing.

Azores and Lisbon route. Imperial Airways was keen to
buy a small fleet of these composite craft, but the concept
was vetoed by the British Government since segregation
of passengers and mail was an unacceptable idea.

There was another alternative to this line of thought,
which involved take-off with a minimum quantity of fuel.
When the aircraft concerned was airborne with a full load
of passengers and mail, it was suggested that an aerial
rendezvous be made with another aircraft carrying fuel.
Experiments were made with two converted Handley
Page Harrows—one of the first monoplane bomber aircraft to serve with the R.A.F.—to enable them to carry

and dispense a fairly large quantity of aviation fuel; one
of these was stationed at Foynes, the other at Botwood.
The flying-boats *Cabot* and *Caribou* were allocated for the
trials, and after a somewhat lengthy and hazardous
process about 800 gallons of fuel were transferred to the
flying-boat, which continued steadily on course throughout the period of fuel transfer. Thus, during the summer
of 1939, *Cabot* and *Caribou* made a total of eight successful round trips over the Atlantic without mishap. But no
passengers were carried on these experimental flights,
brought to a close by the outbreak of war, which meant
that the honour of inaugurating a scheduled transatlantic

The 42-ton Boeing 314 flying-boat with which Pan American inaugurated the North Atlantic passenger service on 8th July 1939. Pan American Airways

passenger service by heavier-than-air craft went, instead, to America.

In December 1937 Pan American had invited tenders for the design and construction of a fleet of long-range transport aircraft. Boeing's flying-boat design was accepted, and when the 42-ton Model 314 was delivered on 24th February 1939 it was the answer to the airline's prayers, for it had a still air range in excess of 3,000 miles. Just over four months later, on 8th July, Pan American started a North Atlantic passenger service to Southampton and Marseilles at a return fare of $675 (£150). It had taken just under thirty-six years of aviation progress to conquer the world's oceans. The improved flying-boats that Imperial Airways had ordered from Shorts were too late to carry the passengers and mail for which they had been designed. Instead they proved invaluable on wartime operations, in a war during which aviation made its most rapid advances.

5

In Full Flight

When, on 3rd September 1939, the British Government declared war on Hitler's Nazi Germany, there were few who realized the achievements and sacrifices that would be made by new generations of aircraft and their pilots, or the effect that all this would have on post-war aviation.

During the progress of the war advances in the technology and equipment of aviation meant that, when an uneasy peace once again settled on the world, the scene was set for an almost explosive expansion of air travel. In order to understand this it is desirable to review briefly the progress that had been made.

First and foremost, the need to carry men and offensive weapons over enormous distances had hastened the development of long-range aircraft capable of lifting loads that were almost a dream before the war. Defence against attacking aircraft and the need to be able to find distant targets in all weathers meant that communications and navigation equipment—in its infancy at the war's beginning—had come of age. Propeller-driven aircraft had been refined to achieve almost their maximum possible speed. The power output of piston engines in general had been almost doubled: for example, the Rolls-Royce Merlin II or III that powered the Spitfire Mk. I was rated at 880 hp, the Merlin 63 installed in the Spitfire Mk. XI produced no less than 1,760 hp. The newly developed jet engine and the first aircraft powered by these new engines had given but a hint of their potential.

There were other factors too that contributed to the rapid expansion of aviation on a world-wide basis. The development of reliable multi-engined long-range landplanes had made it necessary to build airfields with long hard-paved runways to provide the necessary length of run for take-off and landing. These same airfields had also been equipped with the best of navigation and communications equipment. Thousands of airmen had served as aircrew and had learned to use the new aircraft and equipment and, like demobilized aircrew of the First World War, they were, in the main, keen to continue flying in civil aircraft. Last, but by no means least, hundreds of thousands of men and women, civilians as well as members of various armed forces, had become accustomed to travel by air as routine. If airlines could continue to carry them on business or pleasure at fares they could afford to pay, then there was no doubt that they would favour air travel above all other forms of transport.

All of this added up to the end of the flying-boats that had been responsible for almost all of the long-range intercontinental passenger services before the war. The reason was not hard to find for the airfields, which in due course became owned by corporations, charged only a landing fee for each aircraft using the airport and its facilities. An airline operating a service with flying-boats had to face the extremely costly business of maintaining its own moorings, ensuring that the seaway was clear of floating debris, providing 'boat to shore' transport, passenger lounges, refreshment and other facilities, etc. A landing fee was chicken-feed by comparison. There were mourners at the passing of the flying-boats: their one-time passengers. These large and slow craft had provided safe and extremely comfortable, nay luxurious, transport around the world. The converted military aircraft with which many airlines were forced to re-open operations immediately post-war could not compare in any way but one: speed.

The fortunes of war had dealt the American nation the best hand with which to bid for the new passengers and cargoes: and since poker was the national card game they knew how to make best use of the cards in their hand. United States forces had been fighting a war remote from their own shores, which meant that the U.S.A.F., as well as Pan American Airways and American Export Airlines which had both become almost subsidiaries of the U.S.A.F., had been concerned with the carriage and maintenance of troops thousands of miles from home. This, in turn, had meant that the American aircraft industry had to concern itself with the design, development and construction of long-range transport aircraft, which it supplied also to its allies. On the other hand, the European nations, allies or enemies, had perforce to concentrate upon the design and production of combat aircraft and these were, in the main, of short or medium-range capability.

Demobilization and the reduction of military potential on both sides of the Atlantic made large numbers of war-surplus aircraft available to airline operators and these, needing comparatively little conversion to enable them to carry civilian passengers, served as valuable interim aircraft during the period in which airliners with more desirable commercial characteristics were being designed and developed. There were, of course, one or two air-

The Boeing 307 Stratoliner of 1939, first commercial transport aircraft to have a pressurized cabin.

craft that were direct developments of military aircraft, such as the pre-war Boeing Model 307 Stratoliner, derived from the B-17 Flying Fortress. The B-29 Superfortress sired the Boeing Model 377 Stratocruiser, and when Pan American introduced this latter aircraft on the North Atlantic route in 1949 it set completely new standards of passenger travel, and it is significant that the three airlines that eventually equipped themselves with the Model 377 gained a lead over other transatlantic operators which they have maintained to this day.

In due course the first of the post-war piston-engined long-range transports began to enter service, and KLM introduced the first transatlantic Lockheed Super Constellation service in August 1953. This was followed by introduction of the Douglas DC-7B in June 1955, the

DC-7C 'Seven Seas' in June 1956, and by the Lockheed L.1649A Starliner in July 1957. These latter aircraft represented the final stage of development of the long-range piston-engined transport, offering to their passengers safe and comfortable travel, and to their operators a high factor of utilization and resulting good economics. It is interesting to record that in the last twelve months of operations, before piston-engined airliners were superseded on the North Atlantic route, the combined fleets of transatlantic operators carried more than a million passengers as routine over what had once been considered the most hazardous of all intercontinental routes.

The British Overseas Airways Corporation had been forced to comply with the old adage: 'If you can't beat 'em, join 'em.' This had involved big capital investment in

*The 71-ton Boeing Model 377 Stratocruiser created a new
era of travel comfort . . .*
Pan American Airways

*. . . it even had a roomy lower-deck lounge where passengers
could 'go below' to stretch their legs.*

the products of the American industry. Nevertheless they
cherished hopes that things might not always be so.
These hopes were based on the knowledge that, long
before the war had come to an end, leaders of civil
aviation in Britain had looked ahead to the post-war
days, concerned with the fact that the British aircraft
industry—preoccupied with the design and manufacture of combat aircraft—would, unless forewarned
and guided, find itself left on the shelf. And so, during
1942–3 a committee chaired by Lord Brabazon of Tara—
appropriately enough the holder of the first pilot's
licence issued by the Royal Aero Club of the United
Kingdom—met to discuss the development of civil
aviation and the types of aircraft that would be needed
after the war if B.O.A.C. was to retain its fair share of

Two that did make it: a Lockheed Constellation of Qantas Empire Airways, of the last generation of highly developed, efficient and reliable piston-engined airliners...

Qantas Empire Airways

...which remarks apply also to this Douglas DC-7C of the Belgian airline SABENA.

*Two that didn't make it: the Saunders-Roe Princess flying-
boat taxiing out for its first take-off . . .*

*. . . and the Bristol Brabazon 1 seen during taxi tests prior
to the first flight on 4th September 1949.*

Looking almost as antique as the Wright 'Flyer', an early Whittle jet-engine, which gave Britain a lead in turbine technology which she retains to this day.

some had suggested a jet engine: one which would dispense entirely with a propeller and rely upon the discharge of a huge volume of high-temperature gases to thrust the aircraft forward. There was, however, only one person in Britain with the determination to overcome the problems of building such an engine, an officer of the R.A.F., Frank Whittle. Not only did he have to face such challenges as finding new alloys able to withstand the extremely high temperatures and stresses set up within the engine, but had simultaneously to deal with the quite different questions of insufficient capital and official lack of interest. When his prototype engine ran successfully for the first time on 12th April 1937 he must have entertained great hopes that it would be developed in sufficient time to play a major role in the war that thinking people were already beginning to consider inevitable. In fact it was not until just over four years later that the Gloster-Whittle E.28/39 prototype, powered by a more

world air traffic. From the recommendations of this committee stemmed many of Britain's revolutionary aircraft concepts that began development as soon after the war as industry could begin to tool up for peacetime production. Some, like the huge Bristol Brabazon, were but seven-day wonders: and so were the beautiful Saunders-Roe Princess flying-boats that should have been christened far more appropriately Sleeping Princess, for they lay for years in their cocoons near Calshot Castle, awaiting the kiss of re-awakening that never came.

There were others, of course, that betokened the dawn of a new age of air travel, like the Viscount and the Comet; though in their original Brabazon Committee form they might never have become pioneers of new concepts. But above all the Brabazon Committee should be remembered for two most important factors: they strongly recommended the continued development of turbine engines for civil use and they made Britain's aircraft designers aware of post-war needs and started them thinking of the future long before they might otherwise have done so. The original prospect of producing world-beating aircraft had come many years earlier than even the Brabazon Committee. Forward-looking aircraft engineers had realized that there was a limit to the capability of piston-engined propeller-driven aircraft, in terms of speed and altitude. A totally different power plant would be needed to overcome these problems, and

First British jet-powered aircraft to fly—the Gloster-Whittle E.28/39 prototype takes off during its development programme. Imperial War Museum, London

The first of the German jet-powered aircraft, the Heinkel He 178, designed by Siegfried Guenter.

developed form of his engine, flew for the first time. Even then, another three vital years elapsed before, on 27th July 1944, Gloster Meteors of the R.A.F.'s No. 616 Squadron became operational.

The E.28/39 prototype was not, however, the first jet-powered aircraft to fly. Only a few days before the outbreak of war, unknown to the rest of the world, on 27th August 1939 the Heinkel He 178 prototype had roared off the ground, powered by a jet engine designed by Pabst von Ohain. Fortunately for the Allies, production of a jet-powered aircraft did not enjoy a very high rating on Hitler's priorities, so that it was not until very shortly after introduction of the British Gloster Meteor that Germany's Messerschmitt Me 262 went into operational service.

These two aircraft represented the first step in the development of a new type of aeroplane that would, one day, offer completely new standards of travel to post-war passengers. The gap between these and existing types of aircraft was then very wide, and the stepping-stones needed to ford this stream of ignorance were difficult to acquire. One in particular—the problem of compressibility—was so difficult a challenge that there were many who considered it insoluble. Strangely enough it was not peculiar to the jet fighters, for pilots of developed versions of aircraft like the American Lightning and British Typhoon had found that when approaching terminal velocity in a dive their aircraft would often shudder violently and frighteningly: it seemed they might shake to pieces. Unfortunately this happened sometimes; wings or tail units broke away from the main fuselage structure and many pilots lost their lives.

Clearly, if aircraft were to avail themselves of the full potential of new types of power plant, something must be done to solve this problem. Then aerodynamicists discovered that when airflow over the wing of an aircraft

The Gloster Meteor, Britain's first twin-jet fighter aircraft, in low-level flight over the runway at RAF Tangmere, Sussex.

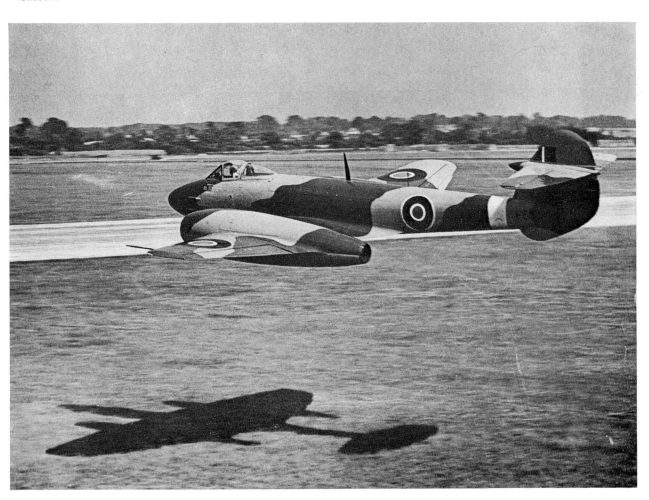

Germany's first operational twin-jet fighter, the Messerschmitt Me 262.

approached the speed of sound (760 mph at sea level, falling to 660 mph above 36,000 feet) the smooth flow ceased; instead, shock-waves were created and it was these that caused the violent shudder, or buffeting. This was the barrier to the very high-speed flight promised by the jet engines. The word 'barrier' itself became bandied around, and it was not long before the press of the world had made everyone conscious of the 'sound barrier'. At the time no one knew whether it would be possible to design aircraft able to fly through this 'barrier' to higher, supersonic flight: they had discovered only that thinner and swept wings (i.e. with the wing leading-edge forming an angle of less than 90 degrees to the rear of the fuselage) would allow an aircraft to approach nearer to the speed of sound before buffeting occurred.

Typical of the highly developed piston-engined fighter aircraft that encountered compressibility problems was the American Lockheed P-38 Lightning.

America initiated research into the problem, and the U.S.A.F. ordered a rocket-powered aircraft from the Bell Aircraft Company. This was built very strongly so that it could, they hoped, withstand severe buffeting without disintegration, and was provided with adequate power to be able to exceed the speed of sound. To minimize the problems of structural weight necessary for a powered take-off, as well as to conserve fuel, the Bell X-1—as it was known—was air-launched at a height of around 30,000 feet from a B-29 Superfortress adapted to carry the rocket-plane beneath its fuselage. After each release its pilot, a young U.S.A.F. officer named Charles 'Chuck' Yeager, flew the X-1 progressively nearer to the speed of sound: at Mach 0·94 (i.e. 94 per cent of the speed of sound) the buffeting was so severe that he, too, had

doubts as to whether it would be possible to penetrate this invisible barrier.

Finally, on 14th October 1947, Yeager was convinced that he could prolong the crawl towards Mach 1·0 (the speed of sound) no longer. He was determined to stake all on a bid for success—if success was possible. When he dropped away from the mother-plane and opened up the rocket engine to full power, his little craft streaked away across the sky, rapidly approaching the critical speed. The buffeting began to build up, gradually getting worse, and Yeager felt that his control of the aircraft was only very marginal. Suddenly, quite unexpectedly, the buffeting stopped. 'Chuck' Yeager was through the barrier into the smooth airflow of supersonic flight, first man in the world to exceed the speed of sound, and to prove that

The Bell X-1 rocket-powered research aircraft clasped beneath the belly of its B-29 'mother-plane'.

a properly designed aircraft could fly safely at a speed in excess of Mach 1. How much in excess no one knew at that time. And so the research programme continued with rocket-powered aircraft until, in October 1967, the last of them, the North American X-15-A2, had carried Major Pete Knight, U.S.A.F., to a height of more than 50 miles to earn him an astronaut's wings, and flashed him through the skies at an undreamed of speed of 4,534 mph.

From research of this nature have been developed combat aircraft able to fly as routine at speeds of Mach 2·5 and it has pointed the way to development of Super-sonic Transport (SST) aircraft able to carry passengers over intercontinental ranges at almost five times the cruising speed of the more advanced piston-engined airliners. The first prototypes of such aircraft, the Anglo-French Concorde and the Russian Tu-144, are carrying out their test and development programmes as these lines are being written. Time alone will show whether they, in their turn, will capture the cream of the long-range intercontinental traffic and give their manufacturing countries a break-through into a market that is virtually an American monopoly.

'Chuck' Yeager became first man in the world to fly through the 'sound barrier' in the Bell X-1, seen here in powered flight. United States Air Force photograph

The North American X-15-A2 rocket-powered aircraft which had flown at 4,534 mph before the research programme ended in 1969.

6

Faster and Higher

Development of the jet engine was proceeding at a tremendous pace, for it was clear that here was a power plant able to offer performance undreamed of with piston engines. Consequently, a completely new generation of military aircraft began to take shape in factories throughout the world. At Hatfield, in Hertfordshire, far-sighted designers of the de Havilland Company had begun work on a quite different project, to take advantage of Britain's lead in jet-engine technology and one that, they hoped, would also give their country a world lead in civil aviation. It was a bold concept and involved far more than wedding the new engines to a conventional airframe, for their aircraft would have a cruising speed nearly double that of all but the most advanced piston-engined airliners. Furthermore, it would cruise at an altitude considerably higher than that of other aeroplanes in airline service, offering much smoother flight, above the worst of the weather. This meant that completely new constructional techniques were necessary, and that in order to allow passengers to breathe normally at a height of up to 7 miles a pressurized cabin would be needed. This involved the design of a structure able to withstand and maintain an internal air pressure of $8\frac{1}{4}$ lb. per square inch. To provide the power necessary to carry this pioneering aircraft, with its thirty-six passengers and crew of seven, four de Havilland Ghost turbine-engines were buried neatly within the wing roots.

This beautiful aircraft, the Comet 1, entered service with B.O.A.C. on the London–Johannesburg route on 2nd May 1952—the world's first jet airliner service—and was immediately an almost unbelievable success. At first considered a wild gamble by the pundits, it quickly demonstrated an ability to operate with trouble-free regularity, and the seemingly amazing reductions in route times it offered, by comparison with piston-engined aircraft, caught the imagination of passengers and operators alike. By the time that B.O.A.C. had extended Comet services to Tokyo, in April 1953, de Havilland had accumulated orders for fifty-two aircraft. The most exciting sale, so far as Britain was concerned,

involved an initial order for three longer-range Comet 3s for Pan American World Airways. It was likely that many more orders would follow if the aircraft proved itself in service and, for the first time, it seemed that a British-built civil airliner might soon be flying with an American international airline.

Then, tragically, two of these aircraft were lost, the second in inexplicable circumstances. When a third Comet, operated by South African Airways, was lost on 8th April 1954, all aircraft of the type were grounded and an urgent and thorough investigation got under way. Remarkable salvage work by the Royal Navy resulted in almost 70 per cent of the fragments of a B.O.A.C. Comet being recovered from the Mediterranean, off the island of Elba. These were taken to the Royal Aircraft Establishment, Farnborough, Hampshire, where scientists and engineers pieced together the huge jigsaw puzzle: by painstaking work they were able to establish that the aircraft's cabin had disintegrated as a result of metal fatigue, caused by repeated cycles of pressurization.

This was one of the most bitter blows that British aviation—and de Havilland in particular—had ever been called upon to bear. Despite it, B.O.A.C. and de Havilland had sufficient confidence in the fundamental design to initiate development of a more advanced version, the Comet 4. Unfortunately for Britain, by the time it became possible for this airliner to enter service on the transatlantic route, the lead over American industry had been lost.

Three months after the loss of the third Comet 1, on 15th July 1954, the Boeing Company had flown the prototype of a jet-powered tanker/transport designated officially Model 367–80, known affectionately to Boeing employees as the 'Dash-Eighty'; it was developed initially as a flight refuelling tanker for the U.S.A.F. Two years after the first flight of the 'Dash-Eighty', on 13th July 1955, the U.S.A.F. permitted Boeing to proceed with commercial developments: on 26th October 1958 Pan American Airways made the first American transatlantic jet-powered commercial flight in what became known as the Boeing 707. However, range of the first production version, the 707–120, was marginal for North Atlantic and other long-distance routes and it was not until the 707–320 Intercontinental entered service in 1959 that this superb aeroplane began to be seen on airports around the world. Powered by four turbojet engines and able to carry up to 202 passengers (–320C), long-range 707s have provided safe, fast and comfortable jet travel, and their success can be measured by the fact that by the end of 1969 major airlines had more than five hundred of these aircraft in service.

The bold concept: de Havilland's Comet 1 jet-powered civil airliner in the insignia of Air France.

The Comet story had been a sad episode for British aviation, and exemplified the hazards of pioneering a new concept. The silver lining to the cloud was the knowledge which accrued to aircraft manufacturers of every nation —knowledge which has enabled the jet airliner to shrink the airlanes of the world and gain for the breed the accolade of giving the highest safety factor of any aircraft type yet constructed.

Fortunately for the British aviation industry they had a second string. This, too, was another pioneering project built around a more economical variation of the jet engine, known as the turboprop, in which the gas turbine drives a conventional propeller through the medium of reduction gearing. The great advantage of this engine concerns its economy of operation by comparison with a pure jet, yet it retains the unique smooth-ness inherent in an engine devoid of reciprocating parts. First production airliner to receive this power plant, in the form of the Rolls-Royce Dart, was the Vickers Viscount 700. This had been evolved from the Vickers VC-2 Viceroy design originally proposed by Vickers to meet the specification of the Brabazon Committee. British European Airways (B.E.A.)—offshoot of B.O.A.C. concerned principally with operations within Europe— had shown interest in the design from the outset. It was they who insisted that the rather cramped thirty-two-seat prototype should be developed as an enlarged and far more comfortable forty-seater. When introduced into service on B.E.A.'s London–Cyprus route on 18th April 1953 it was an immediate success and eventually well over four hundred were built. Most significant was the fact that it was bought by Trans-Canada Air Lines, who

First of the turboprop airliners, and first modern British airliner to break into the American market, a Vickers Viscount of B.E.A. Charles E. Brown

operated the type on their Toronto–New York and Montreal–New York services. This may well have influenced one of the most important sales, sixty Viscounts for Capitol Airlines of America. This represented the first major sale of a British airliner into the American market, and the type eventually served with airlines throughout the world. It was followed by the larger Bristol Britannia, which entered service on B.O.A.C.'s London–Johannesburg route on 1st February 1957, the long-range version plying on the London–New York route in December of the same year. Carrying a maximum of 134 passengers in an all-economy class, the Britannia proved to be another winner for the British industry. It was a winner also for B.O.A.C., having a utilization factor second only to the big pure jets that eventually superseded it.

In parallel with this development of civil air routes for the carriage of passengers, rapidly growing fleets of aircraft were being built specifically for hauling freight, over both short and long ranges. Originally, cargo for carriage by air had fallen neatly into one of three categories: precious, perishable or panic. The first of these groups benefited from the fact that little handling was involved and that once the aircraft was airborne there was no danger of a consignment of industrial diamonds or a fortune in gold bullion being snatched by thieves. In the perishable category came things like cut flowers, cheese, lobsters and exotic fruits to satisfy the demands of new and higher standards of living. In the final category came items like newspapers—for there is nothing deader than yesterday's news—medical supplies and urgently needed spares. The availability of bigger and more specialized aircraft changed all this, and made it possible to carry cargoes ranging from apples to zebras, literally. You produce it, we can fly it, was the motto of the cargo operators and, very often, they could do it more cheaply than by any other route. This was because little handling necessitated only light packaging, and freedom from

The beautiful Britannia, Britain's long-range turboprop airliner that equipped airlines throughout the world.
Shell Photographic Unit

A DC-3 cargo-carrying aircraft of KLM provides a glimpse
of the everyday hardware that goes by air.
Keystone Press

This Canadair CL-44 has a swing-tail to facilitate loading of long or bulky cargo, a typical arrangement with specially developed cargo aircraft.

damage and pilfering produced low insurance rates. Most surprising, perhaps, was the introduction of a car ferry service across the English Channel, started by Silver City Airways in 1948. Fares were higher than by sea at the start, but as the service became popular they gradually got lower. In any event, thousands of travellers on business or holiday were quite prepared to pay a little more for the time saving involved.

The other big trend of post-war development concerned aircraft able to make a vertical take-off and landing (VTOL), and with each passing year this field has grown in importance. That this should be so is immediately clear when one considers, as a simple example, the city-centre to city-centre journey from London to Paris. As surface traffic congestion began to increase, it was not long before the journey by road from central London to London's Heathrow Airport could often exceed the time taken to travel by air from Britain to France, and the same conditions applied at the termination of the air journey. Interestingly, statistics have shown that despite

the enormous advances in aircraft speeds the overall London–Paris journey time had changed little since before the Second World War and that, on occasion, it could be far worse.

Igor Sikorsky who, as already mentioned, had started work on helicopter design in Russia before the First World War, turned to the idea again when he had established his Sikorsky Aircraft Company in the United States. In 1939 he flew his VS-300, the world's first completely practical helicopter, and steady development improved both reliability and performance until the new vehicle could begin to show its paces. The Korean War proved the 'chopper's' ability to carry out tasks beyond the capability of any other vehicle. It could put down or pick up troops in areas virtually inaccessible to surface transport or any other type of aircraft. It was invaluable for picking up wounded men and speeding them to hospital, resulting in a reduction of the death rate from wounds to the lowest figure in military history. And its value in saving lives was not limited to the battlefield:

Rear-loading clam-shell doors of this Breguet Universel shows one solution for rapid off-loading from road vehicles. Air France

The Bristol Freighters of Silver City Airways made cross-Channel journeys easy for car owners.

Specialized aircraft, like this Aero Spacelines Super
Guppy, have been developed to cope with cargo that could
not otherwise be carried by air. The Boeing Company

Igor Sikorsky's VS-300 prototype seen in hovering flight,
the world's first successful helicopter. Sikorsky Aircraft

soon it was rescuing rash holidaymakers cut off by the tide, egg collectors from cliff faces, amateur yachtsmen who had been swept overboard and refugees from floods. The aircraft, for so long associated with death and destruction, was showing that it could also be a dove of peace. Military demands meant that it was not long before helicopters grew in size, to carry more troops or equipment, and this paved the way for civil versions to carry fare-paying passengers. There were, however, some drawbacks to helicopters: they were expensive to operate because vertical take-off demanded engine power far in excess of that required for cruising flight, they were slow and noisy.

Consequently, aircraft designers began to cast about to find other means of achieving VTOL capability, and there were many different approaches. In Britain, Rolls-Royce pioneered jet-lift in 1954, when their ungainly looking 'Flying Bedstead' was shown to be capable of lifting itself from the ground by the thrust of two jet engines. America began to experiment with tilt-wings, in which a more or less conventional wing, on which was mounted the engines, could rotate through 90 degrees. With the engines pointing vertically upwards the pro-

The Rolls-Royce 'Flying Bedstead' which, as early as 1954, pioneered the jet-lift technique.

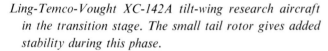

Ling-Temco-Vought XC-142A tilt-wing research aircraft in the transition stage. The small tail rotor gives added stability during this phase.

269

Another form of V/STOL aircraft: the Fairey Rotodyne seen taking off from Battersea heliport.

Sikorsky S-58 helicopter of the Belgian airline SABENA, first airline in the world to provide international passenger services with rotary-wing aircraft.

pellers acted in much the same way as a helicopter's rotor: when airborne the wing was slowly rotated until the propellers were working as normal tractors, with the aircraft's wing providing the lift.

The world's first VTOL airliner was built in Britain by the Fairey Aviation Company, and proved to be a concept far ahead of its time. Virtually a monoplane aircraft powered by two turboprop engines, VTOL capability was provided by a large rotor driven by compressed-air jets located at the tips of the rotor blades. Once airborne, the aircraft flew as normal, except that the rotor auto-rotated and provided only a small amount of lift. With a crew of two and forty to forty-eight passengers, it was designed to have a cruising speed of about 170 mph and range in excess of 400 miles, which would have made it a most valuable aircraft for short-range feeder or cargo operations.

But despite the problems associated with helicopter

Britain's B.E.A. were the first airline to carry passengers by helicopter. Today its Sikorsky S-61Ns offer an exciting start to many a holiday in the Scilly Isles.

B.E.A.

operations there were civil operators who were prepared to experiment and to discover the possibilities and capabilities of such vehicles. They relied in the first instances, as had the embryo fixed-wing airliners, upon the carriage of mail, since this had not the human reactions to being treated as a guinea-pig. Thus, the world's first scheduled rotary-wing service had been started by Eastern Air Lines in the U.S., when experimental mail-carrying operations were initiated on 6th July 1939, using a Kellett KD-1B autogyro. The world's first international helicopter service, again a postal route, was opened by the Belgian airline SABENA on 21st August 1950. Less than a year later B.E.A. carried the first helicopter passengers, on 4th June 1951, but it was SABENA that provided the first international helicopter network, with a steadily increasing route mileage. By mid 1957 they had already carried more than 100,000 passengers.

Private flying was also enjoying rapid growth, particularly in America, where manufacturers like Beech, Cessna and Piper began to produce large numbers of beautifully finished lightweight cabin monoplanes, powered by one or two proven and reliable air-cooled piston engines. The North American continent was an ideal venue for the growth of this branch of aviation. Climatic conditions were, on the whole, fairly reliable: the United States had come out of the war in pretty good financial fettle, and the export potential of her vast manufacturing capacity created rapidly a wealthy nation: above all—no pun intended—there was air space to spare. Production of private aircraft was not limited to recognized manufacturers alone, for with an aviation-minded population separated by great distances the amateur builder began to try his hand. The bulk of these 'home-builts' followed the plans of experienced designers, but many amateurs produced original designs. Some of these looked absolutely right, and proved to be first-class, and in general the standard of finish was immaculate.

In Britain there is not the same scope for expansion, for weather, fuel cost and lack of air space all oppose progress. Some very good light aircraft have been produced with export rather than home market in mind, but sales were pitifully small by comparison with the Big Three in America, Beechcraft, Cessna and Piper: in 1969 Cessna Aircraft Company alone built nearly 6,000 private aircraft, far more than the total number of aircraft of all types built in Great Britain. In 1969 the U.S. aircraft industry produced 14,008 general-purpose aircraft, a category which excludes all civil airliners and all military aircraft.

In Europe, which had problems similar to Britain's, the development of unpowered aircraft—sailplanes—grew rapidly, mainly because geographical conditions favoured soaring flight. In Germany, particularly, the sailplane

Private flying has many aspects, and a beautifully finished aircraft like this Cessna Turbo Super Skylane is often the quickest way to spots off the beaten track.

From private aircraft have evolved air-taxi and third-level airline services. This DHC Twin Otter coming in to a meadow landing exemplifies such operations.

This graceful Fk 3 sailplane manufactured by VFW in Germany is typical of modern development . . .

. . . by contrast, this is the sort of glider that went to war. An American Hamilcar glider swallows a Tetrarch tank.

Charles E. Brown

Besides carrying passengers and fighting battles, aircraft have many peaceful and valuable duties, such as crop-spraying . . .

movement grew to large proportions. This was not surprising, for after the First World War, when Germany was forbidden to build aircraft, her young people still retained a keen appetite for aviation. It was fed by the design and manufacture of sailplanes and Germany soon gained pre-eminence in this branch of aviation.

With the outbreak of the Second World War it might have been expected that the glider would disappear from the scene, for these beautiful and silent craft, soaring and banking on a sun-dappled day could hardly be associated with warlike activities. On the contrary, it was not long before they, too, were enlisted for war service, carrying airborne troops of Allies and enemy alike in some of the most daring exploits of the war. The gliders that went to war were not, of course, the frail-looking beauties that had floated in the summer skies of peace. They had been

enlarged to carry troops and their equipment, and their first major utilization came in Crete, when German Ju 52s towed ten-seat DFS gliders some 200 miles before releasing them to dive down to the carnage below. America and Britain were not slow to follow the German example, and airborne divisions had a vital part to play in the invasion of Normandy, and there can be few who have not read of the heroic but futile airborne operation at Arnhem, in which hundreds of gliders took part. Almost 10,000 airborne troops were involved, carried in gliders or dropped by parachute. In a desperate battle which raged for nine days, some 1,100 of these brave men were killed and more than 6,000 taken prisoner. So failed a bold gamble, one that had offered a chance of ending the war in 1944.

With the end of the Second World War, history was to

274

New Zealand Government photograph

. . . crop dusting . . .

. . . carrying the sick . . .

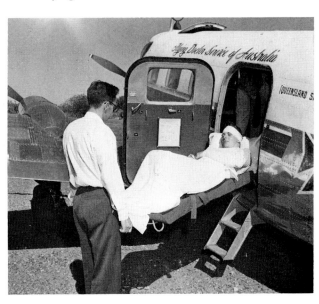

repeat itself, for once again the design and manufacture of aircraft was forbidden to the German people. As before, youthful zeal to participate in aviation quickly revived the sailplane movement. This time, new constructional techniques and advanced materials meant that a much refined breed of high-performance sailplane began to appear and, not unnaturally, their participation in international contests soon raised standards throughout the world and aroused widespread interest in this sport. The West European nations, however, with no restrictions on the development of aircraft, soon began the design and construction of light planes. Nowhere was this more apparent than in France, where there was a complete resurgence of interest in aviation, and this country began to build new and interesting aircraft for the private owner. Unfortunately these nations all suffer

. . . and fighting forest fires by water bombing.

from much the same limitations that have frustrated the growth of private flying in Britain.

In America the annual construction figure of private aircraft began to assume staggering proportions and, as manufacturers gained wider experience of market requirements, they started to develop more advanced versions of their models to satisfy a growing demand for air-taxi and business aircraft, soon a healthy segment of their production. This is logical, because for business or holiday flights freedom from inflexible schedules is important. Furthermore, the light plane designed to have operating economics that would interest a private individual could obviously allow the carriage of fare-paying passengers—few though they might be per load—at realistic fares. The result has been an exciting growth in a completely new area of civil operations.

Business aviation has grown in parallel with civil aviation, for shrinkage of the world by high-speed communications has meant that new markets for the products of the manufacturing nations have been growing all the time. This, in turn, has made for greater competition and the need for more advanced sales techniques. The company that could first get its marketing and technical team in front of a potential buyer were often more than half way to getting a sale. Builders of light aircraft the world over have been quick to appreciate this requirement, and as a result competition has become very keen, with a wide range of attractive aircraft becoming available in the six-to-ten seat category. Typical of such aircraft is the British Hawker Siddeley HS 125 twin-jet executive transport, powered by two rear-mounted Rolls-Royce turbojet engines. Able to operate from unpaved runways, this aircraft accommodates a crew of two and has luxury seating for seven passengers, who are carried in an air-conditioned and pressurized cabin. Maximum cruising speed is 510 mph at 31,000 feet, and range of the latest versions can exceed 1,900 miles.

Even now, we have not covered the broad and colourful palette which depicted the expanding post-war aviation scene. Aircraft of one sort or another were adopted to spray or dust crops, control traffic, make aerial surveys, carry patients to hospital, to fight fires, help nature conservation, promote rainfall, feed starving cattle, inspect fence-lines and power cables, relieve lighthouse keepers, *ad infinitum*. The list is almost endless.

After the First World War Orville Wright had said of aviation: 'What a dream it was, what a nightmare it has become.' It is a pity that he could not have lived to see that the aeroplane, so often harnessed by men to the chariot of war, was capable also of the far wider and wiser peaceful applications of which the pioneers had dreamed.

7
Aviation into the Seventies

A short news item on the front page of the *Daily Mail* on 20th January 1970 carried the headline *Liner for Sale*: it told, briefly, that the 26,500-ton liner *Empress of England* was on the market because competition from air traffic was making its operation uneconomic: a rather apposite illustration of the growth and importance of air transport and an appropriate introduction to a brief review of the aviation scene at the beginning of the seventies.

It will be remembered that, with a magnificent sprint, de Havilland had first taken the lead in the jet airliner prestige race. Other countries were not prepared to let Britain snatch the glittering prize of massive international sales. In the event, the disastrous structural failure of the Comet lost Britain the lead, and by the time she had got back in the running with the Comet 4, both America and Russia were well to the fore.

In the United States Pan American had been first into the jet age, ordering twenty Boeing 707s and twenty-four Douglas DC-8s: both were formidable aeroplanes with almost double the capacity of the most advanced piston-engined airliners and offered ranges in excess of 5,000 miles. Close behind, at the prototype stage, came the Soviet Union's Tupolev Tu-104, a medium-range twin-turbojet airliner that transformed Aeroflot's route times. For example, on the Moscow–Irkutsk route the schedule was cut from twenty hours to just over seven and, quite

Line up at Vnukovo Airport, Moscow, shows an Ilyushin Il-18 at right and a row of Tupolev Tu-104's. These *latter aircraft transformed the whole of Aeroflot's operations. B.E.A.*

naturally, Aeroflot introduced these jets just as fast as they could be built. By the time that the Boeing 707 entered service, on 26th October 1958, Russia had experienced a second revolution—this time an entirely peaceful one—in which the whole country had become overlaid with a network of fast air services. Aeroflot has long enjoyed the reputation of being the world's biggest airline—in 1969 it carried nearly seventy million passengers—but it has also, at times, had to suffer not entirely just criticism as the world's poorest or most backward. Be this as it may, the jets gave the airline a new lease of life, and it has never needed to look back. Traffic increased so enormously that it became possible to compete on level terms with conventional surface travel: in some cases air fares for a given route were lower than those of the snail-slow and often uncomfortable railways.

The Boeing 707 entered service on Pan American's North Atlantic service on 26th October 1958 and immediately showed itself to be an outstanding aircraft, and as advanced versions of the 707 began to appear—offering increased range—the early model was withdrawn from transatlantic services for use on shorter-range domestic routes. The long-range version of the Douglas DC-8 entered service on 27th March 1960, followed by the Convair 880 in January 1961.

At much the same period the French industry produced a remarkable short-haul airliner, the Sud-Aviation Caravelle, which has its two jet engines mounted at the rear of the aircraft, one on each side of the fuselage. This made for a cleaner and more efficient wing and improved take-off performance and provided a far quieter cabin environment for its passengers. An immediate success, the Caravelle quickly dominated short-haul routes throughout Europe. The rear-mounted engine configuration was soon taken up by America, Britain and Russia, the former introducing the medium-range Boeing 727

278

A Douglas DC-8, one of the first of the long-range 'big-jets', in the insignia of Air Canada.

A beautiful aeroplane beautifully decorated with the insignia of Delta Air Lines, a Convair 880.

First of the rear-engined jet airliners was the Sud-Aviation Caravelle. Other nations soon followed suit . . .

with three and Douglas DC-9 with two engines. Britain's contributions were the BAC VC10 with four, Hawker Siddeley Trident with three and BAC One-Eleven with two engines, and Russia was a little later with the Ilyushin Il-62 powered by four, the Tupolev Tu-165 with three and Tu-134 powered by two engines.

The foregoing jet aircraft are representative of the types which today serve the world's airlines. Not only have they reduced flight times around the world, they have also introduced completely new standards of travel and safety and such was the early prestige of the big jets that they automatically attracted the majority of fare-paying passengers. They have, at this period of aviation history, two in-built snags, the first of which is noise. Anyone who lives near a major airport must regard aviation as a mixed blessing. Irritation from this source seems likely to increase unless engine technologists

. . . Britain's variation on the theme was the BAC VC10 . . .

. . . while Russia produced the Tupolev Tu-134 twin-turbofan airliner . . .

Martin Fricke, Zürich

. . . and last, but not least, the highly successful Boeing 727.

*Airbus of the future—today—the Boeing 747 'Jumbo-jet',
designed to carry up to 490 passengers over intercontinental ranges.* The Boeing Company

succeed in effecting a considerable reduction in noise
levels. But since noise has never yet halted progress it
may mean that major airports will become sited even
more remotely from city centres. The second problem is
one that comes under the heading of comfort. The
enormous capital cost of these modern airliners demands
high utilization factors if they are to prove a satisfactory
investment for their operators. This has meant that seat-
pitch and elbow-room have shrunk to an uncomfortable
minimum. Furthermore, operating economics have
dictated cruising altitudes which, unfortunately, coincide
all too often with areas of considerable turbulence. Little
wonder that older citizens refer nostalgically to the
golden days of aviation, when flying-boats offered
standards of comfort that have disappeared into memory.
Perhaps they can wipe those emotional tears from their

eyes and look at the aeroplanes of now and the immediate future which may—if only temporarily—offer
even better standards of comfort, plus far smoother and
less tiring travel at jet-age route times.

The first of such aircraft, operated by Pan American,
made its maiden passenger-carrying flight from New
York to London on 22nd January 1970, and there is
surely no one with the slightest interest in aviation who
cannot be impressed by this huge aeroplane—the Boeing
747 'Jumbo-jet'. Designed to carry no fewer than 490
passengers in an all-economy configuration, current
utilization factors have set a 362-seat layout, comprising
304 economy and 58 first class, which means, for the time
being, spacious and luxurious passenger accommodation,
with room to stretch out and walk around. Furthermore,
the advanced turbofan engines which power the 747,

when fully developed, may enable it to cruise economically at an altitude that will carry it above most of the turbulence. Of course, Boeing are not alone in the development of these giant airliners—they were first: but some industrial leaders are already posing the question as to whether or not they are several years too early. To distort a well-known saying, every silver lining has its cloud, and the 747 and similar aircraft which will follow it into service are no exception. They will impose great handling problems on the ground, with so many passengers and their luggage to leave and join the aircraft. On the apron these mammoth airliners will be surrounded by a mass of equipment seeking to provide fuel, oil, water, food, linen, toilet facilities, in-flight entertainment and other requirements in unprecedented quantities. If the capital cost of these super-jets is to be repaid in a short enough period to save their owners' accountants from stomach ulcers—or worse—the turn-round time is critical. The Jumbo-jet, like any other aircraft plying for revenue, earns money only when it is in the air, comfortably laden with passengers, or cargo, or both. These last eight words are important.

It is not easy to gaze into a crystal ball and assert that this or that will happen, but at the present time there appears to be a case for the development of large exclusively cargo-carrying aircraft. Whether this turns out to be justified will depend largely upon whether or not it becomes economic to carry ordinary consumer goods by air, rather than the more specialized cargoes carried at the present time. A different line of thought has developed

This full-scale interior mock-up of a Boeing 747 gives some hint of the standards of comfort that can be offered in wide-fuselage transport aircraft.

The Boeing Company

transport aircraft with convertible interiors: in this configuration the aircraft can be used for all-passenger or all-cargo traffic and, by utilizing easily removed or folding seats in conjunction with a movable bulkhead, any permutation between these two extremes, to ensure that on every flight the aircraft is economically loaded. It seems possible, however, that developed versions of the new large commercial transports, or new generations of aircraft evolved from them, will have adequate under-floor cargo holds to fulfil the majority of demands for cargo space and that, in the course of time, such aircraft will completely replace the ocean liner. This form of surface transport would then serve only to carry those people who fancy sea air and more leisurely travel.

There is little doubt, of course, that there will always be transport aircraft to lift specialized cargo; for instance, the American-built Aero Spacelines Super Guppy 201. Developed from the earlier Super Guppy—which had been designed to air-lift whole sections of large booster rockets—the commercial model is currently employed in carrying the assembled sections of an entire DC-10 fuselage or the two wings of an L-1011 TriStar from subcontractors to the final assembly line.

The second type of the new generation of passenger aircraft is already flying, too, albeit in prototype form. These are the new Supersonic Transports (SSTs)—the BAC/Sud-Aviation Concorde in Britain and France, the Tupolev Tu-144 in Russia—both of roughly the same size and designed to cruise at above Mach 2. The Concorde, flying at a height of more than 9 miles above the Atlantic, will shrink distance to the extent that London and New York will be only $3\frac{1}{2}$ hours apart. In America, Boeing also planned to build an SST, known as the Model 2707-300. This was to have been almost twice the size of the SSTs born on the other side of what may soon become known as the Atlantic Channel. Unfortunately a recession in the American aircraft industry has made it impossible to finance construction of prototypes of the Boeing 2707-300. If the Concorde and the Tu-144 are successful in airline service they will prove to be very important for the aviation industry of their respective countries. These will be the true Queens of the Air, riding the high skies. Yet they, too, have one rather disconcerting problem, in the form of the sonic boom which is created by any aircraft flying faster than the speed of sound. This may limit overland speeds to below Mach 1, unless the scientists and engineers find some way of eliminating this effect, which can be both noisy and damaging.

Biggest, and possibly the most important, expansion must come in STOL (short take-off and landing) and VTOL transport aircraft, thus allowing them to come

Not a super-carousel at Coney Island, but San Francisco's International Airport. Airliners earn revenue only when in the air, so modern layouts are needed to provide quick turn-round . . .

. . . the TWA Satellite building at Los Angeles Airport provides another example.

close to, if not within, city centres. At the moment of writing Germany leads development in this field with many V/STOL transport projects. The Dornier Do 31, for example, is intended to carry 100 passengers and will have Rolls-Royce turbofan engines for propulsion and lift-fan engines by the same manufacturer for VTOL capability. The Hamburger-Flugzeugbau HFB 600 project, which also relies upon direct jet lift, will be slightly smaller. Of about the same size is the Messerschmitt-Bölkow-Blohm BO 140, but this utilizes the tilt-wing technique described earlier.

Inevitably, of course, such a capability appeals to military planners, for a strike/reconnaissance aircraft able to operate from a base close to the front line without need for a prepared landing strip would be of great importance. Such is the Hawker Siddeley Harrier with which Britain has pioneered this concept, a single-seat close-support and reconnaissance aircraft which can fly close to the speed of sound, and yet is able to take off and land vertically.

One must not overlook the still-developing helicopter which has shown its ability to perform Herculean tasks. For example, the Soviet Mil V-12, largest helicopter yet flown, has set a world weight-lifting record by carrying a 88,635 lb. payload (nearly 40 tons!) to a height of over 7,000 feet. The continuing war in Vietnam has also speeded American thinking and techniques, thus hastening the development of the helicopter. Products of the American industry have demonstrated under the most severe conditions their practicability as heavily armed combat aircraft, fast troop transporters, ambulance aircraft and breakdown 'choppers'. This last category concerns helicopters used to rescue disabled aircraft forced down in enemy-held or remote territory. As an

The BAC/Sud-Aviation Concorde 001 prototype in flight over Paris.

example, by January 1971 Boeing CH-47 Chinooks operating in Vietnam had retrieved no fewer than 10,000 aircraft valued at around $2·7 billion. Helicopters have also demonstrated speeds in excess of 300 mph and there is every reason to believe that this figure will soon be exceeded as a result of intensive research to produce higher speeds, quieter operation and greater economy.

Production of light aircraft, especially in America, has reached staggering proportions, and even the seemingly unlimited air space over North America will soon become cluttered. One wonders how much time will elapse before the demands of safety result in a clash between the differing needs of commercial and private flying. It is now becoming essential throughout the world that private flying comes under the guiding hand of air traffic control, and this means inevitably that the cost of private flying will increase. Pilots will need more specialized training to enable them to operate the costly and sophisticated navigation and communications equipment they will have to carry if they want to share crowded air space with commercial operators who, presumably, will retain prior claim.

Safety in the air is, as always, the prime concern of those connected with aviation at whatever level they may be involved. Since jet airliners have set a superb safety record, we have come to realize that the loss of a very occasional aircraft together with around 100 passengers is an acceptable risk because of its very infrequency. We cannot, however, view with complacency the prospect of losing an airbus with close on 500 passengers. Such thinking will ensure that maximum emphasis will be placed on development of the even more sophisticated navigation equipment that will be needed as the increased population of the air brings aeroplanes travelling at ever higher speeds nearer to one another. A glimpse of the kind of development that may do much to help this situation was given by the news that on 20th October 1969 the national carrier of Finland, Finnair, became the world's first airline to use an inertial navigation system, enabling accurate navigation on scheduled transoceanic passenger flights without a human navigator being carried on board the aircraft. Autopilot and autolanding techniques are the subject of intensive research and development and there is no doubt that landing, still one

*Russia's SST, the Tupolev Tu-144, looks like some strange
bird in this photograph.* Novosti Press Agency

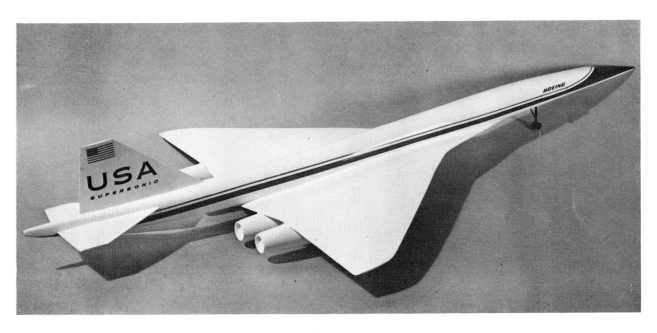

*Model of the larger and faster American SST project, the
Boeing 2707-300, axed by economic recession.*

V/STOL research aircraft, the German Dornier Do 31, in hovering flight. Brian Mackenzie Service

V/STOL operational strike/reconnaissance aircraft, the British Hawker Siddeley Harrier GR. Mk 1, takes off from a disused coal yard in central London.
Hawker Siddeley Aviation

Russian Yakovlev experimental VTOL fighter aircraft demonstrated in 1967. Tass

of the most hazardous areas of the entire flight parameter, due to varying conditions of visibility, will soon be controlled by 'black boxes' that can 'see' in any weather. As long ago as 16th May 1969 a Super VC10 operated by B.O.A.C., with 146 passengers on board, made the first completely automatic landing on a scheduled flight from Chicago and Montreal.

But to put the safety of air travel in perspective it is worth recording that in 1969 the world's scheduled international airlines, excluding Aeroflot, carried close upon 200 million passengers with a fatality rate so low that an individual could make more than a hundred round-the-world flights without raising a single hair in fright. Which makes travel by air very safe indeed.

However, the crowded skies over Britain leave doubts that private flying can or will increase. But for those who still like to see light planes and hear the once-familiar sound of small propeller-driven aircraft there is the possibility that at least one aspect of sport aviation will enjoy a tremendous expansion in the near future. This is air racing, which has become immensely popular in America, and which draws crowds of thousands. Since the event takes place in the air, with the aircraft flying around short pylon-marked courses, it means that the spectators can see everything that happens and the position of their own favourite. Thus it has the thrills of motor racing without the disadvantage of long periods when there is no action. At the moment there seems every prospect that this new aviation-age entertainment medium will spread to Britain, unless the high noise factor goes against it.

This brief picture of aviation in the seventies must close with a glimpse at the gliding movement, offering scope to those who prefer to take an active part. This branch of heavier-than-air flight is currently enjoying a steady growth and more manufacturers of these craft are turning to the provision of powered gliders. This should increase instructional facilities, the lack of which has, until this time, proved a barrier to wider participation in one of the most enjoyable mediums of flight. Banking slowly and majestically in the azure sky, in silent and graceful flight, the glider offers to man the world over an opportunity to experience the dream that inspired the first pioneers, so very long ago.

A US Army CH-47A Chinook helicopter carrying a disabled US Navy T-2A training aircraft.

Typical of the highly professional 'home-builts' which form a large part of American private flying are these D'Apuzzo Senior Aero Sports. Howard Levy

Autoland in action: a BEA Trident landing at London Airport in fog conditions. Hawker Siddeley

First of three prototype Cassutt racers, built in Britain by Airmark, is typical of the aircraft to be seen in exciting air races over England.

8

Man into Space

Most of us have enjoyed fireworks at some time or other, if only by ooohing and aaahing at a grand display on some never-to-be-forgotten occasion and, of course, fireworks have been known for centuries. There is, however, no precise record of when rockets were first used. History tells that they were employed widely some seven hundred years ago, principally for military purposes, continuing in use until the gradual development of artillery and small firearms supplanted them: that is for quite a few years.

At the beginning of the nineteenth century they shed their military connections when a more peaceful application of this projectile was initiated by Henry Trengrouse, who lived in Cornwall, England. The rocky coastline of Cornwall was dangerous to shipping, and rough weather frequently caused vessels to be crippled quite close in to the shore, where wild seas and needle-toothed rocks often made rescue of the crew impossible. Trengrouse's solution was to attach one end of a light line to a rocket, the other to a stout rope, strong enough to provide a means of escape for the men on board the foundering ship. When the rocket carried the line over the ship, it could be hauled in, dragging the heavier rope behind it. The technique was gradually improved and continues to save lives to this day.

It is a long step from Cornwall to the vast country of Russia, the homeland of a man who has become recognized as the father of space flight, Konstantin Eduardovich Tsiolkowsky. As early as 1903 this far-thinking man designed a rocket-powered spacecraft, specifying that the rocket should be fuelled by liquid propellants, similar to those in use today. Tsiolkowsky was also first to realize that a multi-stage rocket would be needed to provide the speed necessary to escape from the Earth's gravitational pull, and suggested that as each stage consumed its propellants it should be made to fall away, thus reducing the total weight to be accelerated to still higher speeds by the remaining stages. A theorist only, he died in 1935 before experimenters of a new generation had proved his ideas to be sound.

Theory advanced a little further under the guidance of the German Hermann Oberth, originally a Hungarian citizen, who published a book in 1923 which explained how a rocket was able to travel in a vacuum and could be used to launch a satellite. His work went beyond theory, for he designed some quite advanced rockets: unfortunately, those that he tested were not very successful. Contemporary with Oberth was the American, Robert Goddard, the most important figure in the early development of rocketry. It was he who carried out early research which led to the construction of a small liquid-propellant rocket engine which ran successfully for the first time in 1923. Twelve years later his work had prospered to the extent that he was able to launch a 15-foot rocket which climbed to a height of $1\frac{1}{2}$ miles and attained a speed of 700 mph. Goddard continued with his experiments until his death in 1945 but, like many pioneers, his achievements were largely unrecognized until many years later.

It was Germany that took the lead, beginning in 1927 with foundation of the *Verein für Raumschiffahrt* (VfR, Society for Space Travel). This was no government organization but a group of enthusiastic students interested in rocketry as a means of travel. Within four years of their first experiments the VfR had developed rockets able to climb almost a mile into the sky.

But by 1934, when the students were beginning to acquire valuable knowledge, the new Nazi regime brought an end to activities and one of their brighter experimenters, Wernher von Braun, found himself working for the German Army. Here, during the course of the next eleven years, he collaborated with an army officer called Walter Dornberger—who eventually rose to the rank of major-general. Together they led a team which developed a series of bombardment rockets, culminating in the A-4, which was tested with complete success on 3rd October 1942, when it attained a height of 50 miles and covered a range of 120 miles. So it was that on the evening of 8th September 1944 mysterious explosions shook the London suburbs of Chiswick and Epping almost simultaneously. Hitler's V-2 reprisal weapon (the A-4 rocket in fact) had been launched against England in the hope of turning the tide of battle. But it was too late and there were too few of them: this new and terrifying weapon was little more than an extension of the annoyance caused by the V-1 'Buzz-bomb'—so far as the British people were concerned—and certainly had no effect on the outcome of the war.

When the Allies swept across Germany as Nazi resistance began to crumble, both East and West scrambled to gain possession of German secrets, scientists and stocks of the V-weapons. Thus, Wernher von Braun,

A modified Redstone rocket lifts off carrying a Mercury spacecraft.

one-time member of the VfR, who had been interested in reaching out to space from his student days, became established in America, and it was not long before he was put in charge of a team of engineers at the U.S. Army's Redstone Arsenal in Alabama. Their first project was a ballistic missile, named Redstone, after its birthplace, and this—with interchangeable high-explosive or nuclear warheads—first became operational in 1956. When, in the course of time, it became obsolete as a missile, it was given a new lease of life as an interim booster rocket, one of the early fingers probing out into space. There was, of course, a lot of probing to be done. The prospect of space flight was exciting, but before America could even begin to consider some of the less heady possibilities it was necessary to gather in a great deal of information. Consequently, a start was made by designing and constructing a number of research rockets to gain knowledge of the upper atmosphere and this led, eventually, to development of the Viking rocket which, when launched for the first time on 3rd May 1949, climbed to a height of 50 miles. This was a satisfying start, but it was not long before other Vikings were showing even greater promise and Viking II, for example, achieved the then record height of 158 miles, carrying 852 lb. of instruments. Clearly, worthwhile progress was being made and American scientists and rocket engineers, with growing confidence, began to talk of putting a satellite into Earth orbit during the 1957 International Geophysical Year.

America was forestalled by the achievement of the Soviet Union which, on 4th October 1957, announced that a satellite called Sputnik I was in orbit. As a result of this Russia gained enormous national prestige and the rest of the world was free to conjecture the implications of this Communist success. Understandably, the Americans were both astonished and disappointed: their astonishment stemmed from the disclosure that the Russian satellite weighed 184 lb., implying the possession of booster rockets of far greater power than any yet developed by them. However, things seemed a little brighter when the first Vanguard rocket—intended as their satellite launcher—made a satisfying first flight on 23rd October 1957. Their elation was shortlived, for the next two Vanguards were complete failures.

A greater shock was to come, for on 3rd November 1957 Russia announced that Sputnik II had been launched successfully, carrying on board the first living creature to travel in space, a dog named Laika. Animal lovers the world over were deeply concerned when, eight days later, Laika was painlessly put to death; the fact was, however, that at that state of the art no one knew how to recover a satellite from orbit.

Close-up of the 'Vostok I' spacecraft which carried Russia's Yuri Gagarin, first man to orbit the Earth.

'Flight International'

What really staggered the Americans was not the news that an animal was travelling around the Earth, but that the payload introduced into orbit weighed nearly half a ton. Defence planners of the Western world viewed this knowledge with great concern; it was clear that the Russians possessed booster rockets of immense power and it suggested that her military rockets might be far in advance of those developed by the West. Immediately the American aerospace industry began to intensify its efforts to get ahead in what the journalists of the world were already beginning to call the 'space race'. So it is not surprising that the successful launch of a Jupiter-C rocket, on 31st January 1958, which put into orbit an 18-lb. satellite named Explorer I, came as something of an anti-climax. In fact, it need not have done, for Explorer I was so advanced—due to American progress in the development of miniaturized equipment—that it was able to supply new and vital information.

Data received from Sputnik II had suggested that there

'Vostok I' attached to its cylindrical instrument section, containing all essential equipment. The 'Vostok I' was released from this before entering Earth's atmosphere after a single orbit.

was little danger to life from cosmic and solar radiation while travelling in orbit. Explorer I had a quite different story to tell, for Geiger tubes placed on board to measure radiation were put out of action. Later space probes, and Explorer XII in particular, were able to confirm the existence of what has become known as the Van Allen belt, a huge belt of radiation surrounding the Earth, running parallel to the equator, with relatively clear areas above the Poles. There was no doubt that the more-cautious approach of the American scientists was proving worth while. The steady launch of space probes provided a wealth of know-how, and as the technique of putting payloads into orbit became more precise it was possible to try out ideas that would offer immediate benefit to the world in general. The first of these, which demonstrated to the ordinary citizen that even he would gain some benefit from the 'king's ransom' being spent on space research, was given the name of Telstar. This was a relay satellite, able to send back to Earth tele-

vision signals that would otherwise be 'lost in space'. Thus, for the first time, television viewers in Europe were able to watch events as they were happening on the other side of the Atlantic.

America continued her steady accumulation of knowledge, sending two small monkeys on a 1,500-mile flight in a Jupiter missile nose-cone, following this, on 31st January 1961, by launching a Mercury spacecraft carrying a chimpanzee. This was the vehicle intended to carry her first man into space and, with no knowledge of Russian progress, it was excitingly uncertain who would be first to achieve this important goal.

It was made abundantly clear who was first on 12th April 1961, when Major Yuri Gagarin, a cosmonaut of the Soviet Union, made a single orbit of the Earth in the *Vostok I* spacecraft, which weighed 10,418 lb. Any disappointment the Americans may have felt at being beaten to this first vital step was offset by their spontaneous appreciation of the Russian achievement. For the first time it seemed possible that competition might become co-operation in space, leading to a better understanding between East and West. Unfortunately, such thoughts were premature.

However, in the following month America recorded a first sub-orbital flight, when astronaut Cdr Alan B. Shepard was launched down the Atlantic Missile Range in a Mercury capsule, attaining a height of 115 miles before dropping back to Earth. As the Mercury capsule neared the sea, its fall was arrested by a parachute, and Alan Shepard was recovered none the worse for his exploit. But for America—and the U.S. Marine Corps—20th February 1962 was the great day, when Lt-Col. John Glenn was carried into orbit by an Atlas booster rocket. He completed an almost trouble-free flight of three orbits in his Mercury spacecraft, *Friendship 7*, before firing his retrorockets to plunge back through the Earth's atmosphere. *Almost* trouble-free, because the automatic control system that should have guided the capsule during re-entry and landing failed, and Glenn had to take over manual control. Following a successful splash-down and recovery, America went wild at her first resounding space success.

American astronaut Alan B. Shepard inspects the Mercury spacecraft 'Freedom 7' after completing his 302-mile sub-orbital flight down the Atlantic Missile Range. NASA

The important and rewarding Mercury programme, during which six of these satellites were launched, terminated on 16th May 1963, following a most satisfactory flight in which Major Gordon Cooper had travelled more than half a million miles in twenty-two orbits of the Earth, setting the stage for America's next step, Project Gemini.

This is anticipating Russian developments, however, for that country had also made considerable progress, including a day-long orbital journey by cosmonaut Herman Titov on 6th–7th August 1961 in *Vostok II*. Just over a year later *Vostok III*, carrying Andrian Nikolayev, had been launched and, on the following day, *Vostok IV* followed it into orbit with Paval Popovich aboard. Before landing, on 15th August, these two spacecraft had approached to within three miles of each other while in orbit, demonstrating that the Russians were getting close to the technique of space rendezvous that was vital before men could think of travelling towards the goal that spurred the efforts of scientists of East and West—the Moon. When the Russians repeated this exercise, in June of the following year, it was a unique occasion because one of the cosmonauts was Valentina Tereshkova, who became the first woman to travel in space.

On 12th October 1964 Russia launched a much larger spacecraft, *Voskhod I*, able to carry a crew of three. It was followed just over five months later by *Voskhod II*, carrying Col. Pavel Belyayev and Lt-Col. Aleksi Leonov. This spacecraft had an air-lock, making it possible for a cosmonaut to leave the craft while in orbit, and this amazing 'first' was achieved when Lt-Col. Leonov 'walked in space', floating alongside the capsule, to which he was attached by a tether. Hundreds of miles above the Earth he was able to operate a small television camera attached to the outside of the spacecraft. Not until June 1965 did American astronaut Edward H. White take a short 'walk' in space.

But the Americans were beginning to claw back the Soviet lead: five days after the launch of *Voskhod II* a Titan rocket put the Gemini III spacecraft into orbit, carrying Virgil Grissom and John Young. They carried out initial experiments to gain information necessary for later craft to rendezvous in orbit. This knowledge was exploited to the full on 15th December 1965 when Gemini VII, which had already been in orbit for eleven days with astronauts Frank Borman and James Lovell on board, accomplished the first-ever rendezvous between two spacecraft, cruising almost alongside Gemini VI carrying Walter Schirra and Tom Stafford. For four hours the two crews remained within feet of each other, and the photographs taken by Stafford were the most

An Atlas booster rocket carrying Mercury spacecraft 'Friendship 7' leaves the launch-pad with Lt-Col. John Glenn aboard, America's first astronaut to make an Earth orbital flight. NASA

dramatic photographs then seen. Gemini VI landed safely on 16th December: when Gemini VII splashed down successfully on 18th December, Borman and Lovell had completed a record 205 orbits and fourteen days in space. Clearly, man could travel in space long enough to get to the Moon and back.

By this time American astronauts had acquired a valuable grounding in essential techniques and the National Aeronautics and Space Administration (NASA), which controlled the whole of the nation's space programmes, had gained a great deal of confidence from the success of the early Geminis. This programme terminated with the flight of Gemini XII, during which Edwin Aldrin spent five and a half hours outside the spacecraft. This was important, determining both man's ability to work in space and the efficiency of the life-support system of his space-suit. America was fast becoming an advanced practitioner of the new art of space technology.

But before man could seriously think about an attempt to land on the Moon, even assuming that the hardware and the know-how to get there and back could be

Astronaut Edward H. White 'walks' in space. He was secured to his Gemini spacecraft by a 25-ft umbilical line and a 23-ft tether line, gold-taped together to form a single cord. NASA

Gemini VII as seen from Gemini VI when these two spacecraft made the first historic rendezvous in space on 15th December 1965. NASA

realized, it was vital to learn a great deal about Earth's natural satellite.

Both East and West began to launch probes towards the Moon, seeking information. Russia's *Luna II* was first to make contact—crashing into the lunar surface on 14th September 1959. This success was followed by an even greater achievement in the following month, when *Luna III* transmitted back to Earth the first photographs of the hidden side of the Moon, taken from a distance of 40,000 miles. America built a series of Ranger spacecraft to find out more detailed information. The first of these craft were set a far too complicated task and failed. When their role was simplified to a simple photographic mission success was immediate and spectacular. Rangers 7 and 8 provided superb close-up photographs of the Moon before they crashed down on the lunar surface, but it was Ranger 9 that thrilled the world. The view seen by its television camera as it sped towards the Moon was relayed on television circuits, and millions of people had their first live view of the cratered and mountainous surface that seemed a rather frightening and remote landing place for man. Ranger was followed by the even more successful Lunar Orbiters which between them photographed almost 100 per cent of the Moon's surface in 1966–7, a total of about fourteen million square miles. But although the photographs were excellent, and absolutely essential, it was necessary to know more about the composition of the lunar soil before a spacecraft could land there. Some scientists had suggested that the surface might be covered with a layer of dust, so deep that a spacecraft would sink in and be unable to take off again.

Russia, however, gained this important first when *Luna IX* soft-landed on the Moon on 3rd February 1966. Once again the U.S. was not far behind, for on 30th May Surveyor I also made a successful soft landing and immediately began to transmit back to Earth thousands of high-quality photographs: this and subsequent Surveyors were able to satisfy NASA scientists that a spacecraft could land safely on the Moon and take off again. By this time the Apollo programme was well under way, its aim being to put two men on the Moon by 1970 and return them safely to Earth. As early as 28th May 1961, a first 'boilerplate' version of the Apollo command module had been launched into orbit, and further launchings with unmanned Apollos continued, to check and re-check the vital components and operations that could only be tested fully in a space environment. Unfortunately, the otherwise successful programme received a tragic setback on 27th January 1967, when astronauts Virgil Grissom, Edward White and Roger Chaffee lost their lives when fire swept through their capsule during ground tests.

So it was not until 11th October 1968 that astronauts Walter Schirra, Walter Cunningham and Don Eisele were blasted off from Cape Kennedy, in Apollo 7, to record America's first manned space flight since the very successful Gemini XII mission of 1966. Just over two months later, Apollo 8 carried Frank Borman, James Lovell and William Anders towards the Moon, and generous television coverage of this exciting event made Christmas Eve 1968 memorable both for Earth-bound mortals and for those bound for the Moon. Seen from an orbit 70 miles above the lunar surface, the alien-looking landscape passed slowly beneath the circling spacecraft. Perhaps for the first time, as they watched television pictures of their own world taken from a quarter of a million miles out in space, ordinary men and women could begin to appreciate something of the marvel that is our universe and understand why—whatever the cost—man has been lured on to seek greater knowledge.

Apollo 9, launched on 3rd March 1969, was given the important task of flight testing the lunar module in

Artist's impression of a Lunar Orbiter: five of these American spacecraft photographed almost the entire lunar surface.

Russia's Luna IX was the first spacecraft to make a soft landing on the Moon and relay back to Earth photographs taken on the lunar surface. Novosti Press Agency

The alien-looking surface of the Moon. A photograph taken by Apollo 11. NASA

Earth orbit, as well as carrying out final checks on the critical rendezvous and docking manœuvres. Thus the stage was set for the dress rehearsal. When Apollo 10 was launched from Cape Kennedy on 18th May 1969, the tension was beginning to build up, for it was clear that a successful Apollo 10 mission could bring a Moon-landing within weeks. It was successful, and Thomas Stafford and Eugene Cernan, descending to within 9 miles of the Moon's surface in their lunar module, must have wished that it was they—so near and yet so far—who could make the first historic touch-down. They could, however, comfort themselves with the knowledge that the techniques they tested so successfully would make the task of their fellow astronauts a little easier.

Finally came the day that thousands had worked for years to make possible, that millions had thought a wild and unattainable dream—16th July 1969, when Neil Armstrong (Commander), Edwin Aldrin (lunar module pilot) and Michael Collins (command module pilot) were lifted away from mother Earth on the great adventure. Four days later Armstrong and Aldrin made their way from the command module, called *Columbia* for the operation, and entered the lunar module *Eagle*, for a series of final checks. Then, at 2011 BST, the descent engine was fired and *Eagle* began the final stage of its journey.

Breathlessly, men, women and children throughout the world watched over the astronauts' shoulders as television brought the drama right into their living-rooms. When, close to the surface, Armstrong took over manual control to avoid an area strewn with boulders and rocks, hearts pounded in and out of this world, and it seemed as if time stood still. Seconds later, in a flurry of lunar dust, *Eagle* settled on the Moon's surface and waiting millions heard the words: 'Contact lights. O.K., engine stop. Tranquillity Base here. The *Eagle* has landed.'

The Americans had made it after all. An alien ship from another world had reached a temporary harbour in the Sea of Tranquillity, and a more appropriately named landfall could not exist.

The Apollo 11 mission ended on a high note of success when, on 24th July 1969, the command module splashed down within about 13 miles of the prime recovery vessel.

On 14th November, Apollo 12 was launched towards the Moon with an all-U.S. Navy crew aboard: Cdr Charles Conrad was the mission commander, Cdr Richard F. Gordon command module pilot and Cdr Alan Bean the lunar module pilot. The mission started dramatically enough, the launch taking place when heavy thunderclouds were overhead, and an on-board power

*A Saturn V booster rocket blasts-off from pad 39A at
Kennedy Space Center, carrying Apollo 11 en route to
the Moon.* NASA

First Man on the Moon! Neil A. Armstrong is setting up a Seismic Experiments package, with the Lunar Module 'Eagle' standing in the background. NASA

An unusual shot of astronauts Alan F. Bean, Charles Conrad and Richard F. Gordon in their Apollo 12 space-craft during a pre-flight checkout. NASA

failure soon after launch caused some concern. Fortunately, the fault was rectified quickly by the crew and from there on things went very much to plan. The Moon landing by the lunar module *Intrepid*, at 1.53 a.m. U.S. Eastern Standard Time (EST) on 19th November, was made with pin-point accuracy in the Ocean of Storms, some 600 feet from Surveyor III which had soft-landed on the Moon in April 1967. Charles Conrad and Alan Bean spent some seven hours on the Moon's surface, setting up experiments and inspecting Surveyor III, removing part of this spacecraft for examination by NASA experts. A highly successful mission ended with a further demonstration of accuracy when splash-down was made at a distance of only three miles from the recovery vessel, U.S.S. *Hornet*.

With this background of two almost routine missions, the third manned launch to the Moon, Apollo 13,

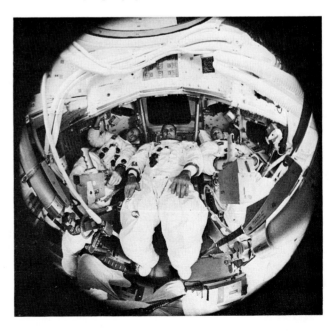

302

Accuracy exemplified. Surveyor III, soft-landed 19th April 1967, examined by Apollo 12 astronaut 20th November 1969. Only about 600 feet away, on the crater's rim, is the Apollo 12 Lunar Module. NASA

aroused little interest from the world at large. In fact, an Italian newspaper summed up the situation with a headline that read: 'Too perfect; the public is getting bored.' Then, on the evening of the third day, when Apollo 13 was some 200,000 miles out from Earth, cruising effortlessly towards the Moon, a sudden and dramatic event focused the attention of the world on these three men far out in space, astronauts James A. Lovell, Jack Swigert and Fred W. Haise. It began when Swigert's voice electrified mission control with the understatement of this, or any other, year: 'Hey, we've got a problem here.'

It was, indeed, a problem and the plight of the three men and their stricken spacecraft gripped the world for three and a half cliff-hanging days. Space will not permit a detailed description of the events and efforts made to secure the safe return of the three astronauts. Suffice it to say that as a result of an explosion in the service module the crew had lost completely one of two essential oxygen tanks and it was soon clear that the contents of the second were gradually leaking away. Prime solution was to use the lunar module *Aquarius* as a space lifeboat, sustaining the astronauts with its essential services, taking in tow the command module and damaged service module, and using the lunar module's Moon-landing and take-off engine as the single life-line back to Earth. The lunar module proved able to cope with the immense task set, and combined with the skill and courage of the astronauts and the superb work of mission control, the rescue operation ended happily on 17th April 1970, at 1.08 p.m. EST, when the command module splashed-down in the Pacific, its descent by parachutes witnessed by what was estimated to be the largest, and most relieved, television audience in history.

Subsequent Apollo launchings failed to arouse much

Artist's impression of what a future space station may look like. Such orbiting laboratories would enable astronomers, doctors and physicists to work in a completely new environment. Douglas Aircraft Company

interest from the general public, with the result that TV coverage was reduced considerably. After only two successful lunar landings the miracle of man on the Moon had already become commonplace. This was a pity, for the Apollo 14, 15 and 16 missions were progressively more rewarding and more successful. Each had incidents and dramatic moments. Solution of the problems that developed during the missions served to emphasize the scope of the astronauts' training and ability and the superb technical competence of the back-up from the NASA team on Earth.

Apollo 14, which lifted off on 31st January 1971, carried a new feature, a golf-cart-like Modular Equipment Transporter which helped astronauts Alan Shepard and Edgar Mitchell in their two EVAs on the lunar surface, during which they collected a total of 96 lb. of Moon rock samples. Apollo 15 and 16, which lifted off on 26th July 1971 and 16th April 1972 respectively, each carried the far more sophisticated Boeing Lunar Roving Vehicle. This permitted surface exploration at distances of up to three miles from the Lunar Module, and during the three EVAs made by astronauts David Scott and James Irwin

This Mariner 6 picture shows a 50-mile-wide expanse of the planet Mars, taken at a height of 2,150 miles above the Martian surface. NASA

of Apollo 15, they collected no less than 170 lb. of samples. Astronauts John Young and Charles Duke of the Apollo 16 mission spent a total of 20 hours 14 minutes on the lunar surface in three EVAs, the longest of which was a record 7 hours 23 minutes. Their sample pick-up was also a record, at some 215 lb.

There was no doubt that the United States had won the 'Moon Race', if the achievement of putting men on the Moon was the deciding factor.

Russia had achieved brilliant success in lunar exploration in two quite different ways. *Luna XVI*, launched on 12th September 1970, made a successful soft-landing on the Moon on 20th September. On the surface, the craft was commanded from Earth to activate a drill to collect a core sample. The drill comprised a hollow tube, with cutting teeth on the leading-edge, and this attained a depth of 1 ft 2 in. The resulting core sample was subsequently brought back to Earth by a capsule which landed some fifty miles south-east of Dzhezkazgan in Kazakhstan on 24th September 1970. This was hailed by scientists the world over as a brilliant technical achievement. It was clear that this technique offered development potential for the collection of rock samples from far more distant heavenly bodies.

Four weeks later, on 10th November 1970, *Luna XVII* was launched to the Moon. It soft-landed successfully on 17th November, and three hours after landing deployed a lunar exploration vehicle called *Lunokhod 1*. This carried two TV cameras, an X-ray spectrometer to study the chemical composition of the surface, and a stamping device to measure the strength of surface rocks. Controlled from Earth by a team of five men, *Lunokhod* travelled some 70 feet on its first excursion and made several trial turns. The next day it travelled a further 300 feet and carried out several experiments. By mid August 1971 this remarkable vehicle had survived nine lunar nights and had travelled a total distance of 6.49 miles. There was no doubt that this was an achievement of prime importance, offering important applications for the exploration of planets inhospitable to man.

Who, then, had really won the 'Moon Race'?

Russian experiments with Cosmos and Soyuz spacecraft indicated that her prime interest was in the construction of large scientific space stations in Earth orbit. An important first step in this direction was demonstrated by Cosmos 186 and 188. The former was launched on 27th October 1967, the latter three days later. With both spacecraft in Earth orbit, Cosmos 186 automatically sought and found Cosmos 188, docking with it and remaining in rigid contact for $3\frac{1}{2}$ hours. When released, by signals from Earth, the two spacecraft moved into different orbits and were recovered subsequently. This was a brilliant technical achievement and further automatic dockings have since been made by Cosmos spacecraft. Another approach has been made by a series of Soyuz manned spacecraft, which has not only involved rendezvous manoeuvres between spacecraft, but also transfer of crews from one to another and extra-vehicular activities that have included welding experiments in the environment of space.

Intelligence sources in the West were reasonably certain that the moment was fast approaching when the Russians would put some form of space station into Earth orbit. When a space vehicle named as *Salyut 1* was launched on 19th April 1971 it seemed that the moment had arrived, and this was confirmed on 24th April when *Soyuz 10* docked with it. However, no transfer of crew was made between the two craft, and it was not until 7th June, when *Soyuz 11* docked with *Salyut*, that a crew transfer was achieved. Cosmonauts Dobrovolski, Volkov and Patseyev remained on board for a record 23 days, 17 hours 40 minutes in space, during which period they carried out a programme involving Earth-resources survey, meteorological, space physics and biological studies.

Their return from space was regarded as routine—and ended in disaster. Their spacecraft suffered decompression during the re-entry phase and all three cosmonauts were found to be dead when the capsule was recovered.

In space travel the margin of safety between life and death is still precariously small, but man is ever ambitious. Already space probes have reached out to Mars and Venus, adding to our storehouse of knowledge, preparing for the day when space travel will be as commonplace as the 8.10 from Surbiton to Waterloo.

It is fascinating to think that in almost sixty-nine years of progress we have come full circle. The spacecraft that have made the first voyages to the Moon are, like the Wright *Flyer*, only a beginning. The writer's only regret is that he will be unable to record the aviation scene some sixty-nine years hence!

Index